T0302133

'Lots of people have been waiting for this book. Angela Espinosa is a noted authority on organisational cybernetics and worked closely with Stafford Beer. Her work deepens our understanding of the "Viable System Model" and offers significant insight into how best to use it in practice.'

– Professor Michael C. Jackson, OBE

'It is a pleasure to recommend this book that brings multiple applications of the Viable System Model (sometimes combined with other systems approaches) to practical problems in society. Too often, new methodologies remain within academia and their potential goes unrealized but this book gives numerous examples of work that combines an empathetic approach to people trying to make their institutions work while maintaining the rigor of the science behind them.'

– Dr. Allena Leonard, Cybernetician, Director Team Syntegrity International, President Metaphorum. Former President of the American Society for Cybernetics and the International Society for the Systems Sciences

'The functioning of our society depends strongly on the functioning of its organizations. Angela Espinosa's book, based on great application experience, shows in a practical way how to apply the Viable System Model so that we can finally make organizations work, however complex and dynamic their environment. A must read for all leaders dealing with organizational issues.'

– Dr. Martin Pfiffner, Board of Trustees Fondation Oroborus

Sustainable Self-Governance in Businesses and Society

Sustainable Self-Governance in Businesses and Society offers a sound introduction to Stafford Beer's Viable System Model (VSM) and clarifies its relevance to support organisational sustainability and self-governance. While the VSM has been known since the early 1980s, it hasn't been always easy to understand and to apply. It explains the self-transformation methodology to analyse the way organisations manage (or not) their complexity and govern themselves.

The work is supported by multiple examples of application in organisations of all scales – from small to multi-national corporations and from organised social networks to communities and national organisations. It clarifies the relevance of Beer's theory to support systemic learning and change in organisations, and to coach them to self-organise and self-govern.

Readers interested in further understanding insights from complex systems and cybernetics theories for designing and transforming organisations will benefit from this book, as it works to offer very detailed insights on how to put the VSM theory into practice. It clarifies how it improves adaptive capabilities, agile and self-regulated structures, more capable of fully implementing corporate sustainability strategies and self-governing themselves. The chapters provide key reading for managers, consultants, practitioners, and post-graduate students working in organisational transformation, governance, and sustainability.

Angela Espinosa is Emeritus Fellow at Hull University Business School, University of Hull, UK.

About Red (in Spanish) Web (in English)
From Impacto Mínimo Series.
Work by Lina Espinosa https://www.linaespinosa.com/impacto-mnimo
Red, Digital print, 53 × 88 cm, 2013, Santa Marta, Colombia

Systems Thinking

Series editor:
Gerald Midgley
University of Hull, UK

Systems thinking theory and practice is gaining ground in the worlds of social policy and management.

The Routledge *Systems Thinking* series is designed to make this complex subject as easy for busy practitioners and researchers to understand as possible. It provides range of reference books, textbooks and research books on a range of themes in systems thinking, from theoretical introductions to the systems thinking approach and its history, through practical guides to the implementation of systems thinking in the world, through to in-depth case studies that are significant for their profound impact.

This series is an essential reference point for anyone looking for innovative ways to effect systemic change, or engaging with complex problems.

Managing Creativity
A Systems Thinking Journey
José-Rodrigo Córdoba-Pachón

Systems Thinking in a Turbulent World
A Search for New Perspectives
Anthony Hodgson

The Hidden Power of Systems Thinking
Governance in a Climate Emergency
Ray Ison and Ed Straw

Buddhist and Taoist Systems Thinking
The Natural Path to Sustainable Transformation
Josep M. Coll

Sustainable Self-Governance in Businesses and Society
The Viable System Model in Action
Angela Espinosa

For more information about this series, please visit: https://www.routledge.com/Systems-Thinking/book-series/STHINK

Sustainable Self-Governance in Businesses and Society

The Viable System Model in Action

Angela Espinosa

Routledge
Taylor & Francis Group

LONDON AND NEW YORK

Cover image: © Lina Espinosa

First published 2023
by Routledge
4 Park Square, Milton Park, Abingdon, Oxon OX14 4RN

and by Routledge
605 Third Avenue, New York, NY 10158

Routledge is an imprint of the Taylor & Francis Group, an informa business

© 2023 Angela Espinosa

The right of Angela Espinosa to be identified as author of this work has been asserted in accordance with sections 77 and 78 of the Copyright, Designs and Patents Act 1988.

British Library Cataloguing-in-Publication Data
A catalogue record for this book is available from the British Library

ISBN: 978-1-138-59079-3 (hbk)
ISBN: 978-1-032-35497-2 (pbk)
ISBN: 978-0-429-49083-5 (ebk)

DOI: 10.4324/9780429490835

Typeset in Bembo
by MPS Limited, Dehradun

To Stafford Beer, whose spirit, wisdom, and unique understanding of organisational complexity has been the major inspiration I have had in my professional and personal life. To Jon Walker, my loving life and working partner who has inspired me to further develop the Viable System Model to address core issues of governance and sustainability.

To Federico Fornaguera, my son, whose unconditional love and support provided me with the strength to develop my passion for cybernetics, despite the sacrifices it sometimes meant for us as a family.

And to Isioma Naya Igwe-Walker, our only (three months old) grandchild, and all the children of this and future generations, hoping we can still contribute to co-create a brighter future for them.

Contents

Figures

Tables

Preface

This is an important book. Its mission is to make an organization theory available, which is of great potential value to professionals in both managerial and academic contexts: The Viable System Model (VSM) is arguably the most powerful organizational theory available today.

The VSM goes back to the cybernetician Stafford Beer. It rests on a very strong theoretical claim: that the model specifies the necessary and sufficient preconditions for the viability of any organization. This assertion implies that an organization is viable if and only if it fulfils the theoretical premises of the model.

Angela Espinosa communicates this theory in a practical way that makes it directly applicable. The components of the model are explained step by step, each one being illustrated with insightful examples. But also essential topics concerning viable systems as dynamic wholes are discussed, e.g., processes of systemic change and organizational learning.

Two important issues raised in the book are worth mentioning especially: First, the author contends that the VSM can and should be a vehicle for creating sustainable organisations, not only in economic terms, but especially in the social and environmental dimensions. Second, she is calling attention to the transformational perspective, drawing on a methodology of self-transformation by Espinosa and Walker. Both issues are worth deepening.

Angela Espinosa is one of the rare authors who has accumulated a long-standing experience in both teaching and applying the VSM in many different contexts. That experience makes this volume precious: The wealth of insightful case studies presented is unique, rendering the opus a valuable companion.

In the last years, several publications have come out that explain the VSM. The present one stands out for presenting the complex topic in a way that is easy to grasp for non-experts. I wish this book the wide dissemination it deserves.

Markus Schwaninger
Prof. Em. Dr. Soc. Oec.
University of St. Gallen, Switzerland
February 2022

Acknowledgements

I want to acknowledge, first of all, my husband, Dr. Jon Walker, who developed with me many of the ideas summarised in this book, over the last few decades. He also has supported me all the way by doing most of the VSM illustrations and doing several reviews of each chapter.

To Gerald Midgley from Hull University, who invited me to write this book, as part of the book series on systems thinking that he was leading at Routledge. Gerald has been always a close academic partner, very supportive of my work, and a close friend from the Centre of Systems Studies.

To Allenna Leonard, Stafford Beer's partner, and Martin Pfiffner, who reviewed the book for me and provided invaluable suggestions for clarification and improvement.

To Markus Schwaninger, who was my first inspiration in developing the Viable System Model (VSM) in the field of sustainability research. Markus also reviewed the manuscript, provided very useful general comments, and wrote the Preface for this book.

To Mike Jackson, who always trusted me and invited me to work at the Business School at Hull University and join the Centre for Systems Studies (now an Institute at the University). He provided me with a rich context to mature my understanding and further develop Stafford's work and contribute to the development of systems science.

To Thom Igwe-Walker and Juan David Alonso, who made the most artistic illustrations that enrich the way of conveying the main concepts through a more creative perspective.

To Lina Espinosa, my dear sister, for sharing her inspiring collaborative artistic work on a fishing community in Santa Marta, Colombia, for the front page of the book.

To my ex-PhD, MSc, and MBA students who have collaborated with me in reporting some of the case studies presented in this book.

- Vladimir Pop (graduated from the executive MBA at Hull Business School), who invited John and I to support a VSM project in the ELF School in Romania his family owns, and then implemented recommendations and wrote his MBA dissertation on reflections of the experience. I used several examples from this case study to illustrate the VSM theory and methodology in Chapters 2, 3, and 5.

- Andrea Martinez, whose PhD projects I supervised at Los Andes University (Colombia) using the VSM to explore issues of sustainable governance in a Mexican corporation. Her work inspired a section in Chapter 4.

- Kartikae Grover (executive MBA at Hull Business School), who invited Jon and i to lead a VSM project in a Local English Health Trust (LEHT) in England, which is introduced in Chapter 4. He also implemented our recommendations and wrote his MBA dissertation on reflections of the experience.

- Gabriela Ramirez, another MSc student from Los Andes University in Colombia, who invited me to support her designing Tinta using the VSM, as described in Chapter 5.

- Alfadhal Al-Hinai (PhD student at Hull University Business School), who invited Jon and I to introduce the VSM to support the design of the Omani Broadband company. We jointly provide a reflection about his use of the VSM in Chapter 6.

- Julija Danilova (PhD student at Hull University Business School), who used the VSM to design strategies for integral supply chain integration in a regional Offshore Wind Industry in England, as described in Chapter 6.

- Carolina Duque, an MSc student from Los Andes University in Colombia, who worked with me on a one-year action research project to support sustainable self-governance in an Amazonian indigenous community, as reported in Chapter 7.

- Carlos Duran (MSc, Externado University–Colombia), who used the VSM to support sustainable self-governance in an Afro-Caribbean community in Colombia, as we jointly report it in Chapter 8.

To John Taborda, Katherine Farrell, and Eduardo Forero, who invited Jon and I to lead a VSM project in Magdalena University in Colombia, which continues to make an impact on its sustainability and organisational strategies – see Chapter 5.

To Bernardus Van Hoof, whose inspirational work in developing a national network of businesses to clean their production in Mexico, is mentioned in Chapter 6.

To Martha Ines Giraldo, ex-director of a National 2nd Generation Broadband Networking Latin-America, who invited Jon and I to lead a VSM project to reorganise the network. This case study is reported in Chapter 6.

To my colleagues in Colombia and England, who contributed to the VSM projects I led in Colombia in the 1990s, reported in Chapter 8: German Bula, Alfonso Reyes, Ernesto Lleras, Roberto Zarama, and Raul Espejo (NAO and NSS projects); Juan Mayr and Martha Giraldo (NES project); and Eduardo Wills, Juan Carlos Palou, Dario Restrepo, and the Reunirse' team (Reunirse project).

To the executive team of the Local English Health Trust (LEHT) – in particular, its chief medical director, where we developed an assessment of the trust's performance during the first two waves of the coronavirus pandemic in 2020. And to the rest of our team on this project, Gerald Midgley, Jon Walker, and Maya Vachkova. An introduction to this project is briefly reported in Chapter 8.

Finally, a special thanks to all the members of the Metaphorum community (a not-for-profit organisation I have contributed to create, develop, and lead since Stafford passed away in 2002, [Metaphorum.org]) whose continuous participation in our conferences and webinar series have been a continuous inspiration and motivation to continue disseminating and developing Stafford's work.

Abbreviations

2^g-B	Second-generation Broadband
BIMCO	Baltic and International Maritime Council
BM	Business Manager
BoA	Board of Administration
BoD	Board of Directors
CAS	Complex Adaptive Systems
CLs	Clinical Leads
CPO	Colombian Presidential Office
CPS	Colombian Public Sector
CS	Corporate Sustainability
D_i	Diagnostic Issue'i" $(i = 1... n)$
DGM	Divisional General Manager
DNA	Deoxyribonucleic Acid
E	Environment
ECM	Enterprise Complexity Model
EIA	Environmental Impact Assessment
FEED	Front-End Engineering and Design
FIDIC	Fédération Internationale Des Ingénieurs-Conseils
FM	Finance Ministry
GST	General Systems Theory
HG_n	Health Group'n'
HR	Human Resources
HS	High School
ICT	Information and Communication Technologies
KG	Kindergarten
KPI	Key Performance Indicators
LEHT	Local English Health Trust
LOGIC	Leading Oil and Gas Industry Competitiveness
M	Meta-systemic Management
MDT	Multi-Disciplinary Team

ME	Ministry of Education
MIT	Massachusetts Institute of Technology (Boston, United States of America)
MLP	Multi-Level Perspective
MSSN	Mexican Sustainable Supply Network
N^2BN	National 2nd-generation Broadband Network
NAO	National Auditing Office
NBS	National Broadband Strategy
NEIS	National Environmental Information System
NES	National Environmental System
NHS	National Health Service
NPO	National Planning Office
NSS	New School System
O	Organisation
OBC	Omani Broadband Company
OCC	Orika Community Council
OSW	Off-Shore Wind
PBL	Project-Based Learning
PH	Concentration of hydrogen ions in a water-based solution
PMS	Performance Management System
PS	Primary School
R&D	Research and Development
R^2BN	Regional 2nd-generation Broadband Network
S1	System 1
S2	System 2
S3*	System 3*
S3	System 3
S4	System 4
S5	System 5
SCI	Supply Chain Integration
SEB	School Education Board
SES	Socio Ecological Systems
SiF	System in Focus
SISP	Strategic Information Systems Plan
SME	Small and Medium Enterprises
SNA	Social Network Analysis
SNM	Strategic Niche Management
SPU_1	Specialist $Unit_1$
SPU_2	Specialist $Unit_2$
SSN	Social Solidarity Network
SSU	Small Service Unit
STM	Self-Transformation Methodology
TM	Transition Management

TS	Team Syntegrity
UK	United Kingdom
UPS	Upper Primary School
V&S	Viability and Sustainability
V_e	Variety of the Environment
V_m	Variety of the Operational Management
V_o	Variety of the Operation
VSM	Viable System Model
WCED	World Commission on Environment and Development
WTO	World Trade Organisation

Contributors

Reviewers

Introduction, Agnieszka Chmielewska, Irena Kossowska, Marcin Lachowski

Dr. Jon Walker
Dr. Allenna Leonard
Dr. Martin Pffifner
Professor Markus Schwaninger

Illustrators
Dr. Jon Walker
Thom Igwe-Walker
Juan David Alonso
Lina Espinosa

PhD, MsC, and MBA Students
Vladimir Pop (MBA – Hull Business School, UK)
Andrea Martinez (PhD – Los Andes University, Colombia)
Kartikae Grover (MBA – Hull Business School, UK)
Alfadhal Al-Hinai (PhD – Hull Business School, UK)
Julija Danilova (PhD – Hull Business School, UK)
Carolina Duque (MSc Los Andes University – Colombia)
Carlos Duran (MSc, Externado University – Colombia)

Consulting Partners
Martha Ines Giraldo, ex-director (National 2nd Generation Broadband Network in Latin-America)
Gabriela Ramirez (Tinta's director)
John Taborda, Katherine Farrell and Eduardo Forero (Magdalena University academic leaders)

Introduction

Shortly after the pioneers of cybernetics developed the mathematical and theoretical foundation of this new science (e.g., N. Wiener, R. Ashby, A. Mc Culloch, G. Bateson, and others), Stafford Beer invented *organisational* cybernetics (originally called managerial cybernetics). He developed the Viable System Model, a theoretical framework to study organisational viability, detailed in '*Brain of the Firm*' and *Heart of the Enterprise*. He was dissatisfied with the the current approaches to management, as he thought they didn't contribute clearly enough with tools to support the management of complexity of organisations.

Most traditional management approaches focused on directing operations by defining organisational policies and strategies, and managing resources, including people. He was well ahead of his time in understanding that organisational and environmental complexities must be well managed, for organisations to adapt to rapidly changing environments, and to offer both theory and tools to deal with organisational complexity.

In the last 30 years – ironically more clearly after his death in 2002 – some organisational researchers have developed new approaches to overcome these shortages, well aligned with the direction set by Stafford and other systems and cybernetics pioneers. But to my knowledge, no one has yet developed a more robust, precise, and practical theory of organisations as complex, self-governed systems.

Complex adaptive systems theory, which is inspired in the same basic principles of systems, neural networks, emergence, and complexity, offers new insights that may be inspiring for managers. But it has not yet explained in enough detail how to put it into practice for designing and managing complex organisations. Meanwhile, Beer's theory has been further developed by a number of academics, consultants, and practitioners from different academic and cultural backgrounds worldwide, and continues to be widely used, as will be demonstrated throughout this book.

It is not surprising that in the current world landscape of turbulent environmental, political, and economic changes, managers are more aware of

DOI: 10.4324/9780429490835-1

their need for improve their adaptive skills, which begins with skills for understanding and managing the complexity of their organisations. The understanding of Beer's pioneering ideas and their implications are now urgently needed and require widespread application.

More than ever, contemporary organisations need to guarantee their long-term sustainability, which implies making sure they use resources in a sustainable way, and respect and protect their local communities and the environmental niches where they work. The difference between a viable organisation (i.e., surviving in a complex environment) and being a viable and sustainable organisation is that in the second case, an organisation actively addresses the challenges and paradoxes of moving into a regenerative rather than extractive development model; and while doing so, develops capabilities for sustainable self-governance.

This book aims to support managers and practitioners in developing self-governed, more effective organisations, capable of continuously learning and adapting, through more agile and balanced relationships within themselves and with the environments they co-evolve with. It introduces my understanding on Beer's VSM theory, which has been influenced by applying and developing it with my partner Dr Jon Walker for the last 20 years. We focus on how the VSM can be used for addressing the core challenges of developing organisational viability, *sustainability,* and self-governance – what I refer to, as the '*viability and sustainability*' (v&s) approach. The v&s emphasizes the idea that, to survive in the long term, organisations need to become more resilient while respectfully co-existing with their business and socio-ecological niches. I acknowledge that we are among a growing number of Beer's followers who are jointly progressing the development of the VSM in fields like sustainability and governance research.

This book aims to explain Beer's original theory in an accessible, straightforward way, without losing its most relevant aspects, and trying to link it as much as possible to contemporary (complex) systems theory and practice. It aims also to contribute to clarifying the VSM implications for sustainable design and governance of organisations, communities, and networks worldwide though several examples of applications. It does so through narratives and stories of a number of applications of the VSM.

All the applications have been developed in an action research mode, with participation from businesses from different scopes and scales, following the 'self-transformation methodology' (STM) (or earlier versions of it). The STM aims to facilitate systemic learning of participants in a VSM project, by introducing the main VSM distinctions, and guiding them in the process of mapping their organisational complexity. As a result, people learn to identify any pathological configurations in their patterns of relationships, and to collectively find effective ways to address them as 'self-transformation projects.' Some of the case studies are the result of consulting projects I have led (some of them with Jon Walker), and some of them are the result of action research I supervised with PhD, MBA, and MSc students.

The first three chapters introduce organisational cybernetics, the Viable System Model, with emphasis in organisational viability *and sustainability,* and the self-transformation methodology with examples from real life applications to illustrate the theory and its application. The following chapters offer a variety of contexts and examples of applications of the VSM. It first offers examples of VSM applications in specific sectors – i.e., the health sector, in Chapter 4, and the education sector in Chapter 5. It then suggests the usability of the theory to design: complex organisational networks in Chapter 6; and to support community organisations to develop sustainable self-governance, in Chapter 7.

Chapter 8 reflects on the idea of systemic change by reviewing several historical VSM applications at the national level in South America and suggesting the usefulness of the VSM to design and implement massive systemic changes at the national level in a country. The final chapter summarises the learning from previous chapters and highlights open research paths to continue developing the VSM theory.

Chapter 1

Towards Self-Governed Businesses and Societies

Systems, Complexity, and Cybernetics Sciences

It's not unusual when working in an organisation to find ourselves moaning about how complex specific tasks are, or how complex relationships or the entire organisation has become. So, what do we mean by a complex task, a complex network of relationships, or a complex organisation? That is what this book aims to clarify: What does it mean to manage complexity in organisations and how do you do it in your daily life?

To undertake this task, we will first explore definitions and theories coming originally from the fields of (complex) systems and cybernetics. Systems thinking emerged in the early 20th century as a transdisciplinary approach for the study of 'systems' of all types. It defined a '*system*' as a set of interconnected components, that share a collective purpose, and that together develop emergent properties that distinguishes them as a whole. According to (Biggart et al., 1998), it was Bogdanov, a largely unknown Russian doctor and scientist, who pioneered systems theories very early in the 20th century, that would later on develop into a new scientific field. Ludwig Von Bertalanffy, an Austrian scientist founded the new discipline, developing further these ideas, into what he called the 'General Systems Theory' (GST) (Von Bertalanffy, 1968).

Before GST was established, a group of scientists were developing a new discipline that Norbert Wiener called 'cybernetics' (Wiener, 1965). He defined it as the study of communication and control in animals and machines. Pioneering cyberneticians were studying the basic mechanisms for learning and cognition in living systems, aiming to learn from them to hopefully illuminate other fields of knowledge such as psychology, anthropology, business management, and operational research. Their discoveries became pivotal to the development of computers, and not too long after, also to the development of the internet.

Following the pioneers, several systemic and cybernetic approaches began to flourish in the second half of the 20th century. They covered a wide

          DOI: 10.4324/9780429490835-2

range of transdisciplinary studies and applications, ranking from the formal representation of abstract models of real systems (systems analysis), the development of software based on such models (systems engineering), the development of machines capable of solving different types of technical problems (computers and electronic devices), the development of highly sophisticated electronic communication systems such as the internet, and the development of machine (artificial) intelligence. Undoubtedly, in the managerial environment, these new inventions began to change radically the way businesses work and relate to each other, the way people communicate among themselves, both inside and outside their jobs, and more generically, the way that industries, economies, and modern societies organise themselves.

But it wasn't only in the technological domain that these new sciences produced dramatic changes and innovations. In the social sciences, as well, their influence has been growing – at a slower but steady pace – particularly in the last few decades. Some of the pioneer cyberneticians were physicists (e.g., Von Foerster, 1981), physiologists (Cannon, 1934), neurophysiologists (McCulloch, 1965; McCulloch & Pitts, 1943), anthropologists (Bateson, 1973, 1980), mathematicians (Wiener, 1965), and biologists (Maturana & Varela, 1980; 1988). Ashby (1962) was a universal scientist who served as a psychiatrist and biochemist, among others.

So, it's not surprising that these new theories influenced several social sciences: Von Foerster led 'systemic family therapy'; Bateson and Mead led their own systemic approach to anthropology. W. McCulloch and W. Pitts developed the first mathematical model of the human brain as a neural network; their work profoundly influenced H. Maturana and F. Varela (1980, 1988), who later developed the 'Santiago School of Cognition,' which opened new paths for understanding biology. And several of them influenced new perspectives on management sciences and economics, as will be discussed in the rest of the book.

Organisational Cybernetics

McCulloch was also Stafford Beer's mentor: Beer took his model of the brain as a neural network and explored the possibility of learning from it to understand alternative models of organisation for complex social systems. Combining McCulloch's inspiration on neural networks with Ross Ashby's theories of complexity and variety, he developed a new and revolutionary model of organisations and management, the Viable System Model (VSM) (Beer, 1979, 1981, 1985).

After successfully using the VSM to redesign a British steel manufacturing company in the 1960s, he further developed the theory through a series of international applications; he most famously used it in the 'Cybersyn' project, which aimed to support Salvador Allende's socialist government to reorganise the state-run industries in Chile through self-regulated worker-owned factories (Beer, 1981, part II). We will revisit this story in Chapter 8, as it set the basis for a cybernetic society, which is still relevant in particular in the context of global and local self-governance for sustainability.

Beer continued developing the theory and related methods all through his life. He became a world-famous consultant, had a number of emeritus positions in universities worldwide, had a gold medal from the UK Operational Research Society, and became president of the World Organisation of Systems and Cybernetics. His work has now been applied and further developed by a wide community of academics and practitioners and continues to be even more widely known and used. Whittaker (2009) offers an anthology of Beer's personal and professional life, as well as a selection of his academic and artistic works.

For those of us who have the privilege to know him and work closely with him, it's not surprising that it took so long for his theory to be widespread and accepted: he was clearly 50 years ahead of his time in understanding that in a complex and sometimes chaotic environment, organisations need to develop adaptive capabilities if they are to survive and become more resilient. And many times, they need to reinvent themselves in order to find their place in a new environment; they need to co-evolve with their environmental niche. The current COVID-19 pandemic has provided a context for thousands of organisations around the world to learn once more this lesson, sometimes extremely painfully.

Complex Systems Sciences

In the 1980s, another group of scientists began to develop new ways of understanding complex systems. Prigogine, working on thermodynamic systems, explained the basic principles of mega-entropy and self-organisation in physical systems. Chaos theory (see Lorentz (1996)) began to emerge as a new discipline exploring chaotic behaviours in complex systems. The invention of super-computers allowed scientists from the Santa Fe Institute in the United States of America (USA) to solve non-linear equations and to run highly sophisticated simulations, which allow them to identify 'strange attractors' in the behaviour of complex systems, from which the idea of 'complex adaptive systems' (CAS) began to emerge (Holland, 1992). Kauffman (1995) and others explained further complex behaviours in biological and social systems. Based on these pioneering theories, many researchers have contributed in the last few decades to the development of complex systems theories. Some of them have provided interesting insights for further understanding complexity and management (Allen et al., 2011).

Nevertheless, there hasn't yet been anyone providing a more robust and comprehensive theoretical framework to fully explain an organisation as a complex system, and to fully describe the implications for managing complexity in organisations (Bohorquez & Espinosa, 2015). No doubt there are several aspects of CAS theory that complement and further develop what Stafford had explained before, but CAS theory has not yet provided the same depth and completeness in its way of explaining organisational and social structures and behaviours when compared to the VSM. We will revisit this discussion in the following chapters and reflect on the benefits and constraints of combining such approaches in the final chapter.

Complexification in the 21st Century

When Stafford Beer first published the VSM theory (Beer, 1979), the internet hadn't been invented: the internet was actually developed based on the same discovery of neural networks that his mentor Warren McCulloch pioneered! Computers and systems were only in an early stage of development, and organisations operated in relatively stable environments. Since those early days of systems and cybernetics, businesses, markets, and societies have all experienced a continuous process of *complexification;* nowadays, they have real-time access to information about changes in the environment, interactions among internal and external stakeholders are not constrained by people working in the same physical space or at the same time, and the availability of online information and communication tools to support the working environment is continuously growing.

Beer (1979) defined a *viable organisation* as one that is capable of in-dependent existence, which means it can learn, adapt, and re-organise as necessary, in order to respond to the changing demands from the environment in which it exists and co-evolves with. Clearly an organisation that may have been surviving 50 years ago may no longer survive in the current business environment: While 50 years ago developing a new international business may have taken several months or even years, in our globalised Anthropocene, it can be done by the click of a form through a webpage. The new technologies have shifted the notions of time and space and we now operate in a highly varied, rapidly changing, and volatile environment. It is in this context that understanding the laws and principles of organisational viability and its im-plications for managing organisational and societal complexities become fundamental. So, it's not surprising that the interest in, and applications of, the Viable System Model (VSM) have continued growing faster and faster in the last few decades, after Stafford passed away in 2002.

Understanding Complexity (and Variety)

What is Complexity and Variety?

Ashby suggested that a system is an abstraction made by an observer of a real situation in which, the observer – according to his or her motives for studying the situation – chooses some variables to focus the study. We can then say that the 'state' of a system is the set of numerical values that its (observer's chosen) variables have at that instant. Then we can define 'complexity' as 'all the possible states that a system can exhibit' and 'variety' as the number of possible states observed by a particular observer. Or, as Schwaninger (2009) explains, variety is a repertoire of behaviours. It's important to realise that the viewpoint of the observer determines completely the choice of variables and therefore the observed complexity of a system. As Ashby (1981, pp. 187) says:

> [I]f two observers differ in the distinctions they can make,
>
> then they will differ in their estimates of the variety.

Beer (1979, p. 36)

> [I]t is the observer who defines the system, and its purposes, and (it turns out) its variety.

For example, if we ask an Inuit person from the Arctic, what is the number of colours of snow, they may say a number close to 20; a foreign visitor, however, may be able to recognise only 1 or perhaps a few snow colours. This happens, as the locals have developed a subtler observation, partly for survival reasons, as there are types of yellowish snow that cover up cracks, so it would be dangerous to step on them. So, you need to distinguish them. In this example, the locals' variety about snow types may be around 20, while for the foreigner it may be only 1.

If we consider the lighting system of our room, it can be either on or off. So, the variety of such a lighting system would be two (2). However, if we ask the same question in a modern teaching or conferencing room, which has a lighting system that can be graduated to produce a wide range of lighting effects, we could consider the variety of such a system to be close to infinite. Rather than giving it a precise number we can say that the latter has a far greater (lighting) variety than the first example.

These examples illustrate that the concept of variety:

a) Is subjected to the observer's cognitive and perceptual capabilities (e.g., a blind person may attribute no variety to either of the previous lighting systems, while an artist may distinguish between multiple states in the second example; and an uninterested observer may hardly notice the difference between the states).

b) Provides an important relational measurement system, rather than a numerical measurement system. So, we can talk about how observer A's variety 'matches' the lighting systems' variety; or whether observer B's variety matches the variety of the lighting system; and we can say that A has a greater variety than B, or vice versa. So, we can talk about observer A's variety compared to observer B's variety about lighting systems, and we can say that A has a greater variety than B, or vice versa.

It becomes clearer that the idea of variety is not a factual, objective measurement, as Ashby (1962, p. 106) said:

Organisation is partly in the eye of the beholder.

Beer (1979, p. 154) reconfirmed this position:

Obviously, for a start, there is no objective reality, as has been

argued passim already in this book. We can account for a major discrepancy of outlook

simply by saying that each group has its own subjective impression of the whole system.

The viewpoint of the observer determines the choice of variables, the way of measuring them, and therefore the observed complexity of a system – see Beer (1979, pp. 32–48). Beer (1979, p. 86) explains that variety measuring is different than naively 'counting states,' but it is about 'matching' state generators; for example, we won't count the variety of a player in a game, but we will observe his capability for generating as much variety as his opponent. We will then say that the varieties of the two rivals are approximately 'evenly matched.' In the context of chess, it is clear that a grand master has far more variety than an amateur, and as such can play several dozen games simultaneously.

Organisational Elements (O, M, E)

According to Beer (1979, p. 89), Ashby's law of requisite variety says: '*Only variety absorbs variety.*' He uses Ashby's Law for developing our understanding of the way we manage complexity in businesses or social organisations. Beer (1979, p. 94) offers a simple language to represent the way we deal with variety in organisations – see Figure 1.1.

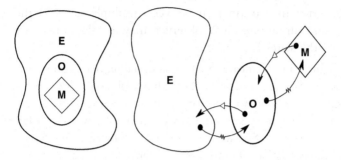

Figure 1.1 Organisational elements: O, M, E

(Illustration by Juan David Alonso)

- An oval to represent an operation (O), which means, a group of people developing a core organisational task (i.e., one implementing the organisational purpose), with some autonomy and enough self-regulatory skills.
- A cloudy shape to represent the environmental niche (E) in which the operation is embedded.

  - It includes customers, suppliers, competitors, communities, ecosystems, and other biological and human agents co-evolving with the organisation in their environmental niche.
  - It is multi-dimensional, and it has hazy boundaries, so we focus on representing all the relevant relationships the operations are engaged with (i.e., customers, suppliers, the market, the local communities, the competitors, etc).
  - Its scope is determined by the nature of the organisation, which will change as the organisation changes: If it decides to export to Bulgaria, then Bulgaria becomes part of its environment.

- A diamond box represents operational management (M). It includes all the roles that support and coordinate the implementation of organisational purpose (i.e., the production of products or services), but which themselves do not add value to them.

It is important to notice that the right-hand side representation of Figure 1.1. is only teasing apart O from M and E, for analytical reasons. In real life, they are embedded within each other (as in the original, left-hand-side representation), and they are all part of the environment they share. Between O and M, M and E, and O and E, there are feedback loops that represent the multiple and (many times complex) interactions at these levels. Beer explained that 'n' people interacting generate n(n − 1) relationships. So, the number of people we interact with would also determine the variety we have to match.

The VSM helps us to analyse recurrent patterns of meaningful interactions between organisational internal and external agents; and to explore effective contexts for such interactive agents to improve the way they manage their complexity. Following Maturana and Varela (1988), human interactions happen through conversations, and it is through language and conversations that we coordinate actions. Structural coupling is the process through which structurally determined transformations in each of two or more systemic unities induces (for each) a trajectory of reciprocally triggered change.

In biology, the *niche* includes those aspects of the total environment where an organism operates, that the organism is "structurally coupled" to, in its realisation of life. In other words, two systems (e.g., organisation and niche) are structurally coupled when they have an interlocked history of recurrent interactions leading to the structural congruence between them. As explained in (Espinosa et al. 2008), it is niche and organisation, together, that lay down the cognitive domain of the social organisation. The niche, therefore, includes all the stakeholders of the organisation.

Ashby's Law of Requisite Variety

Beer's (1979) interpretation of Ashby's Law of Requisite Variety to an organisation begins with the observation that in every organisation, V_e is orders of magnitude bigger than V_o; and V_m is orders of magnitude smaller than V_o – see Figure 1.2.

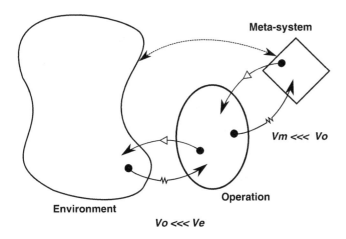

Meta-system

$Vm <<< Vo$

Operation

Environment

$Vo <<< Ve$

Figure 1.2 Ashby's Law of Requisite Variety

(Illustration by Jon Walker)

A group of people undertaking a particular task, and continuously interacting with other agents in their environmental niche, need to continuously learn about external agents, and about the core socio-economic and environmental challenges and opportunities that constitute their context. They need to learn how they can best react to them. Beer calls this (external) environmental variety 'V_e.'

- 'V_o' is the variety exhibited by an operational team 'O' (or by the organisation as a whole) while implementing its core task. In order to do it effectively, people need to know as much as possible how to do their tasks, and find effective ways to interact with each other, to have a mutually satisfying working (or living together, in a community) relationship.

- 'V_m' is the variety exhibited by the management (of the operational team or of the organisation). It depends on the way it interacts with the operational team and how much s(he) understands and knows about the way it implements its task and uses its resources and knowledge to do so.

Over time the organisation (O) learns ways to develop 'requisite variety': each time V_e increases, O increases its own variety, V_o, to match the increased V_e. In other words, O becomes structurally coupled to relevant agents in their niche and learns to co-evolve with its niche. Similarly, the management (M) needs to increase its own variety (V_m) to match an increased V_o. Ashby's Law of Requisite Variety clearly explains why managers always operate facing uncertainty and dealing with limited amount of information and knowledge; management decision making has to deal with navigating uncertainty and ambiguity. It also helps us to reflect on the natural variety imbalances that happen in all organisations when learning to understand their core tasks and to manage their complexity.

Beer explains that any manager, in principle, is unable to deal with the variety of one subsidiary system, e.g., an operational team (never mind all the subsidiary systems) (Beer, 1985, p. 37). According to Ashby (1962), *self-organisation* is the ability of a machine or living organism to change its own organisation. Therefore, self-organisation is the most powerful way to deal with operational variety from a worker's perspective and the best way to delegate responsibility from a manager's perspective. The more a team of workers can self-organise to implement a particular task, the more likely they are the 'doers' and the 'knowers,' so they will learn by doing to do it effectively and timely – they will develop requisite variety. The more they need to get approval for everything they do (the less self-organised they are), the less variety they will be prepared to handle, and the more likely decisions and actions are going to take longer.

In order to be able to manage operational variety, O and M need to create an effective learning context – the double loops in Figure 1.2 – by designing amplifiers and attenuators, to improve information and communication flows. Attenuators are any organisational mechanisms that would reduce the variety of a situation, to make it more understandable for the receiver. Amplifiers are also mechanisms that would increase the scope of the message, so that it can be taken by an enlarged audience at the niche. The following examples further illustrate these concepts.

- If an operational manager has more than seven people to manage (42 relationships to consider), then(s)he can improve her management of variety by:
    - attenuating the operational variety by grouping teams of people in sub-task groupings.
    - amplifying operational variety by devising a rewards system.
- Some 'inelastic variety attenuators' like the organisational chart and job descriptions, may attenuate too much variety – e.g., by over delimiting individual freedom, or preventing spontaneous collaboration and engagement in complex tasks – if not properly designed.
- To attenuate, V_e managers may, for example, classify business sectors in their niche, and appoint sector's representatives, responsible to deal with all the business interactions in a particular sector.
- A very innovative marketing campaign, which may reach much more people than not having one, or than having a very standard and uninteresting campaign, could be potentially a good amplifier of V_o.
- A highly effective variety attenuator between operations and operational manager is *divisionalisation* of tasks: when the manager has a very large operation and begins to feel overwhelmed by its variety, (s)he may decide to create sub-units, and appoint someone responsible for each one, to whom (s)he would communicate directly. The new divisions or subunits reduce importantly V_o, as the new unit's coordinators absorb most of the variety leaving only some residual variety for the manager to absorb.
- A manager can amplify the variety by sending a group mail to all the members of the operational team, suggesting a particular strategy to discuss in the next monthly meeting.

Viability vs Complexity Management

Managing Variety and Learning

Cyberneticians understand learning as a conversational process where we build up shared mental models of complex issues to enhance our variety to interact with them properly. Once we have identified a learning interest, we search for reputable sources of knowledge on this specific field of knowledge, study them, discuss it with our peers, and end up agreeing on a 'mental model' of this topic, which hopefully improves our way of understanding and dealing with this topic and with those we relate to regarding such topic. To develop a mental model, we make '*distinctions*' in language: we '*name*' some '*objects,*' attribute them with some '*characteristics,*' and provide them with some '*explanations*' (Asby, 2021).

In any positive learning experience, we can *learn to learn*, which means to discover better, or more effective, ways of learning individually or collectively, which result in improving our capabilities as critical learners. This means to develop self-awareness, which implies being able to identify our needs for self-development, and learning about ourselves, about our relationship with others, and about our relationship to the environment.

Our understanding of variety challenges traditional views of group learning and knowledge management; taking Ashby's Law into account, individual and social learning are also processes of developing variety. Managing complexity in organisations also requires of creating proper contexts for enabling good communications among people working (and learning) together. Creating a proper communication context for effective learning is always mediated by implicit challenges of human communication. For example, not always can we express ourselves clearly enough when we speak; and many times, other people 'hear' different things from what we aimed to say in the first place.

The consequences of Ashby's Law are paramount for understanding the management of complexity in organisations, as it explains that managers always operate facing uncertainty and dealing with limited amount of information and knowledge. Even with sophisticated information and knowledge management systems, management decision-making always requires skills for information processing, knowledge management, and for managing uncertainty and ambiguity. Managers and organisations are continuous learners, and it is only when this is properly understood, and the structures, processes, and technology are adequately designed to cope with the natural imbalances in variety between them and their environment, and between managers and staff, that more harmonic, effective, and high-performing organisations can be developed.

Organisational Learning and Development

Like other living organisms, organisations grow and evolve in an organic way. A small group of people may start testing and developing an innovative idea, for example by developing and selling a product or service in a niche environment. There will be intense communications among them, for planning and developing their start-up. They will be experimenting, testing, and learning together on the best way to develop it. They will constantly need to clarify the organisational purpose, core tasks, and how to distribute responsibilities to implement them, which are their required resources and expected (and hopefully achievable) outputs.

This implies continuous negotiations and decisions on what precisely each one ought to do at a particular time and sharing experience and knowledge on best ways to do them. If done with cybernetic criteria, this will support development of operational teams as critical learning teams, and workers as knowledge workers. As we explained elsewhere (Espinosa et al., 2008, p. 640), the making of such distinctions (i.e., the identification of difference, what works and doesn't work in a social organisation), is an intrinsic part of human inquiry and is what lays down a cognitive space. Developing our variety is then at the root of developing social cognition, and therefore, organisational intelligence.

Undoubtedly, getting organised as a group always comes with a cost for individuals, which is accepting certain constraints to their freedom to act (e.g., by distributing and clarifying roles and tasks). It also requires learning to learn together, which includes relinquishing some individual freedom to achieve the group's purpose. Power struggles very often come while distributing roles and responsibilities in a group and more particularly when deciding on scales of retributions and rewards. See Figure 1.3 for a cartoon of a learning team.

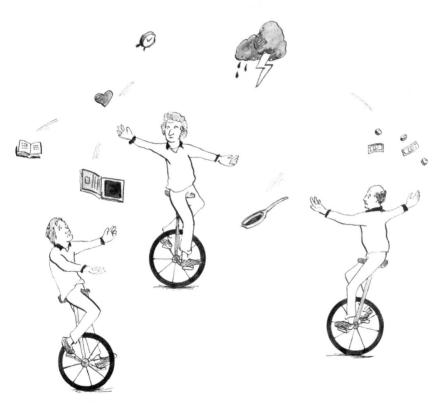

Figure 1.3 A cartoon of a learning team

(Illustrated by Thom Igwe-Walker)

To coordinate actions and align purposes, we continuously develop conversations among 'doers' and managers. We learn how to do tasks, how we assess our performance, and how to improve it. The agreements we reach about each of these basic questions affect our bonding, our ways of working together, and become the substrata (the 'rules of the game') on which organisational and social structures operate and adapt. Over time, some of these agreements result also in formal or informal norms, shared values, agreed roles and responsibilities, process design, or standards. These are all social mechanisms (variety attenuators) to deal with social and environmental complexity. They help us clarify the boundaries between acceptable and unacceptable decisions and behaviours while implementing core organisational tasks. The organisational culture evolves from historical agreements within its members about the values and behaviours that are favoured by the organisation and those that are undesirable or even unacceptable.

As shown in Figure 1.4, systemic (organisational) learning involves learning about us, learning about our relationships with others, and learning about our relationship with our niche. In an organisational context, learning about ourselves in the workplace implies observing our working self, the way we understand and implement our tasks, our own activities' planning, our reactions to events, and to interactions with others. It also contributes to observing (and managing) our own emotions resulting from interactions with others.

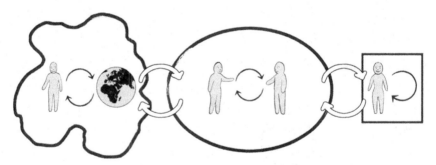

Figure 1.4 Systemic organisational learning

(Illustrated by: Thom Igwe-Walker)

Learning about our relationships with other people in the workplace includes reflecting on our teamwork, our capabilities for communication, coordination of actions and leadership, jointly reflecting with the teams we work with on our teams' performance and in the quality of our interactions with other teams/organisational units. Learning about our niche implies reflecting about the way we use natural resources and dispose of waste in our work, the way our organisation impacts its environmental niche and the communities where it operates, and the way it manages its social responsibility. It also implies learning about our interaction with external social networks we are involved with like allies, intervenors, government institutions, and competitors.

Individual and organisational learning require the development of capabilities. According to Helfat et al. (2009), operational capabilities develop from routinely implementing operational tasks, while 'dynamic capabilities' result from managing operational procedures; and 'learning capabilities' support development of dynamic capabilities. Learning results from experimenting with operational tasks, doing experiments and spotting opportunities for improvement. Continuously self-assessing performance contribute to facilitating organisational learning. It is by being able to identify (and accept) our mistakes, that we learn and develop self-governance capabilities. We may also 'learn to learn' – what some authors have called second-order learning – by critically observing our learning process and outputs, and sporadically assessing our knowledge assets.

The VSM explains that to effectively manage organisational complexity, we should develop adaptive capabilities, and continuously review our processes and structures to deploy requisite variety. As will become clearer over the next chapters, the VSM offers a meta-language to map recurrent patterns of interactions between people implementing tasks: It provides a pictorial language to map the complexity of such interactions and distinctions to assess how well they operate and learn together as a complex organisational system.

Managing Complexity in Organisations

Miller (1956) explained that human beings have physiological constraints for managing different topics simultaneously; he proposed the 'magic number' 7 +/–2 as the maximum number of variables that our cognitive system can manage without generating too much physiological stress (which manifest itself as headaches, lack of concentration, irritability, etc.). This is closely related to the idea of managing variety, which is core to organisational design. When we end up in situations in which the variety of a situation exceeds our capability for dealing with it in a period of time, we experience the effects of variety overload – see cartoon in Figure 1.5.

A non-viable organisation is one where most of the workers and managers suffer continuously from variety overload because they do not have enough capacity to cope with the variety of the tasks they are responsible for and/or the variety of the environment they coevolve with.

Figure 1.5 Variety overload

(Illustration by Juan David Alfonso)

A manager who does not understand her/his niche is decoupled from it, or just ignores all the signals coming from it, and will be unable to react effectively to events that may require an agile organisational response. Failing to do so continuously will impact organisational viability. In other words, a lack of understanding of situations that may affect organisational viability (lack of variety) will threaten organisational viability: or as Beer (1979) said, *sheer ignorance* is the lethal attenuator of variety. The quest for organisational viability is therefore closely related to the quest for handling variety in a way that allows the organisation to adapt rapidly, and implement its tasks effectively, while coupling with its niche in ways that are sustainable for all organisational stakeholders, both internal and external.

As the VSM was inspired by the understanding of neural networks, as an ideal type of organisation to manage complex tasks in turbulent or changing environments, it abandons the traditional understanding of single/individual managers as those having the authority and the knowledge to guide or lead an organisation towards particular purposes. These old-fashioned ideas of leadership are no longer appropriate in the current context of the continuous change and chaos that we live in. Instead, the VSM refers to meta-systemic management (M) as those roles which are there to provide support (e.g., human, technical, financial, legal) to operational tasks, to guarantee they have an optimal context for self-organising to implement the organisational purpose. But they do not directly add value to the operational teams, which are empowered to self-manage and self-govern their processes. They only exercise authority when required to ensure cohesion.

Heinz Von Foerster, another pioneering cybernetician, explained in the 1970s, that an optimal structure of a team of people developing a task, depends on the complexity of the task and of the interaction between team and niche. For simple tasks, and for organisations operating in stable environments, a pyramidal structure where one person coordinates and organises everyone's tasks normally works well – as proven throughout the Industrial Revolution. For more complex, more ambiguous tasks, operating in more fluid environments, more interactions are required between team members to understand and deal with the task; in these cases, a flatter structure, self-organised, with limited central control is normally more effective (Von Foerster, 1995).

But this lesson hasn't yet been assimilated by most contemporary organisations, many of which do operate in fluid, volatile, complex environments trying to implement complex tasks, but are still fixed to very traditional, hierarchical, authoritarian, and rigid structures. Traditional management theories (as in Fayol (1984) and Taylor (1967)) understand organisational structures as hierarchies where the top layer decides on policy, the middle layer decides on strategy, and the lower layer does the operation and produces the organisational outcomes, by following orders from managers. They describe structures as organisational charts which mostly indicate relationships of power and authority.

According to Beer, these are at the core of poor organisational performance; and it could only be improved by adopting a new paradigm of management based in understanding organisations as complex self-organising systems. The VSM suggests a heterarchical model in which organisations operate as cohesive *neural networks,* where each operational network (a strategic business unit) is autonomous self-organised, self-regulated, and self-referenced, while the whole organisational network remains cohesive by sharing purposes, knowledge, and resources and relating to each other and to their niche in a harmonic way – see cartoon in Figure 1.6.

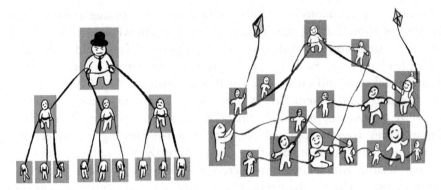

Figure 1.6 Hierarchical vs. heterarchical organisations

(Illustration by Thom Igwe-Walker)

Allowing individual creativity, spontaneous cooperation, and networking creates a richer and more nurturing learning environment, where people can develop themselves, increase their commitment to the organisation, promote innovation, and evolve into more agile and sustainable organisations. Hierarchical structures inhibit innovation and adaptation, reduce development of trusting relationships, and create bureaucratic, rigid, and slow-reacting organisations.

Why We Need to Evolve Towards Sustainable Self-Governed Organisations

When Beer developed the original VSM theory on the 1970s and 1980s, he envisioned a democratic, self-governed organisation, supported by real-time information. Implementing this management model is more likely to succeed if supported by computers and the internet, which were only being developed in those early days. It is only now, well into the 21st century, when we have fully developed the required cultural and technological context to enable a full VSM implementation. We have access now to a fairly robust global communication infrastructure, to real-time information in many aspects of our lives (weather, news, stock exchange, etc.) and we are moving fast to the 'Internet of Things.'

Many companies and governments are beginning to realise the need for flatter, more networked types of structures to deal with the volatility, un-certainty complexity, and ambiguity of the business and societal environ-ments.[2] More than ever, Beer's pioneering theory is inspiring innovative ways to shift into more agile and adaptive organisations. Nevertheless, the progress towards more sustainable self-governed organisations and societies has been slower and less effective than expected, as proven by main negative threats which we are facing currently: (a) the escalating negative impacts of global climate change, (b) the difficulty to deal effectively and fairly with the global pandemics, and (c) the lack of global self-governance to keep human society peaceful, i.e., by avoiding a world war which could well result in our humanity's holocaust.

In Espinosa and Walker (2017), we suggested that a main reason why current attempts to make progress towards more sustainable businesses and societies are not working fast enough is because of our current mindset: Businesses and societies keep using ideas, concepts, and methodologies that evolved in a previous age, and which are no longer relevant or capable of dealing with contemporary challenges and paradoxes. We consider that by better understanding the management of complexity in businesses and societies, we would have a better chance to dramatically change our current practices and beliefs, especially with regard to progressing towards sustainable self-governance. And that it may help us to progress towards the required massive systemic change for our society's sustainability. As Rifkin (2019, p. 211) says:

> The vast majority of cities, regions and nations are still mired in siloed green projects and initiatives, tucked inside the body of an outdated twentieth century fossil fuel paradigm and its accompanying business model and form of governance.

Despite some progress towards stronger approaches to sustainability, there is still a significant gap between theory and practice: even if most businesses are now interested in implementing corporate sustainability (CS), most of them recognise that there is still lots to learn about implementing CS strategies. Regarding both business and societies' sustainability, it is in filling this gap that our research has focused: What is the sort of organisational context that would be more useful to improve possibilities of success when implementing sustainability strategies? As will be argued throughout this book, we believe that a massive adherence to an ethos of sustainability and equity, together with a self-organised and networked approach to organisation provide the best context for progressing towards sustainability. The following chapters will develop these arguments in more detail.

Summary

This chapter has introduced the basic cybernetic laws and principles, on which Beer's theory of viability is based, including Ashby's Law of Requisite Variety, and has introduced a view of organisations as viable and sustainable learning networks. It described the systemic nature of organisational learning, as the cognitive process we experience while interacting with ourselves, with others, and our niche, while co-creating an organisation, and while critically learning about our interactions.

In an increasingly complex society, where the nature of relationships between individuals, families, workers, and institutions has dramatically changed in the last decades, with the appearance of new technologies and the internet, the need for new forms of organising ourselves becomes vital. Old-style hierarchical authoritarian organisations do not exhibit the level of flexibility and adaptability demanded by contemporary businesses and institutions. Many contemporary researchers in business and management have strongly supported the need for a radical shift towards more networked and heterarchical modes of organisation, an idea suggested by the pioneer cyberneticians when explaining the original ideas of self-organisation, variety, and complexity management.

This book aims to contribute to this shift in our way of thinking and managing ourselves, our businesses, and societies, by developing S. Beer's original theory of organisational viability to include sustainability strategy and practice more clearly. In particular, it aims to offer an insightful view of our viability and sustainability approach, including clear and accessible methodological guidelines to put it into practice. This book offers a wide exploration of different fields and scales of application, from the individual to the business, community, and national levels. It offers briefings on current research and practice in fields like education, public management, and community development.

Notes

1 https://orcid.org/my-orcid?orcid=0000–0002-5200–7613
2 This concept of VUCA organisations was developed also in the 1970s and has only recently become popular in the business jargon.

References

Allen, P., Maguire, S., & McKelvey, B. (2011). *The SAGE Handbook of Complexity and Management*. London: SAGE Publications Ltd.

Asby, R. J. B. (2021). *Thinking Systems and a process language for survival*. Charmouth: Triarchy Press.

Ashby, W. R. (1962). 'Principles of the self-organizing system' in Von Foerster, H. & Zopf, G. W. Jr. (eds.), *Principles of Self-Organization: Transactions of the University of Illinois Symposium*. London: Pergamon Press, pp. 255–278.

Ashby, W. R. (1981). 'Requisite variety and its implications for the control of complex systems' in Conant, R. (ed.), *Mechanisms of Intelligence: Ross Ashby's writings on Cybernetics*. The Systems Inquiry Series. California: Intersystems Publications.

Bateson, G. (1980). *Mind and Nature – A Necessary Unity*. Glasgow: Fontana.

Bateson, G. (1973). *Steps to an Ecology of Mind*. London: Jason Aronson Inc.

Beer, S. (1979). *Heart of the Enterprise*. Chichester: John Wiley & Sons.

Beer, S. (1981). *Brain of the Firm*. Chichester: John Wiley & Sons.

Beer, S. (1985). *Diagnosing the System for Organizations*. Chichester: John Wiley & Sons.

Biggart, J., Dudley, P., King, F., & Ashgate, A. (eds.) (1998). *Alexander Bogdanov and the Origins of Systems Thinking in Russia*. Brookfield: Aldershot.

Bohorquez, L. E., & Espinosa, A. (2015). 'Theoretical approaches to managing complexity in organizations: a comparative analysis', *Estudios Gerenciales*, 31, pp. 20–29.

Cannon, W. B. (1934). 'The wisdom of the body', *Nature*, 133, pp. 82.

Espinosa, A., Harnden, R., & Walker, J. (2008). 'A complexity approach to sustainability – Stafford Beer revisited', *European Journal of Operational Research*, 187(2), pp. 636–651.

Espinosa, A., & Walker, J. (2017). 'A complexity approach to sustainability: Theory and application'. 2nd ed. *Book Series on Complexity – Imperial College*. London: World Scientific Press.

Fayol, H. (1984). *General and Industrial Management* (revised by Irwin Gray). London: Pitman.

Helfat, C., Finkelstein, S., Mitchell, W., Peteraf, M., Singh, H., Teece, D. J., & Winter, S. G. (2009). *Dynamic capabilities: Understanding strategic change in organizations*. London: John Wiley & Sons.

Holland, J. H. (1992). 'Complex adaptive systems', *A New Era in Computation*, 121(1), pp. 17–30.

Kauffman, S. A. (1995). *At home in the universe: The search for laws of self-organization and complexity*. Oxford: Oxford University Press.

Lorentz, E. (1996). *The Essence of Chaos*. Washington, D.C.: University of Washington Press.

Maturana, H., & Varela, F. (1980). *Autopoiesis and Cognition: The Realization of the Living*. Dordrecht: Readel.

Maturana, H., & Varela, F. (1988). *The Tree of Knowledge: The Biological Roots of Human Understanding*. Boston: Shambala.

McCulloch, W. (1965). *Embodiments of Mind*. Cambridge, MA: MIT Press.

McCulloch, W. S., & Pitts, W. H. (1943). 'A logical calculus of the ideas immanent in nervous activity', *Bulletin of Mathematical Biophysics*, 5, pp. 115–133.

Miller, G. A. (1956). 'The Magical Number seven plus or minus two: Some limits on our capacity of processing information', *Psychological Review*, 63, pp. 81–97.

Rifkin, J. (2019). *The Green New Deal*. New York: St. Martin's Press.

Schwaninger, M. (2009). *Intelligent Organisations: Powerful Models for Systemic Management*. St Gallen: Springer.

Taylor, F. W. (1967). *The principles of scientific management*. New York: W W Norton.

Von Bertalanffy, L. (1968). *General System Theory: Foundations, Development, Applications*. New York: George Braziller. Revised edition 1976: ISBN 0-8076-0453-4.

Von Foerster, H. (1981). *Observing Systems*. Salinas: Intersystems.

Von Foerster, H. (ed) (1995). *Cybernetics of Cybernetics: Or, the control of control and the communication of communication*. Minneapolis: Future Systems Inc.

Wiener, N. (1965). *Cybernetics or Control and Communication in the Animal and the Machine*. 2nd edition. Cambridge, MA: MIT Press.

Whittaker, D. (ed) (2009). *Think before you think: Social Complexity and knowledge of knowing*. Oxon, UK: Wavestone Press.

Chapter 2

Organisational Viability (and Sustainability)

The Need for more Resilient Organisations and Societies

In the early days of systems and cybernetics sciences, the need for more re-silient businesses and societies was only beginning to be recognised at the global level. Awareness of the human impact on global climate change was still in its infancy at that time. The Brundtland Report: 'Our Common Future,' produced by the World Commission on Environment and Development, provided an original framework for understanding the idea of *sustainable development* worldwide. They defined sustainable development as '*development that meets the needs of the present without compromising the ability of future generations to meet their needs*' (WCED, 1987, pp. 8). It has taken several decades for global acceptance of the need to make fast and dramatic changes in our businesses and society to ensure a sustainable future for generations to come.

Even with clear advances in the right direction, our progress towards a more sustainable global society is worryingly slow. CO_2 and methane emis-sions continue to grow beyond acceptable limits, and global temperature and sea level keep rising at a much faster rate than predicted a decade ago. The number of extreme weather events is higher than ever. The Antarctic, Artic, and the Greenland ice sheets are melting faster than expected (Pritchard et al., 2012). Biodiversity destruction has increased to unprecedented levels, and industrial agriculture continues to produce massive soil degradation. The re-cent coronavirus pandemic is also related to the loss of biodiversity, and we are all aware of the damage it has brought to our individual, working, and social lives. Not to mention the threat of a third World War, launched recently by Putin with his invasion to Ukraine.

These current global trends raise serious alerts concerning the sustainability of our current ways of interacting between industries, human society, and nature, and specifically, about the economic growth paradigm that underlies most of the current global neo-liberal approach to economics. As Beer used to say, the very idea of 'sustainable development' is an oxymoron, as there isn't anything less

DOI: 10.4324/9780429490835-3

sustainable than understanding development as continued economic growth; see Espinosa and Walker (2017, pp. 315–386). To be viable and sustainable, businesses and societies need to accept their 'limits to growth' (Meadows et al., 2004) and learn how to self-govern themselves more sustainably. They can't just grow without constraints, and they must only grow without causing severance from its niche. As Klein (2015, p. 21) says, the only path to more sustainable societies is to invent a new socio-economic order, as *'our economy is at war with many forms of life on Earth, including human life.'*

The lack of faster progress towards sustainability may be partly related to the fact that many organisations still follow what Solow (1993) calls a 'weak' approach to sustainability. Such organisations seem to be more worried about providing evidence that they are complying with basic sustainability standards than about making more long-term changes in unhealthy patterns of inter-actions with their niches, even if it means giving up short-term gains. A strong approach to sustainability requires deep and sometimes dramatic transforma-tions in individual, organisational, and community values, culture, and ethos; in the way businesses manage their production and supply chains; in our ways of interacting within local communities, when using eco-systemic services; and in our way of designing and implementing eco-policies.

On an optimistic note, many of current trends could be reversed or limited, by developing more ambitious and innovative sustainability policies locally and globally. For example, Leclère et al. (2020) explain how biodiversity loss could still be reversed by proper land and conservation policies, massive changes to agricultural policies, and individual changes to our diet. Evidence that this is doable is the European Union's ambitious plans to reach zero carbon emissions by 2050 and a 50–55% cut in emissions by 2030.[2] They aim to move swiftly into a greener economy by redesigning energy generation, food consumption, transport, manufacturing, and construction systems in the next decade.

What is a Viable and Sustainable (v&s) Organisation?

Beer (1979) defined a viable system as a 'system capable of independent existence,' and he identified the necessary and sufficient conditions that any living organi-sation must exhibit to remain viable. He used to say that *'the purpose of an organi-sation is what it does,'* and suggested we focus any viability analysis on the interaction between an organisation and its niche. While the VSM explains clearly the ne-cessary and sufficient conditions for organisational viability, it doesn't emphasize enough the relevance of being also sustainable, which requires from an organi-sation to fully undertake its environmental and social responsibilities.

However, there are many examples of organisations which are viable, but not necessarily sustainable, like the Mafia; or the many corporations which profit from extractive rather than regenerative businesses and don't fully undertake their corporate social responsibility. This is why, over the last decades, some of Beer's followers have been developing Beer's original theory to explain not only how an organisation can be more viable over time by improving its internal organisation, but also how it can be more sustainable and remain viable, without severance to its niche. See preliminary work in this direction in Schwaninger (2003, 2004, 2015), Espinosa et al. (2008); Espinosa and Porter (2011), Espinosa et al. (2011), Espinosa and Walker (2013, 2017), and Panagiotakopoulos et al. (2016).

Following Maturana and Varela (1988), we can describe a *'niche'* as those aspects (subset) of the environment, that a living organism is structurally coupled to in its realisation of life. As Maturana and Varela put it, it is *'organisation in its niche'* what should guide our analysis and thinking, rather than seeing them as two distinctive interacting bodies. Or, as Bateson (1973, pp. 491) said decades ago:

> *'The unit of survival is organism plus environment: we are learning by bitter experience that the organism which destroys its environment destroys itself.'*

Based on Beer's definition of a viable organisation, and considering Maturana and Varela and Bateson's insights we can say that *a viable and sustainable (v&s) organisation* is:

- Capable of independent existence without severance from its niche, or from future generations which will inhabit it.
- Its structural coupling with the niche may result (or not) in access to vital resources and knowledge to effectively implement its identity.
- Is capable of surviving with the resources it has access to.
- Its products or services are welcomed and required by its niche.
- It doesn't result in severance from its social or ecological niche.
- It contributes to improving the quality of life of its members and the communities it interacts with.
- It preserves and/or enhances the biodiversity and health of the ecosystems in its niche.

In other words, an organisation is v&s as a result of healthy patterns of co-evolution with its niche (e.g., with customers, suppliers, communities, competitors, regulators, etc). Its way of developing and delivering products or services is acceptable in the niche's culture and norms and it does not abuse its ecological services. It also takes responsibility for the wellbeing of the local communities it interacts with. Remaining viable and sustainable over time, requires an organisation to perform effectively and efficiently when implementing its purposes, without severance to its niche.

The Physiological Inspiration

As mentioned before, Beer was inspired by the work of Warren McCulloch, explaining the way the brain coordinates physiological operations with the muscles and organs of the body. McCulloch described the workings of the brain-body system, where each of the organs has autonomy in its operation, but collectively shares information and other physiological resources and coordinates body functions through the neural networks of the central and autonomic nervous systems. Beer explained in detail in his book 'Brain of the Firm,' the physiological analogy between the body-brain system and an organisation versus its subsidiaries' interactions (Beer, 1981, p. 131).

Broadly speaking, Beer's identified a structure of the human neurophysiology, which is invariant and is applicable likewise to neurophysiology and human organisations. Inspired by this physiological analogy, Beer designed the Viable System Model as a network of operational, autonomous, self-managed, and self-regulated units, coordinated by meta-systemic management roles. A neural network type of organisation is the most effective type of organisation to cope with the complexity of a continuously changing environment.

Inspired by Beer's analogy, Figure 2.1 illustrates the physiological metaphor with examples of the physiological analogies between operational (S1) and meta-systemic management roles (Systems 2 to 5).

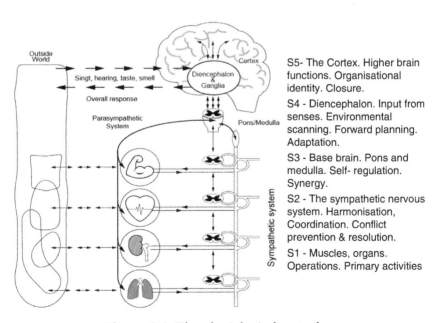

Figure 2.1 The physiological metaphor

(Illustrated by Juan David Alonso)

The Viable System Model

As explained before, the VSM depicts an operation (**O**) as an organisational unit, which is directly responsible to produce products or services, has a certain level of autonomy, and is self-regulated. Together with its meta-systemic management (**M**), it is capable of independent existence in its environmental niche (**E**), which means that it could (potentially) become a separate viable system in its own right. System 1 includes all the operational units (the ovals in Figure 2.2), which are self-managed by operational managers (the little square boxes connected to the ovals). Each element of S1 is potentially a viable system itself: its quest for viability results from effectively producing its products or services, co-evolving and keeping a balanced relationship with its niche, while dealing with its own internal dynamics.

The metasystem (M) supports the operational units and their management by providing them with additional resources, skills, technology, and infra-structure to support them in developing their purposes and core tasks. It provides the regulatory mechanisms to help them becoming more than the sum of its parts (being stronger together). This involves not only support but also restrictions of autonomy where needed for the benefit of the whole. A viable system contains and is contained within other viable systems. Therefore, every organisation can be mapped as an element of S1 of another organisation embedding it at a higher level of organisation. And every operational unit may contain subsidiaries, i.e., smaller operational units, which are the components of S1.

Figure 2.2 represents an example of a viable system with six components of S1 (1a, 1b, to 1f) inside its operational oval. The metasystem is represented by a diamond shape. The five types of meta-systemic management services, that Beer called Systems 2 to 5, will be explained in detail in the following sections. As shown in the figure, each subsidiary is also a viable (and hopefully also sustainable) system, so they are also represented as three smaller nested viable systems. The squiggly lines connecting the three operational ovals represent interactions between the elements of S1.

To assess how *viable and sustainable* is an organisation, we first need to understand its identity and then we need to be able to understand the way the organisation interacts with its socio-ecological niche, before mapping its internal organisation following VSM criteria. The following are broad questions we may want to answer as the starting point of a v&s analysis:

- What does this organisation exchange with its niche?
- What is the value added to the niche as a result of what the organisation has been doing?

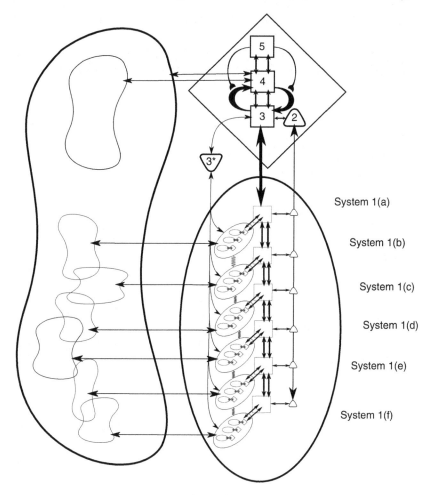

Figure 2.2 The viable system model

(Illustration by Jon Walker[3])

- Or conversely: what is the damage produced in the niche (environmental, social, and/or economic) because of the organisation's existence and operation?
- How resilient and adaptive is it? i.e., how effectively is it co-evolving with its niche?
- Does it develop its environmental and social responsibilities (as a pre-requisite for sustainability)?
- Is it potentially capable of independent existence without severance to its niche, in the middle and long terms?

We can broadly respond to these questions at the beginning of a VSM diagnosis, but a more in-depth and evidence-based response requires a deeper study into the way the organisation is organised: how it relates to its niche and what patterns of interactions it develops among its internal and external stakeholders. These are broad and sometimes difficult questions as they don't have a unique answer, but it is by acknowledging the shortfalls and limitations that constrain organisational learning and adaptation that we can begin to act upon them aiming to develop a more viable and sustainable (v&s) organisation.

The next sections provide the language and criteria to map an organisation as a v&s system in detail, and to explore for evidence to respond to the previous broader questions, at different scales within an organisation. I will use examples of a recent v&s project in a group of eight schools in Romania (ELF Schools) to illustrate the theory.

> *Early in 2019, one of my MBA students, Vladimir Pop (VP) called me to discuss the possibility of starting a v&s project in ELF, a family-owned school in Cluj, Romania, which now includes five kindergartens, two primary schools, and one upper primary and high school, all distributed in different sectors of Cluj. ELF is one of the best private schools in the country and continued to attract many new students every year. The owners, Vladimir Pop and his sister Ana, have accepted the challenge to expand the school, and in order to be ready for it, they wanted to improve the school's resilience. This and the following chapter bring examples from the v&s project we did in ELF in 2019.*

System 1 (S1)

As said before, the VSM is inspired by a model of organisation as a neural network, which means that each one of the network's components should be itself a viable system, therefore self-organised and self-managed. S1s are the operational units that add value by implementing products or services. To be viable and sustainable, S1 should have enough freedom to do so, i.e., enough autonomy and capability for self-management and self-governance while developing products or services, while taking fully its social and ecological responsibilities.

A main characteristic of S1s is therefore what I call their *'responsible autonomy.'* They freely interact with their niches' stakeholders (e.g., customers, suppliers, local community) to make sure they deliver the agreed products or services within the agreed levels of quality and timing and assuming fully their social and ecological responsibilities. Such autonomy is constrained to some extent by the need for *'cohesion' with other operational units at lower and higher recursive levels. And it is also constrained by the ethos of sustainability which would ensure no action is taken that violates basic social and ecological responsibilities.* As Beer (1979, p. 146) says:

> *it's a condition of existence for the operational element that it subsist*
>
> *within a larger whole, containing other operational elements.*

It is the interaction between the operational and the cohesion forces which defines autonomy (i.e., freedom) in a viable system. Undoubtedly, some of this freedom is constrained by environmental interventions (e.g., environmental policies constraining possible use of resources, or regional politics affecting the organisational possibilities for action). Also, it is constrained by interactions with other S1s, and by interactions with meta-systemic management. When the meta-system intervenes (e.g., in the interest of fairness or cohesion within all S1s), it diminishes (or increases) the variety available to each S1.

To ensure viability (and sustainability), the meta-system should minimise its interventions along the vertical axis: it should only intervene by exception to guarantee organisational cohesion or to protect the organisational viability and/or reputation. It is important to note, however, that autonomy and cohesiveness are functions of the *purpose* of the system, and *systemic purpose* is a subjective phenomenon. Therefore, freedom depends on the perception of systemic purpose.

A clear organisational paradox emerges from understanding this theory: meta-systemic management when working to maintain cohesiveness, may end up increasingly 'growing amplifiers' in the downwards path or attenuating too much variety, which results in institutional pain and dismay. This creates an organisational paradox: how to decide between guaranteeing operational autonomy and maintaining cohesion.

At a practical level, once we have understood broadly the organisational purpose, we need to distinguish which are the components of any S1. We can say that an operational unit is a S1 if its products and services are those which implement what the purpose of the organisation states. And, if:

- It is directly responsible for producing:

  - Specific *types of products or services,* OR

  - Products or services for a particular *type of client,* OR

  - Products or services in a particular *geographical niche,* OR

  - Products or services in a particular *time shift* – using shared infrastructure (e.g., a factory or a school).

- Has a clear niche it is embodied in, and it interacts with

- Has some autonomy for managing its tasks and resources
- Has self-management capabilities (i.e., operational management roles)
- Is represented as a profit centre in the organisational accounts
- It has a physical or virtual space shared by its workers and operational management

Figure 2.3. presents a typical representation of a S1 (or of a whole organisation) as a viable system, interacting with its niche.

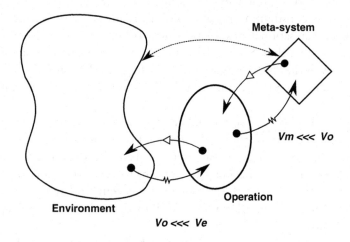

Figure 2.3 System 1 [4]

(Illustration by Jon Walker)

In a viable system, the interactions between operations and operational management, as well as the interactions between operations and their local niche follow the Law of Requisite Variety. The VSM distinctions help practitioners to reflect on a current organisational design, how well it matches its niche's variety, and its capacity to react properly to unexpected changes at each level of organisation.

For a S1 to be v&s it has to develop a balanced relationship with its socio-ecological niche, which means surviving without damaging the possibilities for survival of the future generations, which means working on a regenerative rather than extractive relationship with its ecological niche. And in a socially responsible relationship with its socio-economic ecosystem. To achieve it, a S1 has to have an ethos of sustainability embedded in its policies, culture, strategies, and processes and in the way of observing itself and self-assessing its overall performance. As a recursive theory, a S1 cannot be viable unless the organisation it belongs to is viable. No organisation can survive if its socio-ecological niche loses its own viability. This is why the theory of organisational viability and sustainability is a relational and recursive theory.

> *For example, in ELF – at the operational level, "O" could represent a school's grade including the different courses, and all the students and teachers' interactions. The teachers have both operational (i.e., teaching) and/or operational management roles (i.e., headteachers, managing teachers, and students in a grade). The environment includes the families; suppliers (e.g., of books, technology, food); competitors (e.g., local schools offering same grade of education); educational researchers and innovators; the international educational community; and local, regional, national, and educational authorities. To be viable and sustainable, each grade must develop quality education, and hopefully include in its syllabus developing academic skills and skills for respecting people and its surrounding socio-ecological niche.*

System 2 (S2)

In a viable system, each S1 must be itself a viable system which means it should be as (responsibly) autonomous as possible. Each S1 has its own specific purposes and tasks, and they all naturally share some resources and compete for others (i.e., money, people, technology, and infrastructure). As each S1 has its own pace, timing, and levels of expertise, it is natural that there are always possibilities for conflicts between them to emerge. S2 is there to prevent these conflicts from appearing and/or from escalating and thus becoming an impediment to good organisational performance. Beer (1979) refers to it as an 'anti-oscillatory device.'

A major risk of self-organisation is that by operating autonomously, S1s may end up behaving like isolated units and heading off in their own direction. Therefore, they risk diminishing organisational cohesion and missing opportunities for sharing knowledge and resources. We can refer to this as the *'autonomy. vs. cohesion dilemma.'* This may also result from S1 misinterpreting its freedom as lack of any constraints. To avoid this risk, the meta-systemic management (Systems 2 to 5) needs to clarify the 'rules of the game' (e.g., organisational purpose, protocols, norms, ethos, and values), which are different than command and control. These rules of the game constrain the possibilities for action of S1s while providing a context for them to act cohesively.

S2's role is to prevent oscillations among Systems 1 without exceeding the minimal variety reduction necessary to maintain organisational cohesion. Otherwise, rather than harmonising S1s operations, S2 would take an oppressive role, which in VSM terms is highly undesirable! So here we refer only to S2 managing constraints in terms of ensuring cohesion. An S2 type of role is one that aims to 'damp oscillations' by preventing conflicts: for example, by using timetables in a school to share teaching rooms, sport fields, laboratories, and the theatre; or by distributing the time of a specialised teacher among classes.

S2 also works by dealing with unforeseen oscillations after certain events (e.g., the ambulance coming to pick up a boy who got hurt in a fight at school, and the schoolteachers organising all children to allow space in the fields for the ambulance to arrive). Every S1 is exercising freedom to fulfil its operational responsibilities, while it also needs to behave cooperatively with other S1s to exercise its corporate responsibility. This implies very high variety of interactions between S1s and therefore very high probabilities of oscillations to emerge. This is how S2 evolves: by designing shared understandings, clarifying roles, and implementing practices and tools to prevent any oscillations from escalating and threatening organisational viability.

To deploy requisite variety, an S2 must have a continuous role: it can't deploy requisite variety if designed for example as a sporadic committee. It must be structurally coupled to operations. S2 always happens 'outside the command channel.' as represented in Figure 2.4, as it is *not a control mechanism*, but an anti-oscillatory *service* to S1.

Typical examples of S2 *roles* in a business are those responsible for designing and operating *conversational spaces* to address specific tensions among operational staff. A conflict resolution approach with facilitators promoting dialogue and preventing stressful relationships to escalate would be an example of an anti-oscillatory *mechanism* dealing with emerging conflict. Other examples of S2 *roles* dealing with issues in advance, that is to say, anticipating and preventing oscillations are designing technical and/or process standards and communication protocols (e.g., providing standard ways of recording expenses and incomes, which may avoid (financial) oscillations among operational units). Examples of S2 mechanisms are shared values; recruitment standards; information and communication technology standards to avoid communication breakdowns; quality control procedures to avoid disparate experiences from customers from different branches of the same organisation; and business processes standards among different branches of the same company.

In ELF, even if every school operates at a different location and offers services to children from different age groups, they all have the ELF brand name, they all share the same identity and values. They also share meta-systemic services (people, finances, technology, and infrastructure management); and they are all expected to operate with similar quality standards. Examples of S2 roles identified in ELF were: Managing complaints about students' or teachers' behaviours, implementing teaching quality standards, managing sustainability standards, designing accounting and fees procedures, and designing the annual school calendar. Examples of S2

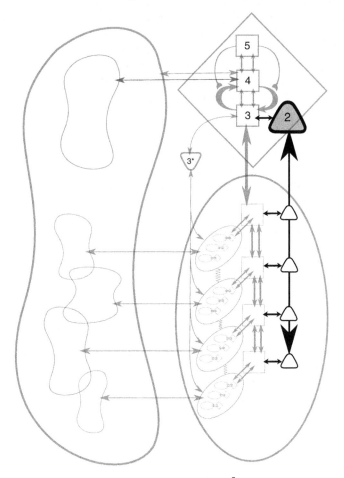

Figure 2.4 System 2^5

(Illustration by Jon Walker)

mechanisms are teaching standards and guidelines, students' academic information systems, headmasters' weekly coordination meeting, and timetabling.

System 3 (S3)

S3 is aware of what is going on 'inside' the organisation and 'now,' in the present time. It represents the 'general management,' including different types of managerial functions (i.e., for managing people, financial resources, infrastructure, and technology). This is different from 'operational management,' which has been described before as the management of each operational unit in S1.

S3: Generating Synergies

As shown in Figure 2.5, S3 facilitates interactions between general and operational management and develops a synoptic systemic viewpoint of operations, operational management, and environmental interactions within S1. By encompassing a systemic view of the entire operation, this meta-systemic management role aims at generating *synergies* among the operational elements. It is from mutual support between operational units that synergistic behaviours emerge. It is therefore a fundamental aspect of S3 to create a context of collaboration to guarantee synergetic relationships among operations. For example, the financial director is a S3 role, seeking to achieve a synergistic use of capital and a business synergy to optimise the cash flow. The squiggly lines in Figure 2.5 represent the interactions between operational units: it is in these interactions that oscillations may occur, and we may need a S2 service to damp them when they arise.

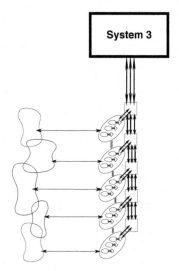

Figure 2.5 System 3[6]

(Illustration by Jon Walker)

It is through maximising autonomy and minimising intervention from the meta-system, while enhancing collaboration and generation of synergies, that a nurturing context for self-organisation is more likely to emerge. A rich context for self-organisation requires each node to be as autonomous as possible and from all of them to share the purpose of the embedding organisation and to act based on clear and shared 'rules of the game.' A required mechanism for allowing self-organisation is to have generalised access to operational information for all the members of operational and meta-systemic units, so that they all share knowledge and can synchronise their decision-making accordingly.

Aligning Meta-Systemic and Operational Management

Figure 2.5 illustrates the meta-systemic versus operational management interactions on the vertical axis: it identifies three types of communication that support recurrent patterns of interactions among general and operational managers, as follows:

- *Resource Negotiation*: periodically, the operational management (S1) meets the general management (S3) to discuss the required resources (money, people, technology, and infrastructure) to achieve its operational goals and implement the agreed tasks. A budget is agreed, which details the level of resources that the metasystem would make available to the operations to achieve their goals. For as long as S1 manages to operate within the agreed resources in a particular period and achieve its agreed goals, there is no need for re-negotiation. This channel is then used when there have been dramatic changes in the levels of service and a re-negotiation is required; or every time there has been changes in the niche which demand self-organisation and adaptation, and therefore re-negotiating expected outcomes and required resources.

- *Accountability*: the relationship between the organisation and each of the Systems 1 relies on all Systems 1 having clear purposes, clear boundaries for defining their operational tasks, in other words a clear '*contract.*' This means that, having agreed on the specific tasks, the operational team is responsible for the expected delivery times and quality standards for the expected results. This channel is used for reaching agreements on these issues between general and operational management, and for verifying the operational teams' performance. In a v&s organisation performance includes achieving organisational goals while fulfilling sustainability standards. To respect operational autonomy, this channel must be designed to guarantee that operational management agrees with general management on the criteria for self-assessing (sustainable) performance, rather than expecting the general management to decide upon it and impose it on operations. This is at the core of the idea of self-regulation, established by pioneering cybernetic theories and distinguishes cybernetic from traditional management.

- *Legal and Corporate Norms*: Every organisation operates within the norms agreed on at upper levels of recursive organisation; for example, a school will act following the educational norms and policies established by the Ministry of Education. A bank will follow the Ministry of Finance's norms as well as the international and national bank regulatory bodies. A manufacturing corporation will follow global sustainability standards. Inside an organisation, this is the channel where the S3 do the checks and balances to ensure that operations comply with corporate, global, and legal policies and norms. For example, *'we will never service these kinds of clients'*; or *'we will always follow these financial bonus policies.'* In general, the meta-systemic management will NOT intervene in the way of doing things by a S1 unless that S1 violates basic norms, and consequently, its actions can threaten the viability (and/or reputation) of the organisation. Only in this situation, S3 intervenes inside S1.

In ELF, we identified several S3 roles for each school and for ELF as a whole, e.g., managing finances, managing information and communication technology, managing infrastructure, managing people, managing suppliers, schools' management (headmasters), and assessing educational performance. Examples of S3 mechanisms are annual grades and teachers' assessments, procedures for negotiating resources for each school, and Educational Secretariat norms for school's assessment.

Complementarity of S3 and S2 Roles

All the common services that contribute to synergy are S3 functions. Nevertheless, it is important to clarify that most S3 roles work jointly with associated S2 roles: S2 is a subsystem of S3, focused on damping oscillations. While S3 develops a broad view of the main issues (performance, resource management, legal and normative context), S2 develops an operational (day to day) view of same issues and provides the supporting heuristics, mechanisms, and/or tools for preventing oscillations, like disseminating values, standards, and protocols; and for managing information and communication on a day-to-day basis on the broader issues dealt by S3.

As the idea of a viable system is to provide as much autonomy as possible – *only limited by the system's cohesion (including synergy)* – then the operational management must work within the level of available resources, within existing corporate and industrial norms, and it must make itself accountable to the general management. Sometimes generating synergies implies a certain loss of freedom but if S1 understands that it will result in improved organisational viability, it shouldn't be difficult to accept. The best way to implement a collaborative S3 management is by co-opting operational managers from S1 to act jointly as a S3.

A clear example of this comes from ELF's five kindergartens: they had two co-ordinators managing two kindergartens each, and another managing one kindergarten. The three coordinators met once a week in a coordination meeting, where they shared their experience with children, teachers, and parents, identified common issues, and addressed them jointly and shared individual solutions and good practice. They, in v&s terms, have created a S3 team, by making joint decisions and acting together in such a way.

The Control Dilemma

Another *dilemma* for managing complexity in organisations arises from the interactions between S3 and operational managers. If the general management creates an autocratic culture and/or has a micro-management style, then (s)he may try to make detailed decisions in the day-to-day operations on behalf of its operational managers. (S)he will therefore not really understand the high variety involved in the interconnectivity operation (O) vs. environment (E), and between each operation (O) and its management (M). There is no way S3 can deploy the requisite variety to make well informed and timely decisions without operational management's inputs.

The more ignorant S3 is, the more information from operational managers (s)he would require. The more information (s)he gets, the less time (s)he has to digest it, to inform her/his decisions, so the less control (s)he has. This is the 'Control Dilemma,' which is one of the most typical pathologies of misman-agement, arising from the lack of understanding of Ashby's Law. It is one of the most common organisational pathologies identified by years of practice of Beer and his followers.

> *From the preliminary interviews we did at ELF we noticed that there was evidence of the S3 suffering from this control dilemma: the headmaster was taking too much direct responsibilities (e.g., dealing directly with teachers' assessments from all schools) and was overloaded by operational variety. The management team began to realise, that they need to address this control dilemma, especially if the complexity of the niche was going to increase exponentially once the new schools were in place.*

A very important aspect of managing complexity in organisations is the de-velopment of trust between people: only if the operational staff and managers feel they are trusted, can they deploy requisite variety. They should be trusted to apply amplifiers to manage their operational variety, and to apply simple rules properly in the interest of legality or synergy.

System 3* (S3*)

System 3* is an alternative channel to capture complementary information from the operational level, to complement what S3 gets through the three channels explained in the previous section. S3* is a non-routine and sporadic audit channel, required to '*take the temperature*' of what's going on at the operational level, both in terms of workers' well- being, working environment, robustness of the existing process, technological infrastructure, and working conditions. It helps S3 to review the way operational processes are managed and resourced, or to alert S3 to identify any other issue that may require its support or advice.

Regarding the management of 'vertical variety' (i.e., the interaction between the metasystem and S1), Beer explained that there are six vertical channels: (i) resource bargain and accountability; (ii) legal and corporate norms; (iii) communications between operational units (squiggly lines between operations); (iv) communications between environmental agents environmental intersects; (v) communications in the anti-oscillatory channel (S2); and (vi) the sporadic audit channel (S3*).

All of the other five channels described above deal with the variety between environmental agents, between operations, and between them and meta-systemic management. However, there is always some variety that is produced at the operational level that can't be easily accessed at the meta-systemic management level, and which may be crucial for alerting or awakening it; for example, when current behaviours are indicative of situations getting out of the control for the operational management.

The purpose of S3* is to sporadically provide fresh information, coming directly from the operational level, which hasn't been 'transduced' by the managerial channels (e.g., the accountability channel), but which can complement formal information flowing through other channels. S3* can provide 'a fresh look' at situations informally, which complements meta-systemic management views on the operational dynamics and behaviours (see channel '*vi*' in Figure 2.6).

Beer (1979, p. 217) explained the need for keeping balances between horizontal (e.g., operations vs niche; and operations vs operational management) and vertical varieties (as in the above figure), as the '1st Axiom of Management.' He suggests that the sum of horizontal variety that cannot be met by the components of S1 (we call it *residual variety*) must equate with the vertical variety (i.e., disposed to the meta-system), required to operate all the vertical channels, to guarantee systems cohesion. A typical example of S3* mechanisms are sporadic, informal audits. Or a complaint box, where staff can leave comments or suggestions, anonymously, to awake meta-systemic management of situations that may be getting out of control and which it may not be aware of through formal channels.

System 4 (S4)

While Systems 1, 2, and 3 can jointly deal with the organisational operation on a day-to-day basis, they are mostly concentrated with the '*Inside and*

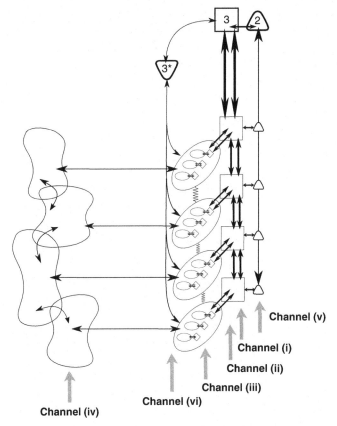

Channel (v)

Channel (i)

Channel (ii)

Channel (iii)

Channel (vi)

Channel (iv)

Figure 2.6 System 3*[7]

(Illustration by Jon Walker)

Now' and thus do not take care of what is emerging in the total external environment. On their own, they can't guarantee long-term viability or sustainability for the whole system (only for themselves)! A v&s organisation needs also to observe and reflect on how changes in its niche (i.e., the larger environment of the whole organisation) may pose opportunities and challenges for its long-term sustainability. It may be either because ongoing niche's changes create barriers to organisational v&s in the long term, or because they bring new opportunities or challenges for re-inventing the organisational future.

Therefore, S4 is necessary: it is the innovation generator and the new ideas incubator. It is responsible for being attentive to the '*Outside and Then.*' It brings new information about developing possibilities in the organisation's niche for continuously re-inventing its future. It needs to be aware of relevant issues in its co-evolution with its niche, that the metasystem should know about, to decide on suitable strategic and sustainability.

The increasing complexification of the global business environment has resulted in new organisational development challenges. A hundred years ago, the rate of change in the business environment was sometimes unnoticeable, so many businesses survived with a very rudimentary S4. But an attempt to do so nowadays would be fatal, as the social, ecological, and technological standards keep rising dramatically. To stay in business requires smart, adaptive, and strategic players. In developing these skills, businesses need to invest time and resources, for developing new adaptive capabilities like innovation, research, scenario analysis, strategy formulation, and sustainable development.

S4 suggests new developmental paths for organisational survival and progress. S4 includes all these roles that directly contribute to clarifying possible and desirable states for the organisation to move forward. This is clearly closely related to what a particular organisation understands by 'progress,' 'sustainability,' or 'development,' and it also depends on the niche's dominant ideologies on business or local development.

S4 role is like the *navigator* in a boat: looking up and above and suggesting changes to the boat's route to get back on track. To do so, the navigator needs to have a clear destination, a clear route – which implies of a good reading of the skies and the natural environment, good driving and steering mechanisms, and very good intuition. Each of these requires developing the navigator's specific skills and capabilities: i.e., innovation and adaptive capabilities. S4 is the organisational navigator, which is different from the captain of the boat. As is evident from this metaphor, a navigator has enormous power. It's therefore not surprising that S4 roles are normally considered senior roles and people are expected to have high levels of expertise.

To develop adaptive capabilities, an organisation must develop enough variety to understand the complexity of its socio-ecological niche and learn to deal with such complexity. The new information and communication technologies (ICTs) have contributed to reinventing our social and professional relationships in our economies and societies. Our interactions with our niche are mediated by a complex technological infrastructure including computers and the internet, which have allowed the emergence of new social and professional web-based networks. Working and socialising through them demands new skills and capabilities, e.g., for using new technologies, for communicating effectively within the emerging digital cultures.

In the search for viability and sustainability, organisations need first to do their best to interact with their niches to satisfy demand for its products or services, and access to the resources to produce them. But they need to learn to do it in ways that are socially and ecologically responsible, and still financially viable. The ethos of sustainability should penetrate every policy, strategy, and process and embed every decision. Acknowledgement of core issues for sustainability should pervade strategy and innovation decisions.

As each S1 should be in itself a viable system, therefore, it needs to develop its own meta-systemic management, including operational management, and its own Systems 2, 3, 4, and 5. It is by continuously doing a particular task that we learn more about the best ways to do it. It is also by aiming to do it better, that we continue exploring the environment for inspiration on new processes, practices, tools, and technologies to better develop our products or services. We need to rethink our processes from a sustainability perspective, and to redevelop them and our interactions with the niche, to co-evolve with it more sustainably. Therefore, each S1 needs to develop its own S4 and its own innovation and adaptive capabilities to improve their resilience in the long term within their own niche.

Figure 2.7 explains the components of S4. According to Beer (1979, pp. 234–236), a key role of S4 is to develop and to maintain an updated model of the total viable system, and a model of the unknown future. These are the main tools of adaptation and must satisfy the requirement for re-quisite variety. S4 must therefore continuously register any changes in the structure, the culture, the processes, and the technology of the organisation as a whole, and continuously map the niche's evolution, to make sure the organisation is prepared to coevolve with it, in as close as real time as possible.

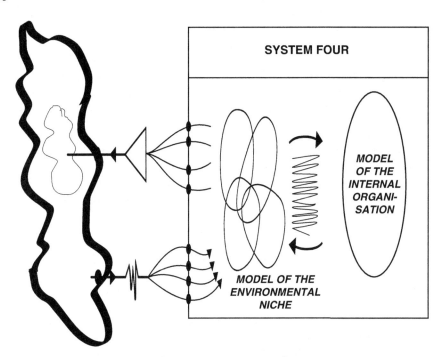

Figure 2.7 System 4[8]

(Illustration by Juan David Alonso)

In ELF, an example of a S4 amplifier was an Erasmus collaborative research project that the kindergarten coordinators attended in Sweden, to learn from educational innovators, how to operate in a learning by doing approach with children, inspired by nature-based projects. This project acted as an amplifier for developing more adaptive capabilities by retraining other teachers who didn't attend the initial Swedish training for becoming proficient in project-based learning.

S4 needs to have requisite variety to match the environmental variety and it implies choosing the best available opportunities for learning and growth. It implies also designing proper communication channels with the environment with requisite variety and proper transducers. To comprehensively understand structural coupling with its niche, S4 needs to continuously learn about: a) the local niches of each S1; b) the problematic environment of the organisation as a whole (the complete cloudy shape in Figure 2.7); and c) the unknown future environment (the smaller cloudy shape at the left of S4 in Figure 2.7).

Analogically speaking, an individual human being has a S4 for dealing with its perceived cosmos, which is larger than the sum of each of its organ's perceptions of its biological environment. Each of us takes account of our problematic environment when we ask ourselves: shall I do this? shall I go this way? In other words, we have foresight: we contemplate the consequences of alternative actions before we make decisions. Similarly, the organisation may decide to engage in forecasting activities (a typical S4 activity), to plan its future action paths.

S4 is an interactive learning system, which includes a model of itself and a model of the niche. It operates in a context of proliferating variety, so it needs to integrate all the elements relevant for its learning. Such integrated views of the environment and the developing organisation constitute what Beer calls the 'kernel' (the interactions between all the components of S4 described in Figure 2.8), which provides *focus* to the innovation and developmental activities. The decision of who would take responsibility for the activities suggested by the kernel and how they will do it is very important for S4.

Beer provides an example of a kernel as the development directorate, which is a decision-making space, supported by performance management systems summarising the state of essential variables for viability and sustainability. It provides visualisation tools that allow decision makers to focus on the most significant changes in these variables that may require of immediate action.

S4's role is exploratory and requires innovation and creativity. S4 can operate at the edge of chaos; it creates awareness of new opportunities for organisational development. S4 roles are responsible for exploring new products or services, new processes, technologies, markets; organisational development approaches and techniques; strategies for the long-term financial viability; strategic

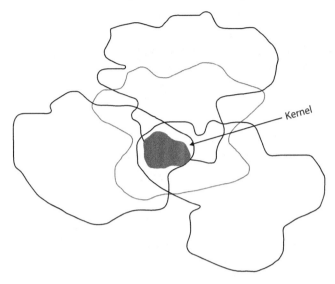

Kernel

Figure 2.8 System 4 integrated elements

(Illustration by Juan David Alonso)

partnerships; and environmental, political, and economic hazards and opportunities. Typical examples of S4 roles include innovation; research and development; financial planning; market research; strategic positioning; strategic information management; benchmarking; and corporate social responsibility.

> *At the preliminary v&s diagnosis at ELF, we identified several S4 roles, some of them developed rudimentarily, others more robustly. For example, producing teaching innovation; planning yearly events; shaping the community expectations; nurturing the school's networks; leading educational events and conferences; Erasmus Projects; designing new processes and procedures; reviewing the curriculum; forming, training; infrastructure development. Most of these S4 roles were developed by the same headmasters and teachers in their own time and, when possible for them, once covered other more urgent and immediate tasks.*

There is a clear difference between having an explicit S4 in a small or in a large organisation. In a small business the manager many times assumes S3, S4, and S5 roles, as there is no need for an independent person to occupy these roles full time, and this may work well enough for a while (depending on the complexity of the environment). The larger a corporation, the more likely it is to find several specialised roles (or even departments) taking full-time responsibility for S4 roles. Chapter 8 offers examples of using the VSM at a state level, which illustrates how different institutions are responsible for S3 and S4 roles required by the state.

Even while some S4 roles may exist in large organisations, sometimes they are not well integrated, or even integrated at all, which create dilemmas when making strategic decisions for the organisation. For example, the organisational development unit may be leading a project to redesign strategic business processes, while at the same time the strategic information unit may be leading a project to redesign strategic information systems. And the two projects may be unaware of each other, following disjunctive – or even disruptive – approaches and even duplicating the same jobs (like modelling strategic business processes with different approaches).

A powerful tool for integration of S4 activities is 'focus': the VSM provides a map to clearly plot all S4 activities in full variety, without blurring each one. S4 provides the inputs for the strategy development process, in which both S3 and S5 participate. If it manages to provide integrated, systemic strategies, there are better possibilities for collective learning, and for closing the organisational learning loop. S4 provides the information for forming a strategic position, and for inspiring organisational policies, and later on for facilitating strategy implementation.

System 5 (S5)

The nature of S5's role is clearly related to the legal nature of the organisation. For a private organisation the Board of Directors – together with the owners – will play a clear S5 role; for a cooperative, the Members Assembly will be performing a S5 function. For a school, the school board would be an S5. S5 is responsible for maintaining or revisiting the organisational identity, providing closure, developing the core values and ethos of the organisation, and defining policies. According to Beer (1979), S5 must represent the will of all people in the organisation, and it is the ultimate authority. Closure is a self-referential process: it is the snake eating its own tail. Providing closure means reflecting about the organisational identity and purpose and adjusting it according to recent organisational trajectories.

It implies observing itself and learning from its way of interacting with its niche, rethinking, when necessary, the organisational boundaries and clarifying organisational rules as well as creating a corporate ethos – an atmosphere. The only way an organisation can be v&s is if S5 manages to embed the sustainability ethos in the values of each operational (and meta-systemic) unit and roles, so strategic decisions are filtered by sustainability criterion. Closing the learning loops needs to be done continuously over time, for the organisation to be viable, as any time lags between facts and related decisions are dangerous to the entire operational system.

Every organisation (and every S1) must produce itself: it means it must continue being itself through balancing internal and external relationships.

This is the basic criterion of viability. To do so, it needs a mandatory investment for S1 to produce itself (both in terms of people and money). S3 will invest whatever is required for S1 to produce itself, and S4 may need extra resources to develop capabilities for adaptation. As a result, the power equation between S3 and S4 is always complex. Their interactions need to exhibit requisite variety. It is S5's role to be the S3/S4 balancer, which means to provide a balanced context for this interaction, which guarantees each one's (sometimes opposing) views are taken fairly into account when deciding the development path for the organisation.

S5 role is highly complex and includes lots of thinking and debate to reach an agreement. Beer calls S5 'the Multinode' (Beer, 1979, p. 265). Rather than being a hierarchical boss, S5 should include representatives of management, shareholders, investors, and even representatives of workers or trade unions. S5 should represent the will of the people (Beer, 1983a). As in every human organisation, there are always a multiplicity of viewpoints, sometimes conflicting and opposite. S5 is subject to the dynamics of power, which span variety through time in wholly unpredictable ways. Balancing variety requires of balancing power. Unless implicit tensions coming from power imbalances are surfaced and dealt properly by S5, there is no hope to reach agreements on policy and strategy required for effective self-governance.

The arrows connecting S5 with the S3 and S4 loop in Figure 2.9 mean that S5 monitors communications between S4 and S3 when making strategic decisions, e.g., about a new organisational development path and the required adjustments to policies. S5 should make sure that S3 and S4 counterbalance each other, e.g., by making sure there is a balanced representation of S4 and S3 roles supportingpolicy and strategy decisions; and by making sure S3 and S4 contributions to decision making are fair and even.

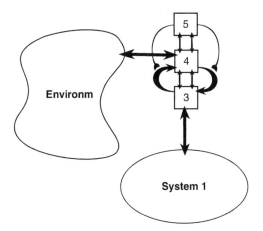

Figure 2.9 System 5[9]

(Illustration by Jon Walker)

> *In ELF, the Board of Administration is a clear S5. It meets once a year and includes a representative from the owners, all six headmasters: three teachers representing primary schools and high school, one local city council representative, and three parents. In VSM terms, the Board of Administration should contribute to close the loop on issues of identity and policy (S5), innovation and development (S4), and the school's performance (S3) and is a clear example of ELF's S5.*

A typical dilemma for achieving sustainable self-governance comes from a S4 aware of the need to invest more on achieving sustainability standards and a S3 putting pressure on short term economic gains. If S3 is too powerful and S4 too weak, S5 needs to rebalance their interaction, by strengthening S4 and constraining S3 ambitions for only short-term gains. This will only happen in S5 has fully embedded sustainability ethos and is prepared to pay for the costs of fully becoming a sustainable organisation. S5's ultimate role is supplying closure: As Beer (1979, p. 260) explains:

> *Closure is the snake eating its own tail. Closure is what makes the language complete, self-sufficient. Closure stops the entire system from exploding in shattered fragments to the end of the universe. Closure turns the system back into itself, to satisfy the criteria of viability, at its own level of recursion. Closure is the talisman of identity.*

The Recursive Viable System Theorem

One of the core characteristics of viable systems is that they exhibit recursive patterns of organisation: each S1 of a viable system is itself a viable system, which means it is 'capable of independent existence.' Therefore, each S1 should comply with all the criteria and principles for managing complexity explained in this and previous chapters. Beer explained this as the *'Recursive System Theorem'* which says:

> *In a recursive organisational structure, any viable system contains,*
>
> *and is contained in, a viable system.* (Beer, 1979, p. 118; Beer, 1985, xi)

Similar ideas of holarchies,[10] or fractal organisations,[11] have been suggested by other systems researchers. Nevertheless, Beer's idea of recursive organisations is the only one that explains a recursive organisation as one exhibiting *structural patterns of interactions* that recur at different levels of embeddedness. This concept has been compared with the Russian dolls: each doll being inside other identical dolls. Figure 2.10 offers an illustration of the idea of recursiveness.

Figure 2.10 Recursive organisation

(Illustration by Thom Igwe-Walker)

In a recursive organisational structure, each component of the system may have several sub-components embedded, each one of which could potentially have an independent existence, i.e., could be a viable system itself. Figure 2.11 shows an example of an organisation showing three levels of embedded sub-organisations, each of which is also represented as a viable system. We call the organisation as a whole, level 0; and the lower levels, levels 1, 2, etc. Each level shows the embedded sub-organisations in more

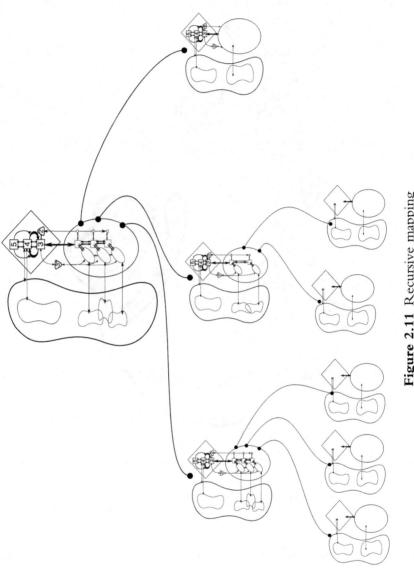

Figure 2.11 Recursive mapping

(Illustration by Jon Walker)

detail, as if looking inside it with a magnifying lens. Recursive analysis is a technique that aims to map the viable systems (operational units) contained in and containing other viable systems (operational units) in an organisation (more in Chapter 3).

When applying the VSM to support an organisation becoming more adaptive and resilient, we start by 'mapping' the organisational complexity, by identifying System 1 and the levels of recursive organisation (recursive analysis). And then by mapping *at each level of recursive organisation*, the viable systems at that level, including their related meta-systemic roles (S2 to S5).

Once the roles responsible for the five systems at each level of recursive organisation are identified, we observe how balanced the patterns of re-current interactions among the roles are. We observe if there are recurrent breakdowns in relationships which maybe pathological, and symptomatic of inappropriate management of complexity. Next chapter will explain in detail the recommended stages and tool for developing a full v&s project. Beer's (1979) Axioms and Principles of Organisation offers more detailed criteria to assess how balanced the different types of interactions (S1/S2/S3, and S3/S4/S5) are in any organisation; see Beer (1985, p. 30) and Beer (1979, pp. 99, 101, 258). The next chapter will offer detailed methodo-logical guidance to apply the VSM for supporting organisations to be more resilient, adaptive, and capable of sustainable self-governance.

Managing Complexity: Organisational Principles

According to Beer, the VSM explains the necessary and sufficient conditions for organisational viability. Requisites for organisational viability include: the existence of operational roles capable of dealing with the variety of their local niches; meta-systemic roles capable of dealing with the variety of the opera-tions (S1); and the organisation as a whole capable of dealing with environ-mental variety, which requires of being capable of being adaptive and resilient. Adaptation and resilience are the pre-requisites for self-governance. There follows more detail on the organisational principles suggested by the VSM to manage organisational and niche's complexities.

Responsible Autonomy

The interaction of *S1s vs. niches* is the horizontal axis of the VSM: it's precisely there, where managing variety is most challenging, according to Ashby's Law, which explains that the niche's variety is the largest the or-ganisation needs to learn to recognise and to deal with. We can increase the operational variety by providing more autonomy to S1 – i.e., by developing operational capabilities for self-regulation. Having more autonomy, operational teams avoid unnecessary delays in decisions going up and down the hierarchy of middle managers. Therefore, they can respond more quickly to environmental changes, co-evolve with them, and therefore adapt without having to lock anyone up!

But operational autonomy also has constraints, like working within the organisational (and environmental) rules, norms, and policies. This is particularly relevant for a v&s organisation, as environmental regulations bring even more constraints to operational autonomy. But in the long term, it provides a healthier and more resilient way of co-evolving with its niche. To operate responsibly within these constraints is to develop *responsible autonomy,* which means developing capability for making its own operational decisions, for taking full responsibility for them and for its results, and for making itself accountable. Beer (1981, p. 158) summarises S1s limits to autonomy, as follows:

- S1s must work within the organisational legal and corporate requirements.
- S1s should welcome the stabilising influence of S2 – to prevent conflict which may damage the whole organisation.
- S1s must respond to the synergetic efforts of S3.

To create a right context for organisational v&s, S1 also needs to limit its autonomy by embedding environmental and social responsibility values and norms in the operational ethos – metaphorically speaking, in *the operational DNA.*

Self-Regulation

Beer calls the roles responsible for taking care of the organisation's *'Inside and Now,'* the *Self-Regulatory Mechanism (S1/S2/S3).* Self-managed operational units naturally absorb most of the variety they generate in their interaction with their niches. The meta-systemic channels S2, S3, and S3*absorb the residual variety not managed by the operational units interacting with their niches. This is what Beer (1979, pp. 216) calls the *'1st Axiom of Management':*

> *The sum of horizontal variety disposed by 'n' operational elements*
>
> *equals the sum of vertical variety disposed on the six vertical*
>
> *components of corporate cohesion.*

More traditional management approaches see hierarchy as the natural way of making decisions. Hierarchical management massively attenuate variety by expecting individuals to do what they are told and supress often more knowledgeable individual variety. On the contrary, the VSM assumes that it is only by providing a rich learning context where individuals can contribute, learn, and grow, that self-organisation and self-governance will happen. This brings clear challenges for managing complexity in the vertical channel such as finding ways to:

- Allow as much autonomy as possible to the S1, while guaranteeing cohesion among S1s.

- Distribute the required resources and information for effective tasks implementation among S1s.

- Generate a culture of mutual support to encourage synergies.

- Develop a meta-understanding of the issues under consideration at each moment between operational and general managers.

- Limit meta-systemic interventions to only those required to maintain system cohesion.

Addressing these challenges can be done by proper design of the self-regulatory mechanism, by developing a culture of trust and responsible autonomy, distributing responsibilities for self-regulation to lower levels of recursive organisation and promoting agile and effective performance management systems.

Agile Management

To be viable, an organisation needs to learn to be *agile* – that is, to be alert, well informed, and capable of real-time decisions and actions. This idea of real-time management, pioneered by Beer, is now getting widely spread under the brand of '*agile*' approaches to management. Beer (1979, pp. 225–366, 499–509) explains the requirements for an agile decision environment, a *real-time* management culture, and robust performance management tools.

Core to self-regulation is to develop *sensing capabilities* to monitor internal and external performance, and the development of an effective performance management system (PMS). A robust performance management system should be capable of sensing the behaviour of key performance indicators and producing *alerts* – in *real time* – when any of them is behaving in unexpected ways. A critical aspect in organisational design is the design of decision-making mechanisms exhibiting requisite variety. It means capable of sensing in *real time* any significant changes to the organisational essential variables and taking agile decisions.

Morlidge (2007) summarises Beer's criteria to support a '*cybernetically sound*' performance management system (PMS) and an '*agile*' decision environment as follows:

- Each S1 is able to self-manage any performance issues most of the times without meta-systemic management intervention.

- To do so, S1 – at each level of organised complexity – must identify its *'essential variables'* and measure its key performance indicators (KPIs) to observe its behaviour in real time.

- S1 must have an effective PMS, capable of producing *'early alarms.'* These should be accessible by meta-systemic management in – as close as possible to – real time.

- Only 'by exemption,' the meta-systemic management would intervene to support or precipitate decisions from S1. This may happen when:

  - S1 doesn't have the resources or skills to deal with a situation. Then it requests from S3 to activate a support network.

  - S1 is in a situation that is out of control and may affect the organisational v&s and/or reputation, then it should activate an algedonic signal to alert S5 directly.

A *'cybernetic PMS'* focuses on sensing the *'essential variables'* – that is, the variables that need to be kept under strict vigilance to guarantee the organisational systems' viability. Analogically speaking, the essential variables of a person are those that need to be kept within physiological limits to keep a person alive – e.g., the body temperature and level of oxygen in the blood. If any of these were below the critical level, the person would be at risk of death. To decide on essential variables, we need clarifying which aspects of the interaction between an operational unit and its niche are vital for effective delivery of its core products or services. The key performance indicators are clear and practical ways to observe the behaviour of these 'essential variables' over time.

Measuring Performance: The Triple Index

Performance is a core measure of the viability of a system. A good performing system is a viable system, while an organisation continuously underperforming – or developing a poor relationship with its niche – is risking its viability. Beer (1981, pp. 268–278) suggested a performance measurement system, 'the *Triple Index*' based on three levels of measurement for performance indicators: *actuality, capability,* and *potentiality.* It includes three generic performance indices: productivity, developmental capability, and overall performance. '*Productivity*' is the ratio between actuality and capability; '*latency*' is the ratio between capability and potentiality – it measures developmental capability; and '*performance*' is the ratio between productivity and latency (or between actuality and potentiality) (Beer, 1981, p. 164).

Managing Algedonics

Algedonic comes from the Greek: 'aldos' for pain and 'hedos' for pleasure. Algedonic signals are early alarms on situations that are pivotal for organisational viability: they are produced at the operational level (S1) to report – directly to S5 – extremely negative (painful) or positive (joyful) events which would impact performance. Beer also suggests designing both a robust PMS and complementary channels to produce '*algedonic signals*' when a situation has gone out of control and needs immediate action from S5. See Figure 2.12.

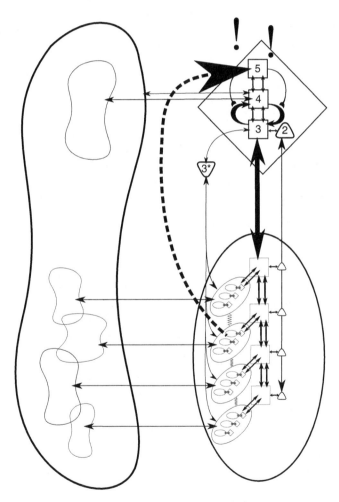

Figure 2.12 Algedonic signals

(Illustration by Jon Walker)

He considers that S5 needs to be alerted when there is instability emerging at lowers level of the organisation, which is not identifiable by traditional management information systems. If S5 is unaware of emerging crisis, it will become unresponsive and will *'go to sleep'* if nothing worrying is happening. But if the situation is serious and bring risks to organisational viability, sustainability, or reputation, then:

> *if we are not very careful then sleep may turn into coma,*
>
> *and coma becomes death.* (Beer, 1979, p. 406)

A viable system cannot remain viable if it goes to sleep in the middle of crisis. This is why we need to design algedonic mechanisms, capable of transmitting algedonic signals to alert S5 when there are operational crises at lower levels of recursive organisation. Algedonic signals should constantly bypass the official management information systems filters because of the extremely lethal risk of a spurious *'metacalm.'* Algedonic signals should then be organised to break through recursive levels of organisation.

> *Beer's most famous application of the VSM was the Cybersyn project in Chile in 1971–1973, supporting Salvador Allende's government to design a cybernetic system to support self-regulation of the Chilean industry.*[12] *Beer and his team designed a Cyberfilter, a software to observe and measure the key performance indicators from each (workers managed) factory and industrial sector. The Cybersyn team trained managers in cybernetic principles, designed and measure the KPIs and fed the Cyberfilter. Using Bayesian time analysis series, The Cyberfilter analysed stability or dramatic changes in the behaviour of performance indicators and produced algedonic signals when there were anomalies on historical behaviours. At each level of recursive organisation, those responsible for S3/S4/S5 tasks would agree the acceptable levels of sensitivity and the acceptable 'elapsed times' before generating an algedonic signal to the 3/4/5 Homeostat at the next level of organisation. In the Cybersyn project in Chile the 'Operations Room' was the decision-making space, supported by the Cyberfilter software, where decision makers would meet to analyse (real time) early alarms and decide on possible actions to deal with them.*

Adaptation

While S1/S2/S3 address all the 'Inside and Now' decisions, S3/S4/S5 do the same around 'Outside and Then' decisions. Beer refers to those S3/S4/S4 roles as the 'adaptation mechanism.' The S4 has its eye on the niche, and alerts S3 and S5 of evolving trends and emerging scenarios from the complex web of interactions in the business or societal ecosystems embedding the organisation.

Emergence is welcomed and expected as it is only through emergence and sometimes chaotic behaviours that innovation happens. Emergent patterns of interaction between S1s and their niches may result in the need for a new organisational level at a higher or at a lower level of recursion, or the need for new strategies or product design, and/or for development of new capabilities.

A robust strategic decision-making space should include a balanced representation of both S3 and S4 viewpoints to agree on both creative enough (S4) and feasible enough (S3) strategies. In a context where the decision makers have requisite variety, there are better possibilities for well informed, creative, and feasible decisions to be made by the '*adaptation mechanism*'; see Figure 2.12. S5 makes sure that Systems 3 and 4 absorbs each other's variety and that their interaction is smooth, so they won't end up in an uncontrolled oscillation.

Naturally, S4 has more curiosity and skills for creative, and exploratory research and innovation. Naturally S3 has a 'down to earth' nature, being more aware of the existing workforce's capabilities and limitations and of the availability of financial and other resources. S3/S4 viewpoints naturally diverge (as both criticise each other), but also complement each other. S5 aims to create a more balanced context for making informed decisions by balancing the S3/S4 interaction.

> *At the ELF project, we noticed early on that while S3 of the school was handling massive amount of variety, S4 was only handling sporadic activity and had limited variety. Thus, there was an imbalance between S3/S4. The residual variety left for S5 to absorb was far greater than the capability of S5 to absorb it. We then decided to redesign S3/S4 and S5 to have a more balanced adaptation mechanism.*

Balancing the varieties of S3, S4, and S5 is core to organisational viability. Beer (1979, p. 298) explains it as the second and third axioms of management:

2nd Axiom of Management:
The variety disposed by System Three resulting from the operation of the First Axiom and the variety disposed by System Four, are equivalent.

3rd Axiom of Management:
The variety disposed by System Five is equivalent to the residual variety generated by the operation of the 2nd Axiom.

There is undoubtedly a massive complexity implicit in strategic decision making in large organisations. To address this with a concrete and practical tool for collective decision making on complex issues, Beer (1994) last invention was the design of 'team syntegrity' (TS), a cybernetic tool to facilitate creative and cohesive decisions by large groups operating in the 3/4/5 Homeostat (more on TS in Chapter 3).

Self-Governance

Viability is all about maintaining balanced relationships between an organisation and its niche, which results in it being more resilient and adaptive. To adapt to their niche, managers and operational staff need to continuously check and balance information about their niche and their interactions with it. If the operational units have a balanced and creative relationship with their niche (including their customers and suppliers) then their possibilities for survival are much higher. If an organisation manages to keep a stable internal environment even while the external environment is undergoing deep change, then it has developed '*internal homeostasis*' (Beer, 1985, p. 17); see an illustration of the idea in Figure 2.13.

Figure 2.13 Homeostatic balance

(Illustration by Thom Igwe-Walker)

Adaptation to the niche may involve continuous self-transformation, i.e., by changing as needed the internal organisation, and processes to adapt to emerging landscapes in the niche. Being able to do so requires self-awareness and readiness to change. It also needs operations and the meta-system to be able to facilitate changes in the directions agreed, and to maintain a balanced (homeostatic) relationship between themselves even amidst change and turbulence. Homeostatic balance is the dynamic equilibrium achieved in such interactions, that when maintained over time, results in self-governance. Self-governance is the pre-requisite for organisational viability (and sustainability).

Viability is always related to individual and organisational learning. Viability can be enhanced by creating proper learning contexts where innovation is enhanced. Critical thinking is expected, and information is openly and transparently managed and available for all the learners and doers. Nurturing the operational environment to create and maintain an effective group learning context is a powerful variety amplifier to support an operational team to manage its tasks' complexity more effectively.

Beer suggested the need to design proper structures, processes, and technology to manage natural imbalances of complexity. It includes the design of *homeostats*, which are mechanisms that support the maintenance of balanced and productive behaviours in the interactions between specific types of roles. Homeostats help to manage the variety of roles' interactions, in a range of times, by responding rapidly to (anticipated and unanticipated) perturbations.

A crucial part in a VSM diagnosis – see next chapter – is to check how well balanced the different homeostats are. What we mean by 'balanced' in this context is that the interactions are working well for both parts and they are manageable and amenable to them. Figure 2.14 identifies core homeostats, which operate between: (A) operations and the environment; (B) S1 and S3; (C) S4 and the environment; (D) S3 and S4; and (E) between S3, S4, and S5.

Homeostat A balances interactions between operational units (S1) and their niches, by keeping the value of essential variables for survival within physiological limits. This balance includes addressing environmental and social responsibilities, to develop a sustainable relationship with its socio-ecological niche. Homeostat B preserves internal homeostasis, as described above. Homeostat C does futures research by exploring organisational responses and models to adapt to possible configurations of the environment. It includes also fully addressing social and environmental concerns in the broad organisational niche when deciding on strategy and innovation.

Homeostat D drives the adaptation organ (S3/S4) by searching for balance between the Outside and Then (S4) and the Inside and Now (S3); for example, by designing and driving organisational self-transformations. Homeostat E oversees these adaptation dynamics to guarantee that S3 and S4 contribute to their best to identity and policy decisions. The following chapters will offer examples from case studies illustrating diagnostic issues on the different homeostats, at different levels of recursive organisation, and ways to address such issues.

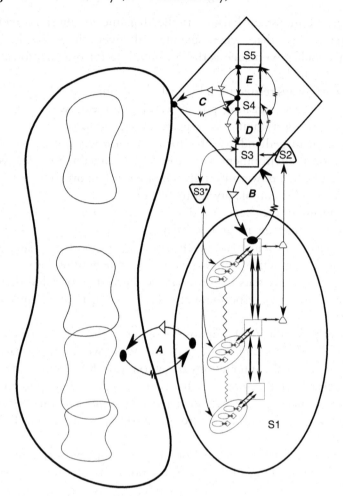

Figure 2.14 VSM types of homeostats

(Illustration by Jon Walker)

Sustainable Self-Governance

To be *viable and sustainable*, an organisation needs to change unsustainable patterns of interaction with its niche when they arise by reorganising itself and redesigning its processes accordingly. Viability and sustainability are relational characteristics and can't be valued independently of the contexts where organisations exist. The path towards sustainability is a long- term path, which has to begin in every individual organisation, but needs to influence other organisations in the same localities, or the same industries, or sectors. It is a process of continuous (recursive) transformation towards a new way of living and relating that has at the heart of its values a deep and profound respect for others and for nature. This is what we call *'sustainable self-governance.'* The ability to continuously adapt to changes in the niche, in a sustainable way that rather than 'extracting' resources from it, uses resources in a regenerative way and contributes to generate social capital in the communities where it operates. Developing sustainable self-governance is a long-term undertaking an requires of sustainable self-governed systems at each level of recursive organisation.

> For example, when observing an eco-region as a viable system (see Espinosa & Walker, 2017, pp. 256–267), we can't have a v&s community, if neighbouring communities are highly unsustainable (i.e., by continuously polluting a shared river basin). It is not good enough to have a few agents in a supply chain cleaning their production process, if they rely on parts produced unsustainably by other members of the supply chain network. (Espinosa & Walker, 2017, pp. 280–299)

Leaving Behind Earlier Critics of the VSM

It should be clear by now, the strengths of the VSM theory. It is a robust, complete, and deep way of understanding how to deal with complexity in organisations. It has become more and more popular in the last few decades and many of its core principles have been adopted and continue to be developed by increasingly large number of followers around the world.

Not surprisingly, during my more than three decades' experience in teaching and applying the VSM (and the v&s) in several countries, some of my students and clients have asked why, being such a powerful systemic approach, is the VSM is not more widely used? A typical response is that the VSM, while being a highly robust approach, was not the easiest approach to learn and to apply. Several of Beer's followers, including myself, have worked hard to make this knowledge more understandable and more widely available. Nowadays, there are hundreds of examples of VSM applications available worldwide, which shows that we have achieved some success.

Another detrimental factor to broader dissemination of the VSM were the criticisms that it attracted when first pioneered by Beer, *many of which would not stand to a deep scrutiny* (i.e., they were based on an incomplete understanding of the contexts of his work or a cursory reading of one or two books or articles). For example, Checkland (1986) misunderstood Beer's theory, by assuming he trusted systems to be real-world phenomena, rather than perceptions and interpretations from observers. He seems to have missed Beer's opening statements when explaining the VSM:

> So where does the idea of Systems in general have a purpose
>
> to come from? IT COMES FROM YOU! It is you, the observer of
>
> the system who recognises its purpose. (Beer, 1979, p. 8)

Also, Ulrich (1981) and Jackson (1991) originally classified the VSM as a functionalist approach that underplays cultural, political, and coercive aspects and which could be used to support authoritarian management. In his response to Ulrich's critique to his work in Chile, Beer clarifies that rather than ascribing a purpose to an organisation, for him, the organisation is what it does. And the responsibility for what the system is observed to be doing is relative to the observer (Beer, 1983a). The growing range of published work interpreting the VSM from a second-order cybernetic perspective (the cybernetics of the observer) demonstrates Checkland and Ulrich's understanding of the VSM was limited (e.g., Harnden (1989), Espejo and Reyes (2011)).

According to Morlidge (2007, pp. 187–217), other traditional criticisms of the VSM that do not stand up to scrutiny included Stacey (2003), a British guru on complexity sciences, suggesting that cybernetics systems cannot learn, demonstrating ignorance of cybernetic models of learning. Also, Ackoff and Gharajedaghi (1996) believed that the VSM does not allow exercise of free will from people constituting an organisation. They seem to have missed that Beer (1983b) clearly explained the VSM's idea of autonomous, self-organised individuals exercising their free will, while accepting basic organisational constraints.

Golinelli (2010) and several colleagues in Italy, have developed the 'viable system approach,' as what they claim is a (substantial) development of Beer's work, by focussing more on external than internal relationships, and arguing that Beer's is an 'static model.' As explained in this chapter, the core of the VSM is to design an agile, adaptive, and resilient organisation capable of matching the variety of its niche, which wouldn't be possible if it wasn't a dynamic system. All the main principles Golinelli mentions come from Beer's original theory, but he fails short of understanding the recursive and adaptive nature of the VSM. He does offer a more detailed analysis of stakeholders, which complements the original theory, but does not constitute as he claims 'a substantial development' of Beer's work.

Other critics have argued that the biological analogy has limitations, a criticism recognised by (Beer, 1981, p. 161), when he explained that the physiological analogy is used as the inspiration and basis for building up the model, but it is through iterative application in real organisations from different scales that the theory was tested and perfected over time. According to Allena Leonard, Stafford's partner:[13]

> it should be understood that much of Beer's early work was performed while working in the British steel industry, and later among a variety of commercial, governmental, and non-profit organizations. As a consultant, Beer did address explicitly many of the cultural and political aspects of his contracts although, for privacy reasons, most could not be publicized. See, however, the case studies in Heart of Enterprise. (Beer, 1979)

Figure 2.15 Stafford's response to critics

(Illustration by Thom Igwe-Walker)

She also explained the reason why Stafford didn't respond to many of these criticisms; see Figure 2.15.

Most of these old criticisms are now fading away, as it is becoming clearer over time than most contemporary VSM applications, such as the ones discussed in the next chapters, understand the VSM as a humane and emancipatory approach that challenges autocratic management structures and empower workers and citizens. It fully respects and promotes cultural and ethical values and recognises their pivotal influence to achieve viability (and sustainability). Hopefully the readers of this book will find enough evidence that the VSM not only promotes autonomous, self-motivated individuals, decentralised, agile, and democratic self-governance systems, but also distributed control and enhanced 'responsible autonomy' among individuals and subsidiary organisations.

Notes

1 https://orcid.org/my-orcid?orcid=0000–0002-5200–7613
2 European Commission. (2019). The European Green Deal. European Commission. Available online on February the 4th, 2021 at: european-green-deal-communication.
3 Inspired by S Beer's work, with permission from Malik on Management. Permission to include it from Metaphorum.
4 Inspired by S Beer's work, with permission from Malik on Management. Permission to include it from Metaphorum.
5 Inspired by S Beer's work, with permission from Malik on Management. Permission to include it from Metaphorum.
6 Inspired by S Beer's work, with permission from Malik on Management. Permission to include it from Metaphorum.
7 Inspired by S Beer's work, with permission from Malik on Management. Permission to include it from Metaphorum.
8 Inspired by S Beer's work, with permission from Malik on Management. Permission to include it from Metaphorum.
9 Inspired by S Beer's work, with permission from Malik on Management. Permission to include it from Metaphorum.
10 Koestler (1967) explained the idea of holarchy, which also refers to whole systems embedding other whole systems; but he didn't explain the way embedded systems reflect a fractal structure, as Beer does in this theorem. Also, the concept of fractality has been further developed by Complex Adaptive System researchers, but it doesn't reflect the idea of recursive patterns of organisation as Beer does.
11 This is often included in Complex Adaptive Systems theory (e.g., Holland (1992)).
12 Chapter 8 will review the Cybersyn project, which pioneered these ideas at the Chilean national level, as well as several case studies also applying Beer's theories at the national level in Colombia, in the 1990s.
13 Personal email communication with the author.

References

Ackoff, R. L., & Gharajedaghi, J. (1996). 'Reflections on systems and their models', *Systems Research*, 13(1), pp. 13–23.
Bateson, G. (1973). *Steps to an Ecology of Mind*. London: Jason Aronson Inc.
Beer, S. (1979). *Heart of the Enterprise*. Chichester: John Wiley & Sons.
Beer, S. (1981). *Brain of the Firm*. Chichester: John Wiley & Sons.
Beer, S. (1983a). 'The will of the people', *Journal of the Operational Research Society*, 34(8), pp. 797–810.
Beer, S. (1983b). 'A reply to Ulrich's 'Critique of pure cybernetic reason: The Chilean experience with cybernetics', *Journal of Applied Systems Analysis*, 10, pp. 115–119.
Beer, S. (1985). *Diagnosing the System for Organisations*. Chichester: John Wiley & Sons.
Beer, S. (1994). *Beyond Dispute: The Invention of Team Syntegrity*. Chichester: John Wiley & Sons.
Checkland, P. (1986) 'Review of 'Diagnosing the System'', *European Journal of Operational Research*, 23, pp. 269–270.

Espejo, R., & Reyes, A. (2011). *Organizational systems: Managing complexity with the viable system model.* London: Springer.

Espinosa, A., Harnden, R., & Walker, J. (2008). 'A complexity approach to sustainability – Stafford beer revisited', *European Journal of Operational Research*, 187(2), pp. 636–651.

Espinosa, A., & Porter, T. (2011). 'Sustainability, complexity and learning: Insights from complex systems approaches', *Learning Organization*, 18(1), pp. 54–72.

Espinosa, A., Cardoso, P. P., Arcaute, E., & Christensen, K. (2011). 'Complexity approaches to self-organisation: A case study in an Irish eco-village', *Kybernetes*, 40(3/4), pp. 536–558.

Espinosa, A., & Walker, J. (2013). 'Complexity management in practice: A Viable System model intervention in an Irish eco-community', *European Journal of Operational Research*, 225(1), p118–129.

Espinosa, A., & Walker, J. (2017). *A Complexity Approach to Sustainability: Theory and Application.* 2nd edition. Singapore: World Scientific Press.

Golinelli, G. M. (2010). *Viable Systems Approach – Governing Business Dynamics.* Padova: Kluwer/ CEDAM.

Harnden, R. (1989). 'Outside and then: An interpretive approach to the VSM' in Espejo, R. & Harnden, R. (eds.), *The Viable System Model: Interpretations and Applications of Stafford Beer's VSM.* Chichester: John Wiley & Sons, pp. 383–404.

Holland, J. H. (1992). 'Complex adaptive systems', *A New Era in Computation*, 121(1), pp. 17–30.

Jackson, M. (1991). *Systems Methodology for the Management Sciences.* New York: Plenum Press.

Klein, N. (2015). *This Changes Everything.* New York: Simon & Schuster.

Koestler, A. (1967). *The Ghost in the Machine.* London: Arkana.

Leclère, D., Obersteiner, M., Barrett, M. et al. (2020). 'Bending the curve of terrestrial biodiversity needs an integrated strategy', *Nature*, 585, pp. 551–556.

Maturana, H., & Varela, F. (1988). *The Tree of Knowledge: The Biological Roots of Human Understanding.* Boston: Shambala.

Meadows, D., Randers, J. & Meadows, D. (2004). *The Limits to Growth: The 30 Year Update.* London: Chelsea Green Publishing.

Morlidge, S. (2007). 'The Application of Organisational Cybernetics to the Design and Diagnosis of Financial Performance Management Systems'. *PhD Dissertation.* Hull: Hull University Business School.

Panagiotakopoulos, P., Espinosa, A., & Walker, J. (2016). 'Sustainability management: Insights from the Viable System Model', *Journal of Cleaner Production*, 113, pp. 792–807.

Pritchard, H., Ligtenberg, S., Fricker, H. et al. (2012). 'Antarctic ice-sheet loss driven by basal melting of ice shelves, *Nature*, 484, pp. 502–505.

Stacey, R. D. (2003). *Strategic Management and Organisational Dynamics.* Harlow: Pearson Education.

Schwaninger, M. (2003). 'Long over short term: The example of ecological management', *Organisational Transformation and Social Change*, 1 (1), pp. 11–27.

Schwaninger, M. (2004). 'What can cybernetics contribute to the conscious evolution of organizations and society?', *Systems Research and Behavioural Science*, 21, pp. 515–527.

Schwaninger, M. (2015). 'Organizing for sustainability: A cybernetic concept for sustainable renewal', *Kybernetes: an International Journal of Systems and Cybernetics*, 44 (6/7), pp. 935–954.

Solow, R. (1993). 'An almost practical step towards sustainability', *Resources Policy*, 19(3), pp. 162–172.

Ulrich, W. (1981) 'A critique of pure cybernetic reason: The Chilean experience with cybernetics. *Journal of Applied Systems Analysis*, 8, pp. 33–59.

World Commission on Environment and Development. (1987). *Our Common Future.* Oxford: Oxford University Press.

Chapter 3

A Methodology to Support Self-Transformation Towards Viability and Sustainability

Although VSM theory has long been available, its application only began to be more widely undertaken in the 21st century. This is not surprising, giving that a thorough application of the VSM requires a complete shift in management paradigms: from a centralised, hierarchical approach to a self-regulated, networked, and heterarchical one. The hierarchical management paradigm prevailed over the 20th century and is still the one most used in business and governments around the world. However, communities, NGOs, businesses, and even public organisations are beginning to experiment with flatter, more networked structures.

It is only recently that this new management paradigm has begun to be recognised as highly desirable and feasible, given an increasingly widespread access to the global internet network and increased awareness of the advantages of flatter and more democratic structures. Evidence that this paradigmatic shift is now well underway is reflected in the growing number of innovative examples in the literature of network-like organisations, like holocracy (Robertson, 2015), agility (Sherehiy et al., 2007), scrum (Cervone, 2011), teal organisations (Laloux (2014), and sociocracy (Rau & Koch-Gonzalez, 2018).

VSM theory and methodologies have been critiqued for being inaccessible because of highly technical visual representations and difficult language creating substantial cognitive barriers (Lowe et al., 2016). We have responded to this criticism by offering a detailed epistemology and the constitutive rules for the VSM from a practitioner's perspective (Lowe et al., 2020). In my experience, the VSM and related methodologies are powerful systemic tools to inspire and guide self-transformations in organisations at all levels. But even if there are lots of published applications of the VSM, we still need clear practical guidance and examples on how to use it. This chapter summarises my attempt to respond to this request, by explaining in detail my methodological approach.

 DOI: 10.4324/9780429490835-4

On VSM Methodologies

Beer (1985) suggested generic guidelines on how to apply the VSM to diagnose and/or redesign an organisation, but they still left many open questions for VSM consultants and practitioners wanting to learn in more detail how to apply his theory. A few of his followers, including myself, have tried to address this gap in VSM practice, by offering a more comprehensive and intuitive way of using the VSM. Espejo developed 'VIPLAN' (Espejo et al., 1999), and has extensively applied it (Espejo and Reyes, 2011). Schwaninger (2009) suggested the 'systemic management control' approach inspired by the VSM. He has also pioneered the use of the VSM to support corporate sustainability – see Schwaninger et al. (2015).

Other VSM methodologies widely used include viable systems diagnosis (Flood & Jackson, 1991), viable boundary critique (Yolles, 1999), viable knowledge management (Achterbergh & Vriens, 2002), and holistic management approach (Christopher, 2007). Hoverstadt (2008) offers a very practical approach for using the VSM, with many examples of application but with little emphasis on methodology. Pérez-Ríos (2012) also offers some methodological guidance to using the VSM with diagnostic and representational tools. Lassl more recently has published a trilogy of VSM books with a very detailed and thorough presentation of the VSM theory and very clear guidance to apply it in a business context (e.g., Lassl, 2019). Pfiffner (2010, 2020) and Lambertz (2018) offer detailed VSM theory and methodology and examples of applications in the European Union.

Other researchers have taken their own stance departing from VSM theory and developed specialised perspectives like the viable system approach (VSA) (Golinelli, 2010), which focuses on applications to marketing and service science. His colleagues use VSM criteria to support strategy forming and implementation for sustainable business management (Dominici and Roblek (2016); Dominici and Palumbo (2013); Barile et al. (2014). They emphasize contextualisation with the environment by identifying external stakeholders as the basis to design a VSM-inspired organisational structure.

There have been different reviews of the current VSM landscape recently that demonstrate in the last few decades that the number of published VSM papers continues to grow exponentially. Vahidi et al. (2019) brief on such developments through a recent Scopus search exploring a sample of more than a hundred papers contributing to VSM research. The final chapter will reflect on the current landscape on VSM theory and applications and the open research fields. The following sections explain the author's methodological approach to support organisational transformations towards viability and sustainability.

Developing the Self-Transformation Methodology (STM)

My own journey in developing and using the VSM started during my PhD at Aston University, when I suggested a VSM methodology, inspired by Beer (1979, 1985) and by Espejo's VIPLAN methodology, originally intended to support strategic information management. I tested it through a case study when developing the strategic information management plan at the Colombian President's Office (Espinosa, 1995) – see Chapter 8. Over the last two decades, I have adapted the original methodology to use it in the context of large organisations, communities, and networks aiming to become more viable, but also more sustainable.

The work I have done with Dr Jon Walker, my partner and a very experienced VSM practitioner in cooperatives, has influenced and shaped my current version of the methodology and my current understanding of VSM practice. I have also coached several PhD, MSc, and post-doctoral students in contributing to the original VSM theory and methodology, in the context of their own research and practice. The following chapters will reflect on selected consultancy and research projects with different collaborators, which I hope will inspire VSM students and practitioners, and support their methodological and practical learning.

I have named the current version of the methodology, the 'self-transformation methodology' (I will refer to it as the STM throughout the book). It supports an organisation to learn to observe its current patterns of interaction, identify organisational pathologies; and self-transform those roles or mechanisms that are dysfunctional or weakly designed according to VSM criteria. The STM is offered as a learning device to coach organisational members in learning about organisational complexity. I have realised that by coaching users in embedding VSM distinctions in their organisational life they become more capable of mapping their co-evolving organisations, and continuously deciding on required adaptations.

The STM has proven to be a useful framework to learn about our ways of organising; to observe and assess our (first and second order) learning about what we do, why we do it, and how do we get organised to do it; and to improve our capabilities for critical and systemic organisational learning. It contributes to creating a collective mental model of the current and desirable organisation, which creates a robust context for self-organisation, self-regulation, and adaptation.

The following sections first explain the way I have described the '*constitutive rules*' of the VSM – basically the minimum types of enquiries related to implementing the VSM in an organisation. Then I explain each stage of the STM and its suggested analytical tools, using examples to illustrate such recommended tools, from a recent self-transformation of the ELF schools in Romania (see an overview of this project in Chapter 5).

The Ontology of the Observer

As explained, my way of understanding an organisation and its need for managing complexity resonates with Maturana and Varela (1988)'s second-order cybernetics, which describes the role of language in the development of intelligence and cognition in living beings. They suggest that our brain's ability to deal with complexity is embedded in our ability to make distinctions in language and to socialise them, by engaging in fruitful conversations with those with whom we share our personal and professional lives.

Some researchers have used the VSM from a functionalistic perspective, by understanding functions versus structure, with am emphasis on knowledge, performance, and information management, e.g., Flood and Jackson (1991), Jackson (2003, 2019), Achterbergh and Vriens (2002), Schwaninger (2009), and Christopher (2007). On the contrary, the STM is clearly rooted in the ontology of the observer, a posture we have clarified elsewhere (i.e., Espinosa et al., 2008; Espinosa & Walker, 2017).

In v&s language, organisations evolve through networks of conversations between the doers in System 1 and their counterparts in the corresponding environmental niches, between them and their (meta-systemic) managers, and between (meta-systemic) managers and their counterparts in their particular niche. The STM aims to support the learning and adaptation of a group of observers to address the main paradoxes and dilemmas of their organisation and to develop their capabilities for systemic individual and organisational learning (Teece, 2012; Zahra et al., 2006).

A learning organisation is a co-evolving configuration of roles and tasks, which is mutually agreed and revised each time it is required, by its members, to adapt to a continuously changing environment. The VSM provides a meta-language for developing a shared mental model of the organisational structure, and for critically reflecting on its internal and external dynamic co-evolution. By mapping recurrent patterns of interactions using VSM distinctions, people begin to share a collective mental model about who they are, in an organisation and the outside world, and how they handle – or not – the complexity of their tasks. Under the guidance of the STM approach, this allows them to discover for themselves better ways to address structural shortcomings in their organisation.

The STM is a systemic framework to facilitate collective agreements for mapping the ongoing configurations of roles and activities, and to assess the healthiness of such configurations, using the VSM criteria described in previous chapters. Revisiting the STM stages of analysis becomes a continuous learning process. Whatever agreements are made at a particular time, they need to be revisited over time, again and again, as an organisation is continuously coevolving with its niche and needs continuous adjustments and adaptation. This way, the STM contributes to enhancing our learning about organisational complexity, while abandoning any aspiration to end up with a unique 'best' model of how an organisation should behave in a particular landscape of organisational dynamics.

The STM: A Systemic Methodology to Facilitate Organisation Learning

A complex system is unpredictable, messy, and has too many components and interactions between them, so analysing it completely, fully identifying root causes for problems, or predicting future behaviours is not always possible. To address complexity in organisations, the best we can do is to progressively learn by producing systemic snapshots of the inherently complex interactions between its components (internal complexity) and between them and their niche (external complexity).

Most traditional methodologies of organisational change assume that consultants are experts on specific change management issues (e.g., organisational behaviour, organisational performance, process redesign, organisational strategy.) Their role in an organisational transformation project is to lead an organisational transformation, which implies being responsible for mapping the organisation, clarifying a strategic direction, producing an organisational diagnosis, and suggesting a portfolio of organisational change projects.

On the contrary, a v&s project is an organisational self-learning project, creating a space for reflection and representation on our way of getting organised, our learning difficulties, and our possibilities for improved (first- and second-order) learning. The role of a v&s consultant is to facilitate collective learning on how to deal with organisational complexity. We understand that the organisational members are the 'knowers,' the only ones who can and should identify their main learning constraints, and creatively find ways forward to overcome them.

The STM involves coaching people on v&s theory, while reflecting on their current organisation and its constraints for effective organisational performance. The v&s analyst supports the judgments made by any participants when undergoing diagnosis and ensure they are correctly using the v&s criteria to inform their self-diagnosis. The collective learning process raises the level of group consciousness and the development of adaptive capabilities and collective intelligence. To develop and embed these capabilities in the structure and the culture of the organisation in the long term, we coach people to understand the theory and to effectively use the suggested analytical tools.

This way, they will be prepared to continue identifying required changes, implementing them, and assessing their impact on an ongoing basis, without support from trained analysts. The result of the learning process is improved autonomy and resilience of each of the working groups, improved communication among roles and teams, and improved capabilities for understanding and affecting the organisational contexts influencing organisational performance. As a consequence, organisational performance is improved in the medium and long terms.

In other words, the STM aims at generating a continuous approach to learning about our organisation: not only first-order learning (i.e., being capable of adjusting the design of processes and roles), but also second-order learning (i.e., being able to question why things are done in a particular way or by particular roles) (see Argyris and Schon, 1996; Gharajedaghi, 2007). The ideal is to develop a culture of continuous adaptation to a changing environment, which means that the v&s criteria for effective organisation must become part of the DNA of the organisation.

On VSM Epistemology

Learning how to fully apply the VSM has always been a main aspiration for practitioners. Some academics have argued that VSM is a complex theory and therefore difficult to learn; however, we could argue that it is the organisational and social world that is highly complex: and the VSM is only one (quite an effective one though) of many attempts to usefully map and understand organisational complexity. If it didn't manage to depict complexity, then it would be better rated as a theory of organised simplicity. Or, as other critics who don't appear to grasp its underpinnings, (e.g., Snowden & Boone, 2007), as a theory of complicatedness rather than a theory of complexity.

My own experience over more than three decades teaching and applying the VSM has been highly enriching and fulfilling. I believe that this has also been the experience of most of the students and organisations whom I have mentored. I believe that by understanding the theory from the perspective explained in this book, and by clarifying its inherent epistemology, it has been possible to ease the path for managers and practitioners as they learn how to manage complexity in organisations.

In a recent research project, with M. Yearworth and D. Lowe, I suggested the VSM constitutive rules and epistemology (Lowe et al., 2020, p. 1019). We understood epistemology as the forms of knowledge and knowledge creation that a methodology uses and its forms of representation in modelling. Then we explained their significance for practitioners, through comparative case studies. Drawing mostly from Beer (1979, 1985) and Espinosa and Walker (2017), I suggested 14 elements, grouped by 3 sequential phases of inquiry, as a comprehensive epistemology for the Viable System Model.

As the epistemology is grouped into three phases of inquiry, it provides a performative description of what a VSM consultant needs to be doing that is specific to the VSM application (as opposed to generic for any systemic approach). The three phases of enquiry are:

I   To define the system in focus, which implies: 1) clarifying the organisational identity; 2) mapping the levels of recursive organisation, i.e., the subsidiary organisations directly responsible for implementing core products or services; and 3) deciding on the 'system in focus' for the analysis.

II Identifying and mapping the five VSM systems at each recursion level of the system-in-focus. To provide a more intuitive understanding of the five systems, we agreed on the following labels: operational units (S1); harmonisation (S2); self-regulation and synergies (S3); monitoring (S3*); adaptation and external communication (S4); and identity and closure (S5).

III Assessing the balance in the interactions between the different (homeostatic) systems: resource bargaining (S3–S1); operational vs. general management (S1–S2 – S3–S3*); strategy development process (S4–S3); maintaining balance (S5–S4–S3); recursive governance – interactions between the (S5–S4–S3) systems at different levels of subsidiarity; and producing algedonic signals.

The rest of this chapter explains in detail how the STM addresses each phase of enquiry, and the suggested analytical tools and methods at each stage.

The Self-Transformation Methodology in a Nutshell

The original version of the self-transformation methodology (STM) was initially developed and used within the scope of my doctoral research, to analyse the process for designing the strategic information plan, while I was leading the Informatics Secretariat at the Colombian President's Office (1990–1992). Since 1992, I have had the opportunity to lead several academic consulting projects that applied this methodology and resulted in adjusted/improved versions. In the following chapters, I will reflect on applications that demonstrated significant challenges of organisational learning at different scales (from designing a start-up company, to redesigning highly complex organisational systems).

Figure 3.1 presents the stages of the STM methodology: The first stage aims to clarify the organisational identity, the nature of the challenges it faces in its internal and external interactions (with its niche), and the internal and external stakeholders. The second stage suggests doing a 'recursive analysis,' to explore

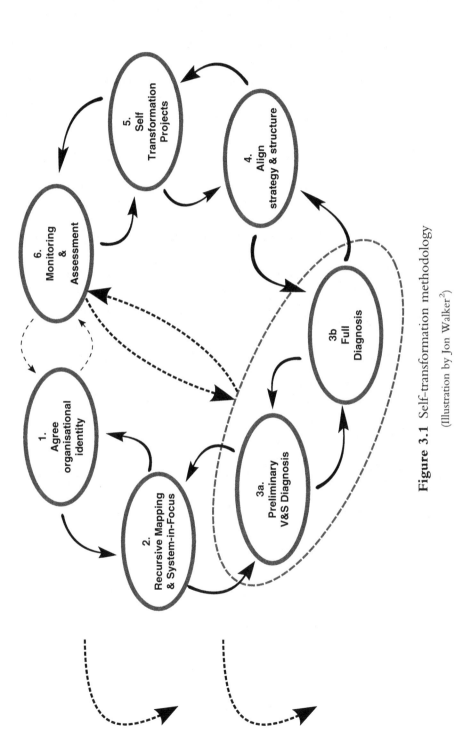

Figure 3.1 Self-transformation methodology
(Illustration by Jon Walker[2])

the levels of segmentation or recursive organisations, and to define the 'system in focus' for the analysis. The third (3a and 3b) stage is the most complex one that fully develops an organisational diagnosis of each viable system within the system in focus (SiF). It recommends doing it with representatives from each one of the viable systems within the SiF. The STM suggests to always starts by analysing the S1 within the system in focus and its patterns of interaction with its niches (including the organisation as a whole in recursion level 0). If several S1s develop the same product or service (e.g., at different locations), a representative sample of them can be included for detailed analysis. Doing this preliminary viability analysis normally takes some time, both in the mapping and the debate around these issues.

Stage 4 suggests exploring the current strategic positioning of the organisation, reflecting on ways of aligning it with the current structure, and identifying the required capabilities for strategy implementation (e.g., new roles or responsibilities at different levels of organisation). It may include another sub-stage to identify any requirements for improving the existing information and communication infrastructure to support strategic information management. Stage 5 aims to summarise all the agreements from the diagnosis as a portfolio of self-transformation projects, clarifying each project's leading roles, required resources (including developing of capabilities, and any new ICT developments), and implementation timing. Once the project team has agreed on details of a project in the portfolio, they can begin implementation.

The final stage assesses the quality and effectiveness of performance management systems and the way they support strategic decision making. As shown in the figure, it normally starts when doing the diagnosis by reviewing (and/or designing) key performance indicators and clarifying (if required) the mechanisms for assessing operational and organisational performance. At the final stage these KPIs are reviewed continuously, to assess the impact of the self-transformation projects on organisational performance.

Table 3.1. explains the way the STM addresses the stages of enquiry from the VSM epistemology. The following sections offer recommendations on how to design and conduct a v&s project and explain in detail the suggested analytical tools for each stage of enquiry using examples from a recent v&s project.

Designing and Starting a v&s Project

Once a decision has been made in an organisation to initiate a v&s project, *we* (the v&s consultants) meet with the leaders to understand the current situation of their organisation, its history and recent organisational developments, and the reasons for undertaking such a project. Jointly, we decide on the purpose, scope, and methodology for the project, and begin to identify key

Table 3.1 Self-transformation methodology versus epistemology

Epistemology – phases of enquiry	STM Stages	Analytical Tools
Defining the "System in focus"		
Organisational identity	Agreements on Organisational Identity	Rich pictures TASCOI analysis
Levels of recursive organisation:	Recursive Analysis	Identifying levels of recursive organisation (current vs. desirable forms of S1's segmentation) Agreeing on the system in focus (SiF) for the analysis
Identifying and assessing the sub-systems of the system-in-focus		
Operational Units (S1)	VSM Diagnosis	Analysing S1 roles, mechanisms, and patterns of interaction with their niches
Harmonisation (S2)		Analysing S2 roles and mechanisms
Self-Regulation and Synergies (S3)		Analysing S3 roles and mechanisms
Monitoring (S3*)		Analysing S3* roles and mechanisms
Adaptation (S4)		Analysing S4 roles and mechanisms
Identity and Closure (S5) –		Analysing S5 roles and mechanisms
Identifying and assessing the interactions within the system-in-focus		
Resource bargaining and corporate intervention (S3/S1)	Managing resources and capabilities	Resource negotiations Clarifying rules and norms

(Continued)

Table 3.1 (Continued)

Epistemology – phases of enquiry	STM Stages	Analytical Tools
Operational vs general management (S1 – S2 – S3)	Self-regulatory mechanisms and processes	Assessing resource negotiation vs. accountability Assessing KPIs and performance management systems
Strategy Development Process (S4 – S3)	Adaptation mechanism and process (1)	Identifying alternative, desirable forms of S1's segmentation. Aligning strategic and operative planning and strategy with structure Strategic information management
Maintaining balance (S5 – S4 – S3)	Adaptation mechanism (2)	Self-transformation projects
Recursive governance	Monitoring performance	Monitoring projects' implementation Monitoring KPIs Interlinkage between all S3s and S4s and S5s on different recursion levels

representatives from the main organisational areas that need to have their voices and perspectives heard in the project.

This preliminary stage is exploratory and aims to produce a snapshot of the current organisational structure, performance, and challenges. We explore the organisational purpose, history and its current strategy, products and services, values, and norms; understanding what has been changing in the organisation, and when and why with what success is fundamental as a starting point.

Developing a broad picture of the organisation is fundamental: the organisational chart, processes, and role descriptions; the number of employees; political, economic, and environmental contexts and position in the market; recent annual reports; general budgets; current ICT infrastructure; key performance indicators; and any previous efforts to adjust then organisational structure, culture, and Information and Communication Technology (ICT)'s infrastructure.

Normally we use both, secondary sources (e.g., the website, the annual report, formal documents explaining organisational structure, current strategy, financial reports, etc.) and primary sources. We interview key stakeholders, e.g., representatives from managers, workers, customers, and suppliers. It is good practice to start the project by running a preliminary diagnostic survey to begin to identify broad organisational strengths, as well as core structural pathologies and their resulting dilemmas and paradoxes.

We normally design a steering committee, where political and economic decisions on the project are taken, and sporadic monitoring of the learning and outputs are reviewed. We also establish a technical committee, which includes a sample of representatives from both operational (system 1), and meta-systemic (systems 2 to 5) levels, from each viable system within the system in focus. The technical committee will fully participate in every stage of the STM.

Agreements on Organisational Identity

Once we have understood the current organisational landscape, we run a first workshop, including representatives from all the operational units (those developing products or services), and core meta-systemic services, to jointly make agreements on: a) the way people currently understand the organisational identity and products or services; and b) the main organisational bottlenecks, dilemmas, or paradoxes to manage the complexity of their tasks. The following tools are recommendable at this initial stage of the STM to support this type of enquiry.

Rich Pictures – The Organisational Landscape

At this stage, it is very useful to collectively develop a 'rich picture' or a cartoon-like representation of the messy or complex situations the organisation is facing. As Checkland and Poulter (2006) explained, there isn't any single or optimal solution to complex or messy situations, as they require progressive and continuous learning. So rather than looking for a single way to *solve* a complex situation, we can look for ways to *dissolve* it. This is more likely to happen if we manage to shift the observers' perception of the problematic situation, into something which makes the problem easier to deal with.

Humour has proven to be one of the most effective approaches to collectively shift our shared perceptions, as it has a cathartic effect. Many years of working with students and clients with this technique have only reinforced my belief that it is worthwhile. Not only does this work in conveying the fundamental issues, but it is very creative and entertaining as a group exercise, which creates a more relaxed and creative environment from where people can start a collective and truly participative reflection on their organisation.

The technique for developing a rich picture is quite intuitive: You ask the participants to put themselves in a creative and relaxed mood and to identify complex messy issues they are aware of in their organisation. You explicitly ask them to find humorous ways to think about them and to find pictorial (and hopefully very creative) ways of representing them. You can use symbols of people doing specific things, thinking in particular ways, or relating to each other in particular ways. The more you immerse yourself into the situation, the more details you bring into the picture and the more creatively you can represent them, the better. Figure 3.2 offers an example of rich pictures in ELF.

> During the first week of the v&s project in ELF we explained the STM and jointly developed the first two stages. We worked in two groups, and each produced their own rich pictures. The first cartoon – see Figure 3.2 – shows a happy stage in the 20-year-long ELF's journey sorting out several 'foggy times.' The new school developments are represented with wheels. Each of the headmasters and school coordinators is dressed up in particular ways suggestive of their attitude and approach to current schools' needs. The whole environment looks very positive with excellent results from both the school inspectors' and the parents' point of view. The continued success of the school recognised by parents and inspectors has driven a clear need for expansion. Apart from an occasional threat (e.g., a dead cat), the working environment looks challenging and promising for everyone.

Statement of Organisational Identity

Beer famously said: The purpose of an organisation *is* what it *does*. Sometimes it looks abundantly clear what the organisation does, so agreeing on its identity shouldn't be too complicated. However, different people often see the same organisation from different perspectives, depending on their role, beliefs, and background. The identity *in use* sometimes is different form the *desired* identity; even when there are formal documents describing, for example, the organisational vision and mission, there is no guarantee that every member of the organisation knows them, or even that they would agree with them or that they would embed such values into their ongoing decisions.

Organisations are always co-evolving with their niches, which means that they are continuously reinventing themselves. What they agreed they were and the things they were focused on a few years earlier may radically change if there were important changes in the niche within which they operate; or if

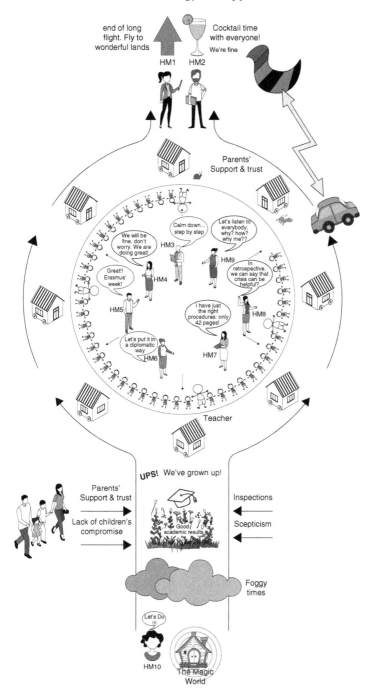

Figure 3.2 A rich picture at ELF

(Illustration by Juan David Alonso)

they start operating in different niches. So rather than assuming that there are ratified agreements about the organisational identity, this stage guides participants to jointly revisit their views on the organisational purpose (i.e., its expected transformation), and to produce a systemic statement about it.

A recommended tool for this stage is doing a 'TASCOI analysis' (Espejo & Reyes, 2011) to help clarify the organisational actors producing the main organisational transformation (**T**): **A**ctors, **S**uppliers, **C**ustomers, **O**wners, and **I**nterveners. Once identified, the different elements in the TASCOI mnemonic can be linked into a statement defining the organisational identity.

Recursive Analysis

As explained previously, in a viable system each one of the subsidiary organisations is itself a viable system, which means it is autonomous, that is 'capable of independent existence.' Recursive analysis (Beer, 1979) is the recommended technique to provide a pictorial mapping of the main embedded (subsidiary) viable systems in an organisation under analysis.

The recursive analysis diagram is not a hierarchical diagram: Organisations at level 0 are not *directing* organisations at the following level, but *'embedding'* them, e.g., by offering meta-systemic support to guarantee they have all the resources, information, and knowledge required to effectively implement their tasks and to cohesively implement the main organisational purpose.

While co-evolving with its niche, an organisation may develop a process of complexification, which means that there may be emergent organisational units resulting from its co-evolution with its niche over time, while others may be disappearing. Any new (or disappearing) organisational unit brings with it new levels of complexity, which need to be absorbed as much as possible at the operational level. Meta-systemic management roles also need to adapt, as they should get ready to respond to the residual variety added by the new operational units (or even by old units disappearing). In v&s terms, we will say that there are emerging levels of recursive organisation, which should (over time) be composed of viable systems in their own right.

Beer recommended using ovals to represent each viable system at the different levels of the recursive organisation: The organisation as a whole is represented by an oval, at the recursion level '0.' We first represent the whole organisation as an oval, and inside, we identify and name each one of its subsidiary System 1s. The embedded S1s are connected by (non-directional) arrows (see an example in Figure 3.3). The *recursive analysis* aims to uncover the way an organisation has grown and developed its operational complexity, by mapping such operational complexity using the above conventions. It doesn't map any managerial or technical support roles. They will be mapped in the next stage while doing VSM diagnosis.

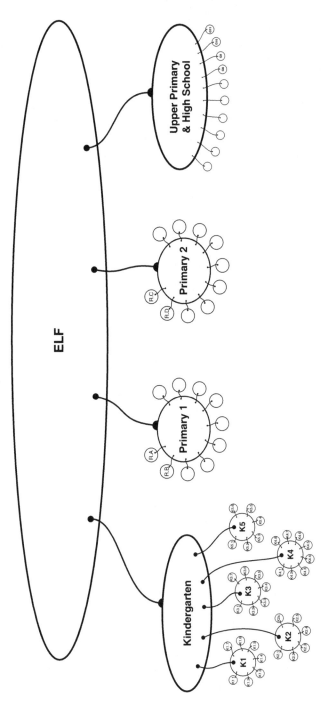

Figure 3.3 A possible recursive mapping of ELF

(Illustration by Jon Walker)

What we mean by a System 1 is an operational unit, directly responsible for implementing the organisational purpose or primary tasks, which:

- Has a team of people responsible for doing the primary tasks.
- Has some kind of operational management.
- Is usually a profit centre.
- Has access to enough (people, financial, technology, physical) resources to implement primary tasks.
- Has enough autonomy to implement its tasks and respond to changes in its niche.

The ovals in this diagram do not represent meta-systemic management units (e.g., strategic planning, finances, information and communication technologies (ICT), human resources management (HRM)). The different types of responsibilities taken by meta-systemic roles are classified as Systems 2 to 5 and are excluded from this recursive analysis diagram. For example, strategic ICT may be a System 4 type of role, while ICT support may be a System 2, and ICT management may be a System 3. Patterns of interaction between meta-systemic roles and S1s will be analysed later, when doing the VSM analysis.

Once we have identified the operational units at level '1' of recursive organisation, we should continue identifying operational units at the next level. Each operational unit (as an element of System 1) is or can potentially become a viable system in its own and should be represented as an oval. This is normally the case for subsidiary organisations distributed by:

- Geography.
- Time shifts.
- Types of products.
- Types of customers.

A first broad diagnosis that emerges at this stage is to assess if the current segmentation of S1 is appropriate at all? And if so, how appropriate is it? Could it be designed in a more (cybernetically) effective way? This assessment implies exploring potential other more ideal forms of S1 segmentation. Learning from experience, it is quite common to find out that core organisational paradoxes come from an inadequate balance in the segmentation of S1s (and their management teams), which had evolved over time for sometimes quite political reasons, resulting in detrimental or ineffective broad organisational design.

If during the recursive mapping, we realized that the way the organisation or any S1 is segmented does not support strategy implementation, then, ideally, we should promote the desirable adjustments to the structure before going further into the diagnosis and design. This is a major check in a VSM diagnosis, because, if the S1 is segmented badly (and that's quite often the case) it doesn't make sense to go on with them in the diagnosis. In such case, a major re-structuring may be recommended as any differently segmented S1 will bring up different tasks for the senior-/metasystem-management. To design it, we should compare the development strategy with the current organisation (including current segmentation) and suggest any necessary structural changes and adjustments in the way of providing meta-systemic support to the newly segmented S1s (see Section 3.9.1) before deepening into the VSM diagnosis.

Figure 3.3 shows the recursive analysis of ELF, as agreed on in the first workshop. Reaching agreements on this mapping of System 1 required several workshops and even by the end of the project we were still considering a better way to represent the evolving complexity of ELF, once the new (projected) schools were developed and working. After eight different attempts – see Figure 3.3 showing one of the attempts we discussed that week – we finally agreed on the final version presented in Figure 3.4.

In some ways, this was the way that ELF was operating at the beginning of the project: There was a very clear meta-system at the level of the school, which was coordinating operations in each of the schools. All the meta-systemic activity was centralised, and the individual schools concentrated on the educational services, only requesting extra administrative or technical support when required. However, the second diagram had the most support from the various teachers and headmasters. They saw ELF as composed of two distinctive organisations, the kindergartens, and the schools offering specialised services according to the age of the students. The former is composed of five geographically separate kindergartens each with between six and eight classes. The school has three units – two primary schools and the combined upper primary and high school – each with 10 streams.

The STM recommends that once we draw a complete recursive analysis diagram, we should specify 'the system in focus' for the analyses. The system in focus may be the organisation as a whole – as exemplified in Figure 3.3 – or an area of the organisation dealing directly with the complex situations we aim to focus on a v&s project. We normally represent the system in focus by surrounding it with dotted lines and signalling it as the 'SiF' (system in focus).

ELF currently includes five kindergartens and the school, which includes two primary schools and one upper primary and high school. At recursions 0 (ELF) the complexity is unfolded by type of product (kindergarten and school). At recursion 1 (5 kindergartens and 3 schools) each of the five kindergartens and each of the three schools is at a different location in the city so the unfolding of complexity at this level is geographical. At recursion level 2 each kindergarten and each school have an

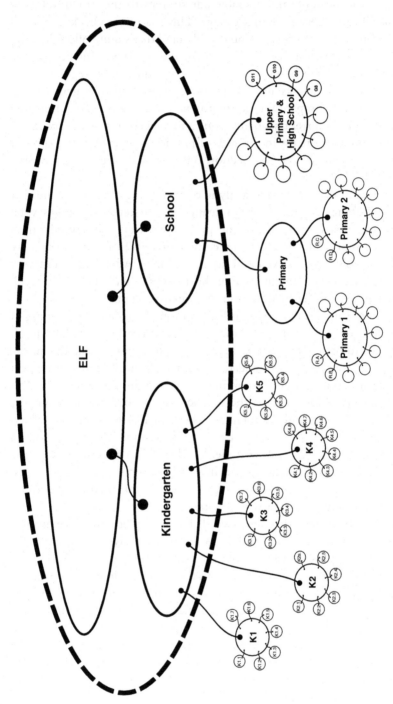

Figure 3.4 Agreed recursive analysis – ELF

(Illustration by Jon Walker)

average of 200 children and is organised in grades (between 6 and 7 grades each). At this level, unfolding of complexity is by type of service as each grade provides educational services at different grades (to children different age groups).

In a small company the recursive analysis undertaken will depict only one level of VSM diagnosis (level 0). In the above example, we could do recursive analysis at levels 0 (ELF school as a whole), level 1 (kindergartens and schools), followed by a VSM diagnosis of each one of the five kindergartens and each one of the three schools. In total, we could develop 11 specific VSM diagnoses over the project's lifecycle. We could go even further, to do a VSM analysis of each one of the grades, and even at each one of the class levels – which we also prototyped during the project. The recursive analysis of a very large organisation – i.e., a region or a nation – will display several layers of recursive organisations. The next chapters present examples of recursive analyses of more complex organisational systems.

VSM Preliminary Diagnosis

Once you have undertaken a recursive analysis, have agreed on major diagnostic issues identified in the recursive analysis, and have identified your system in focus, then you can then progress the v&s diagnosis for every viable system at every level of recursive organisation within the system in focus. The following sections will offer criteria to deepen a v&s diagnosis, and examples of v&s diagnosis in ELF at different levels of recursion.

Mapping the Viable System of the System in Focus

Once you have decided which system in focus to analyse, then you should produce a VSM diagram of the SiF,[3] as follows:

- Start always by drawing the System 1 at the lower level of recursion of the chosen system in focus, as a series of ovals following a typical VSM diagram; then represent – on their left – their environments as cloudy shapes.
- Draw the metasystem for the entire S1, as a diamond shape above the System 1, and add the boxes for Systems 3, 4, and 5. Draw the triangle shapes to represent System 2 on their right and System 3* on their left.
- Draw the whole environment as an amoeba-like shape including all operational niches and link it to the metasystem.
- Draw the connections between the different systems (1 to 5) following VSM conventions, as illustrated in the following system in focus from ELF, in Figure 3.5.

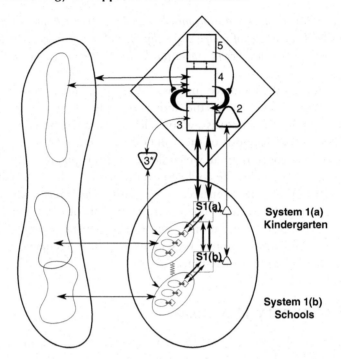

Figure 3.5 VSM of ELF (recursion level 0/1)

(Illustration by Jon Walker)

Now you are ready to start filling it with relevant information for the VSM diagnosis.

Doing a VSM Preliminary Diagnosis

Once you have a broad understanding of the organisation (rich picture, identity statement, and recursive mapping), you can explore in more detail the problematic issues identified. To start this preliminary analysis, you can use a v&s survey and/or v&s interviews with people occupying key roles from the system in focus. The survey provides generic questions and can be done to as many people as possible within the whole organisation. With a survey it is possible to gather views from larger groups of people than through interviews. However, as questionnaires are always a strong variety attenuator, as they predefine potential questions and answers, it is re-commendable to balance the results with additional open interviews (high variety) with specific roles later on without pre-setting the interview's agenda.

You can do individual interviews with representatives of all System 1s and all meta-systemic roles, within your system in focus. To prepare for the interviews, you can tailor specific questions for the interviewees, according to their roles, to expand/clarify broad responses from the surveys, if you have done them. The interview provides more precise information as well as insights into different worldviews co-existing in the organisational ecosystem.

In ELF, we started the VSM analysis by first running a survey with most employees of the school (about 100 participants responded to the survey; and then having individual interviews with each one of the projects' participants (we did around 20 interviews)). Once we collected information from the v&s survey and interviews, we tabulated them in a v&s diagram. We colour coded the answers as a very happy face (brown), a neutral face (blue), and an unhappy face (green). This way we managed to have a first broad and intuitive perception of the main balances and unbalances they were experiencing.

Complete VSM Diagnosis

To progress the organisational diagnosis, you can summarise the responses to the VSM survey, and interviews, and run v&s workshops (or alternatively virtual focus groups) with a selected sample of participants from the SiF, to further explore the preliminary diagnosis. Our experience shows that starting by doing v&s, coaching is the best way forward, as the project's participants can better engage when they understand the v&s language. It allows people to map and assess their own roles and interactions and fully contribute to the diagnosis.

There are normally important pre-diagnostic issues emerging from the initial stages of the STM, like uncovering, when reviewing the organisational identity, or the recursive analysis what we call 'organisational archetypes,' which are typical organisational pathologies that VSM practitioners have found systemically in many organisations of different types and scales, worldwide – see more details in (Espinosa &Walker, 2017, pp. 485–492; Cardoso-Castro & Espinosa, 2019). For example, *'identity'* archetypes include ill-defined organisational identity; tasks which do not correspond to the agreed identity; underdeveloped primary activities; a support activity acting as a primary activity; too frequent changes in identity; and divergent perceptions of identity. Also, it is not uncommon to identify serious problems of segmentation such as a missing recursion level.

Mapping v&s Roles and Mechanisms

Once the skeleton of a VSM diagram is drawn, we start plotting the roles and mechanisms in use for dealing with the organisational tasks (internal complexity) and their interactions with their niches (external complexity). We then organise a workshop to further understand existing roles and communication schemes, aiming to analyse who does what; who is responsible for each type of task; how they interact with each other to implement primary tasks; and which mechanisms and tools they use to communicate and coordinate actions.

Given that not always there are enough time and resources for running these types of workshops inviting all the desirable participants, deciding on representatives from each S1 and meta-systemic roles to attend them is fundamental for the success of these workshops. If possible and convenient, the same workshop can be run in parallel with different groups of representatives.

A good starting point for mapping roles distribution in a v&s diagram is to ask each of the participants, to fill in a table by writing down their different roles, one per row; classifying them using v&s distinctions (S1 to S5); and estimating the amount of time they devote to each one. We aim to assess at this point if operational staff mostly concentrate on operational rather than administrative tasks; or if they spend too much time resolving administrative requests, leaving too little time for implementing their primary tasks.

> *During the 1st workshop in ELF in 2019 we asked the participants to fill in such a table and then use stickers with each one of their roles and their names to place them in the VSM mapping. We made sure all the main roles were properly represented by addressing any doubts the participants had when interpretating their roles in VSM language. For example, we found at the kindergartens, a very well-balanced distribution of time for the coordinators between teaching and management tasks, even if they felt not enough time was devoted to S4 tasks.*

Identifying and Mapping Diagnostic Issues

While asking diagnostic questions during the interviews and/or workshops, you get engaged in conversations about the way that things are done in an operational or managerial unit. This way you begin to uncover recurrent breakdowns in specific relationships, and to diagnose structural problems which would require further investigation. You can represent the most significant (positive and negative) issues discussed in different VSM mappings, at the right level of recursion within the system in focus.

As mapping all the diagnostic issues identified may become too complex to represent inside the VSM mapping, we usually produce a Table coding the issues discussed as diagnostic points (D_1, D_2, ... D_n) and explaining them in detail. Then we include the diagnostic codes in the right place at the VSM mapping. As a diagnostic issue implies a value judgement (i.e., how well the situation described mirror v&s criteria), it is important to be able to provide evidence to support it, if required. By the end of these analyses and agreements, you will have produced a collage picture of the current situation. Figures 3.6, 3.7, and 3.8 offer examples of identified diagnostic issues, at recursion level 0 (ELF), and recursion level 1 (schools and kindergartens).

System in Focus : ELF Schools.

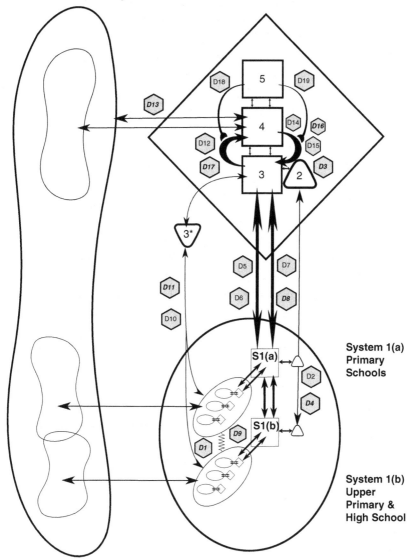

Figure 3.6 VSM of ELF schools (recursion level 1/2)

(Illustration by Jon Walker)

At recursion level 1/2 (ELF Schools), Figure 3.6. shows that to improve synergies between schools we agreed to share information about students' performance (D1) and to promote cross-fertilisation in academic innovations (D9).

S2 required of improvements in existing anti-oscillatory mechanisms (i.e., Google Drive and Adservio) (D2); further alignment among PSs and UPS and HSs

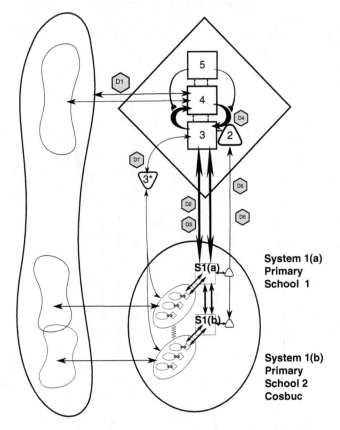

Figure 3.7 VSM diagnosis in the primary schools

(Illustration by Jon Walker)

standards and procedures (D3); and the design and implementation of an inventory management system (D4).

Regarding S3, it was agreed to clarify mechanisms for negotiating and managing each school's resources (people, technology infrastructure) (D5); operational budgets (D6); reviewing teachers' assessments (D7); and agreeing on improvement plans (D8). Regarding S3* need to decentralise the way of managing complaints from parents to each school headmaster (D10); and to redesign the existing scheme for monitoring teachers (D11). Regarding S4, need to redesign the teachers' mentoring program (D12); promote teaching innovations (D13); invite schools' participation in curriculum planning (D14); clarify procedures on plans for infrastructure development (D15); promote development of systemic education projects (D16); and design and implement environmental policies in education management and infrastructure (D17).

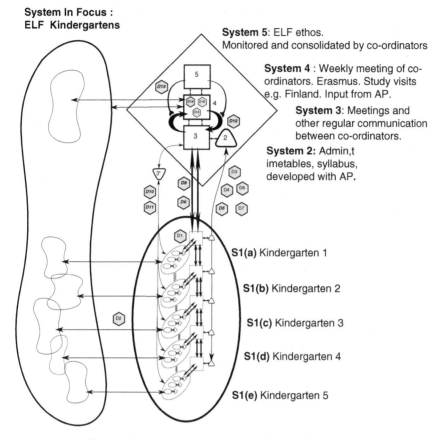

Figure 3.8 VSM diagnosis in the kindergartens

(Illustration by Jon Walker)

For S5, we agreed that each school will have a clear input for preparing the annual school report for the educational authority (D18); and for developing the digitalisation policy and strategy (D19).

At recursion level 1/2 (ELF Primary Schools), Figure 3.7. offer the following examples of diagnostic issues:

D1   *Headmaster directly attending parents and teachers requests and complaints for all schools.*

D2   *Headmaster managing recruitment, admissions process, payroll, purchasing and acquisitions, and open days for every school.*

D3   *Lack of shared information between schools on parents with more than one child in the schools.*

D4   *Uneven distribution of academic innovations among PS (e.g., program on socio emotional skills).*

D5   *Need to improve shared academic information (i.e., Google Drive).*

D6   *Overwork in coordination among school's headmasters (e.g., 10 pm WhatsApp talks).*

D7   *Need to rethink current monitoring system from a controlling to a mentoring role, with full teacher involvement.*

At recursion level 1/2 (ELF Kindergartens), Figure 3.8 offer the following examples of diagnostic issues:

S1   *To design a better recruitment and admissions system (D2); and a better approach for liaising with school inspectors (D1).*

S2   *To further promote and disseminate the ongoing Erasmus Project implementation (D3); standards and procedures (D4); quality control (D5); curriculum implementation and assessment (D6); and to co-design a new inventory management system (D7).*

S3   *To design a clearer procedure for resource negotiation (D9), and to review current approach to teachers' assessment (D8).*

S3* *To design better mechanisms for monitoring fee collection (D10), and for ensuring academic quality (D11).*

S4   *To design more incentives for teaching innovations (D15); to clarify mechanisms for deciding on the teachers' allocation plan (D12); the strategic direction for the school council (D13); and curriculum planning (D14). And to promote nature related projects at all levels (D16).*

Learning to identify diagnostic issues in each viable system (or interaction between systems) is one of the core VSM learning skills; sometimes at the beginning of a v&s project, people have many doubts concerning what type of viable system(s) a particular role or situation refers to. As the VSM distinctions are generic in nature, they are subject to interpretation. There isn't normally a unique way of interpreting roles or situations, so the facilitators' expertise provides important help in the participants' learning process. But it is when people feel confident enough with the VSM distinctions to start using them in their daily life, that they can get deeper and deeper into their learning from this approach.

You will notice how, by practising this type of analysis, that the participants in a v&s project begin to develop a 'cybernetic instinct.' This will alert them later (following the departure of external analysts or consultants), when they are experiencing any dis-functional relationships. And it is this alertness that creates the right context for self-reference and self-organisation to emerge. This is where the possibility for double-loop learning also emerges as a result of embedding in the organisation capabilities for self-reference.

Once you have identified the roles (and mechanisms) for each of the five systems, you can then progress to the next stage of enquiry, which focuses on looking at the way the five systems interact. The next sections provide some guidance and examples on how we can further explore people's perception of their current interactions with other roles and their own performance; and the main challenges or difficulties experienced when delivering their tasks.

Assessing System 1's Interactions

According to Ashby's Law of Requisite Variety, the biggest challenge for managing complexity in organisations comes from addressing the natural variety imbalance between the operation (O) and its environmental niche (E), and between the operation (O) and operational management (M). How to design proper processes and mechanisms to attenuate the niche's variety and to amplify the operational variety is central to operational performance. To analyse S1 vs E interactions, we must enquire if S1 operates with 're-sponsible autonomy,' and if it has enough skills and proficiency to de-monstrate good operational performance. This means having autonomy to take decisions quickly and effectively when required, resources and knowledge to implement their decisions once taken, and respect for legal and resource constraints.

If an operational team works well, develops the expected level of pro-ducts or services with the expected quality, effectively uses the available resources (including information and knowledge), is capable of adapting to its niche when it changes, and leaves its customers satisfied, while respecting organisational values and constraints, then we can say this S1 is viable. If they also do it without severance to their socio-ecological niche, and sup-porting their local communities, then we can say they are viable and sus-tainable. This is why interrogating the external stakeholders' perceptions (e.g., the customers, suppliers, competitors, local communities) about the organisation is a central aspect to S1s' assessment. A positive external sta-keholders' assessment means that the operational team is dealing well with its internal variety and managing properly the variety of its interaction with its management.

Proper variety management is normally related to having harmonic and balanced internal and external relationships. Clear evidence of unbalanced in-ternal interactions can be seen when there are recurrent breakdowns which are affecting operational (or even organisational) performance. To progress the diagnosis at this level we must investigate problems of poor performance; lack of autonomy; lack of people, financial, physical, or technological resources; poor or delayed communications with operational or meta-systemic management; and effectiveness of the administrative and technical support to operations.

We must also interrogate representatives from S1 on how balanced and healthy their interactions with their customers and suppliers are (e.g., addressing their concerns and requests effectively, informing them of new products or service developments); if there are clear commercial policies; how robust are their marketing and advertisement strategies; if there are effective mechanisms for assessing customer satisfaction; and how robust is the operational processes design. Based on answers to these enquiries, we can at this point assess the core structural weaknesses of each S1, and represent any diagnostic issues found in the VSM mapping at the right level of recursion.

The Inside and Now (Systems 1, 2, and 3)

The diagnosis at this level aims at finding out the quality of interactions between operations and meta-systemic roles, focusing on the 'Inside and Now' (S1/S2/S3/S3*), which means to assess how well prepared the meta-system (S2/S3/S3*) is to do its job properly of: (i) generating synergies between operational units; (ii) supporting S1s to be responsibly autonomous and self-regulating; and (iii) addressing any major breakdowns if any of them breaks basic legal, organisational, or industrial rules.

To make progress in this analysis, we continue engaging with representatives of operational and meta-systemic roles to explore whether there are any gaps in their ways of interacting and/or their processes' design in the light of VSM criteria. Developing awareness of the existence of structural problems, and preparedness to address them quickly and effectively, is the basis for promoting effective learning loops.

Firstly, we investigate S2's effectiveness: If there are clear roles and mechanisms for conflict resolution; if the organisational ethos and values are embedded in people's daily decision making; if there are effective standards and quality control systems; if the sustainability criteria are embedded in day-to-day operational decisions. We also aim to explore how effective is the interaction between operational and general management (S3). For example, if S3:

- Provides enough autonomy to S1s and promotes synergies among them.
- Provides S1s with the required skills and resources.[4]
- Has effective mechanisms for resource negotiation, accountability, and legal or normative issues.
- Has effective monitoring systems for checking people's wellbeing, appropriateness of technical and physical infrastructure, and any emerging troubles in operational processes.
- Use sustainability standards (e.g., for managing services, deciding on technologies and suppliers) to guide decision making.

- Is able to resolve conflicts between operative units should they arise.
- Sets the boundaries for strategic (S4) and operative (S3) planning within System 1.

The Outside and Then (Systems 3, 4, and 5)

S3, S4, and S5 interact to address issues of the 'Outside and Then.' They are the organ of adaptation, the ones responsible for agreeing on the most suitable and creative organisational development path. S3, from the *Inside and Now* perspective, and S4, from the *Outside and Then* perspective, support S5 decisions on strategies or policies. S4 continuously explores the 'Outside and Then' by bringing information from the niche about opportunities for innovation or about emerging threats. It also manages the communication loops between the organisation and its niche. On the other hand, S3 continuously provides a well-grounded, synoptic view of what is going on inside the organisation and how the S1s are interacting with their internal and external stakeholders in the production and delivery of products or services.

The S3/S4/S5 interactions are the most complex ones in an organisation, the ones where power imbalances have a huge impact on the developmental decisions taken. S5's main role is to facilitate the conversations and decisions between S3 and S4, by generating a balanced context for decision making (e.g., by inviting similar numbers of S3 and S4 roles to participate in strategy and policy decisions). If there were too many S3 and too few S4 roles, the decisions made are prone to be too down to earth, more conservative, and risk avoiding, therefore sacrificing creativity and innovation.

Alternatively, if there are too many S4 roles and too few S3 roles, decisions may be very innovative and sometimes far too risky, and unrealistic, with little grounding in the organisational capabilities, strategies, and policies (which may bring in more implementation risks). S5 should create a rich context for the S3/S4 interaction, by making sure that there is a balanced representation from each type of role in strategy and policy decisions, so that they can absorb each other's variety. Also, S5 ensures everything is within policy constraints.

For analysing the Outside and Then, we first identify the S4 and S5 roles that lead policy, innovation, and strategy decisions and the mechanisms they use for making such decisions. Then we assess if the mechanisms where strategy and policy decisions are taken (boards, councils, forums, etc.) can manage the variety of the topics to be decided upon (e.g., by including balanced representation of S3, S4, and S5); in other words, whether the participants and agenda for the meetings, the information brought in advance to enrich the context for decision making, and the way meetings are conducted provide enough variety for rich and agile decisions making.

To support the diagnosis of existing S3/S4/S5 interactions regarding strategic and innovations' management, we need to explore whether all the relevant S3/S4 and S5 roles have requisite variety to contribute to strategic decision making. For example, how well S4 does environmental scanning; how responsibilities for innovation among people at different S1s are distributed; how effectively innovations and sustainability strategies get implemented; and any need for improvements in operational performance, and how much they contribute to strategy forming. Also, the diagnosis should show whether there are effective knowledge management systems in place; and if the operational strategies are aligned with organisational strategies.

We also should investigate the effectiveness of self-governance structures. For example, if S3 and S4 have an opportunity to contribute their viewpoints to strategy and policy decisions by being properly represented in strategic decision-making spaces, and by being allowed to speak and influence decisions. Also, if these roles making strategic decisions have requisite variety to manage the complexity of the issues to be decided upon; and if there is a participatory, democratic, and transparent culture for strategic or policy decision making. S3/S4/S5 diagnosis should also identify and assess where there is space for improvement e.g., by developing adaptive capabilities for mapping the complexity of the niche vs. the complexity of the internal environment. Or by improving the variety in managing communications with the external environment.

> In ELF, we had identified in the previous workshops that headmasters needed to allocate more time to fully develop their S4/S5 roles (people's development, educational development, physical and technological development, and organisational development). Also, they had understood the need to design more robust strategic decision- making spaces as many decisions were still made in an informal and centralised way without proper participation from lower organisational levels. More inclusive and timely ways of preparing the formal annual school report to be discussed (or just signed) at the Board of Administration (BoA) were agreed.

A result of this analysis is to assess the need for adjustments in the decision-making spaces, agendas, or types and numbers of participants; in the culture and dynamics to make strategic decisions; in the tools to support decision making; and in the quality of the information to support strategy and policy decisions. In the following chapters, we will review different case studies with varied examples of organisational pathologies, which include pathological situations in the S3/S4/S5 interactions, risking organisational v&s.

Aligning Strategy, Structure, and Information Systems

The previous sections offered criteria and guidelines to perform a full VSM diagnosis. During the recursive analysis, core issues of segmentation were addressed (and hopefully agreed if major changes were required). At the diagnosis stage, we should have identified a range of diagnostic issues that need attention. In order to get ready to think about possible self-transformation projects, this analytical stage suggests the need to: a) revisit the current organisational strategy and analyse whether the current structure provides the required capabilities for implementing it; and b) assess any needs for improvement for existing information and communication systems, resulting from the organisational diagnosis and/or from any additional requirements for effectively implementing organisational strategies.

> *In ELF, when we started the project the school's owners had already bought some land on the outskirts of the city and were in the process of getting planning permission and of designing a new school. They had decided this new school will aim to receive hundreds of new students from upper primary to high school. Their plans were to build it in the next few years once they got all the needed permissions and resources. As all the other headquarters were rented, this new headquarter would be the first and only one owned by ELF and some of the services for all schools will move there (e.g., catering). To prepare for the new school, they needed to prepare the future headmasters, teachers, and administrative team to be ready to cope with the increased complexity.*

Aligning Strategy and Structure

We assume in the STM that an organisation will have periodically agreed on a developmental strategy, using the – hopefully systemic – approaches and methodologies they prefer,[5] so in this stage we aim to review requirements for structural improvements to implement the agreed organisational strategy. Atkinson (2006) explains that quite often there is a gap between a portfolio of agreed strategies and what gets finally implemented; he calls it the 'implementation gap.'

Following v&s criteria, the implementation gap can be further explained if the 3/4/5 homeostat is unbalanced or doesn't work well, such as in the following scenarios:

- S4 is weak in the strategic decision-making space (e.g., too many S3 roles, too few S4s) and its recommendations are not fully understood or considered thoroughly in the final strategy decisions.

- S4 has the power and resources to decide on the organisational strategy but it doesn't understand existing resource constraints (people, financial, technological) that may deter success in strategy implementation.

- S3 isn't supportive of creative strategies, due to its focus on existing constraints in resources or capabilities or on avoiding risks.
- S3 fails to convince operational units to implement agreed strategies, as they compete with more and immediate challenges they need to consider.
- S1 is segmented badly!

At this analytical stage, we want to make sure that the organisation has (or will develop) the required capabilities and the technological infrastructure to avoid the implementation gap. This requires revisiting the current organisational structure, in the light of the agreed strategy, and identifying any new operational units/roles, or additional skills, capabilities, or technological support required for successfully implementing the agreed strategies.

It may be recommended at this stage, to follow again the first and second stages of the methodology in 'design mode.' This means to review the organisational identity based on the agreed developmental strategy, checking if the '*identity in use*' remains valid when implementing the organisational strategy, or if there is a need to agree on a new, '*desirable identity.*' Also, implementing the organisational strategy may bring forward changes in the existing segmentation of operational units. In any of these cases, we would need to produce:

- A new statement of 'desired identity.'
- A revised recursive analysis, based on the desired identity, including any emergent units required for implementing the 'desired identity.'
- Revised VSM mappings for the system in focus, adjusted to the revised recursive analysis.
- A comparison between these new recursive analysis and v&s mapping with the current ones, to clarify the differences (i.e., required new S1s, or new meta-systemic roles required in the existing structure).
- A list of desirable adjustments in the current roles and structure, as well as the new capabilities required for implementing the new strategy.

Based on the above analysis, we must complement the existing developmental plan to ensure the right roles and capabilities are going to be deployed to guarantee an effective organisational context for implementing the agreed strategies.

Strategic Information Management

At this stage, we analyse the strategic information management needs of each of each one of the S1s of the system in focus and develop a plan for addressing them. To identify strategic information management needs, a review of the existing software and communication infrastructure should be conducted with the specialist ICT units in the organisation. Also, the v&s diagnosis can be used to check which roles need additional ICT support at each level of organisation. All identified needs can be summarised as a strategic information management plan. Implementation of the strategic information systems plan should be aligned to the self-transformation projects.

In ELF, several diagnostic issues were identified regarding the use of ICT both for administrative and academic purposes. Responsibilities for exploring and implementing ICT improvements and innovations were clarified and during the lifetime of the project most of these initiatives were successfully implemented. It included an adapted version of the Kinderpedia software (students' and parents' information system) successfully used in the KGs, which was then developed and implemented in PSs. They also purchased new computers and tablets for the children and teachers in PSs and continued with existing efforts to develop creative use of state-of-the-art technologies in the classroom (i.e., drones and robots).

Self-Transformation Projects and Plan

At this stage, we need to suggest and prioritise self-transformation initiatives to address each one of the diagnostic issues at each level of organisation in the system in focus. Also, we must identify the required responsibilities, resources, and timing for implementation. Once formulated, the different initiatives can be clustered into different types of self-transformation projects, and for each one, a project leader may be appointed. In some cases, one self-transformation project may address several diagnostic issues, all of which originate in one structural pathology.

The project's leaders should review, clarify, and assess the relevance of the suggested initiatives, and complete any omissions. They should be fully responsible for detailing and specifying each project: required adjustments to roles and processes, development of new required capabilities; required ICT support; and required improvements to infrastructure (if at all). The detailed projects should then be put together by the project leaders, as the self-transformation plan.

The technical committee for the implementation stage should include all the project leaders and should meet to discuss and decide on the final details of the self-transformation plan. As mentioned before, strategic development decisions are generally one of the most political and complex decisions for an organisation, as they imply using some of the financial surplus or developmental funds – if there were available – or finding other types of funding for implementing the self-transformation plan.

There are normally negotiations between the project leaders and the meta-systemic management (S3/S4/S5) that finally result in an agreed developmental plan, with proper timelines, clear responsibilities for each project, and agreed sources of funding. Once agreed, this technical committee should meet periodically to assess progress in implementing the self-transformation projects, and to review improvements in performance.

> For example, some of the self-transformation projects in ELF included: to begin operating strategic councils in each school, where they have been discussing in a more organised and effective way strategies and policies for people syllabus, physical and technological developments. To create a new sustainability strategy role and to begin to design clearer environmental and sustainability policies and strategies. For example, they strongly promoted and disseminated pioneering efforts to educate students as responsible citizens by actively participating in city projects (i.e., for creating awareness and tools for disposing waste in a more sustainable way in the neighbourhood of each school).

Monitoring and Assessing Performance

While it is now common practice in most business and public organisations to implement performance management systems, (e.g., balance score card); not all organisations manage to have robust KPIs, or to keep their control boards updated to support agile and robust decision making. This is normally the case if the KPIs are not designed according to v&s criteria, i.e., if they:

- Are not focused in observing 'essential variables' for operational units.
- Represent too many or too detailed issues to be measured and analysed.
- Present serious challenges for data collection.
- Can't be maintained with updated (hopefully real time) information.
- Are badly represented (not using size, colour, relations, and trends).

In such cases, the control boards may end up including a large battery of mostly outdated and not that useful KPIs, so they are not fit for their purpose of supporting strategic management decisions. Therefore, it is recommended at this stage to fully review the existing KPIs using the above criteria, and to identify required improvements.

Each S1 in the system in focus should first identify or review its own key performance indicators and assess existing procedures for collecting and analysing performance data.[6] They should agree on a 'cybernetically sound KPIs design.' Beer (1979, pp. 279–306; 367–394; 409–509), (Espejo, 2009), and Morlidge (2007) assess operational and organisational performance. If the organisation does not have a proper set of KPIs and/or an effective performance management system, then it is recommendable to set up a project to design it at this stage, as part of the self-transformation plan. The following steps help to check if there is a 'cybernetically sound' performance management system.

- *Number of KPIs*: According to Miller (1956), the optimum number of control variables that we can handle within physiological limits is $7 +/- 2$ (*the magical number*). In practical terms, this imposes constraints to any users of a performance management system (e.g., those responsible for the S3/S1 homeostat). To keep attention focused, it is best to continuously observe the behaviour of *the magical number of* KPIs; otherwise, users won't be able to follow up each one of the indices' behaviours effectively. Therefore, the first thing to review is whether the number of agreed KPIs for each primary activity and for each level of complexity is within the range of *the magical number.*

- *Mapping Operational Units*: Even if a nalanced score card was already in place, it is recommended to review existing KPIs by mapping them on the VSM of the organisation. We aim to make sure that only a limited number of KPIs — those that are core to observing performance of operational units, at each recursive level — are continuously observed and measured. In some cases, the same KPIs would be recursively nested, so that 'aggregates' can be produced at higher levels of organisation (e.g., the number of students succeeding to 'pass' a grade level at different levels in a primary school, in a particular period of time).

- *Reviewing the Measurement System*: Ideally a new measurement system, based on Beer's ideas of actuality, capability, and performance, should be put in place, as it allows historical data analysis and therefore a long-term mapping of operational and organisational performance.

- *Assessing Recursive Governance Structures*: Not only do we need an effective performance management system (PMS) and culture at each level of recursive organisation, but we also need well connected, cohesive, and responsive inter-organisational PMS. We should assess existing PMSs at each level of recursion. If they speak to each other; if the sum of the strategies in S1 is the same as the strategy of the metasystem; if they do fit together; and if the operative plans are cohesive and well assessed.

- *Establishing the Impact of Self-Transformation Projects:* Once the KPIs have been agreed or reviewed, an effective way to measure and assess them needs to be put in place from the beginning of the project's implementation cycle to monitor the impact of the self-transformation projects on organisational performance.

In ELF we examined the schools' self-assessment system and the headmaster's capabilities for providing strategic performance information in preparation for the annual school assessment. The existing school assessment system was intended to respond to all the official educational authorities' accreditation criteria and even if very complete and well-structured it mixed up operational performance and meta-systemic assessments. It didn't include measuring key performance indicators in core educational areas. It was agreed to redesign KPIS, based on operational performance, and to align the way academic and operational assessments were produced and discussed in each school.

This stage of the STM methodology should be initiated when analysing S1's performance, during the full diagnosis stage. This is why in the STM diagram, there are doble loops arrows connecting stages 3 and 6. This analysis can be completed in this final stage with the definition of technical and financial requirements for developing or improving the current performance management system (PMS). Once a robust performance management system has been designed, adjusted, and put into operation, it should be used to support real time decisions in the S1/S2/S3 homeostat, and in the S3/S4/S5 homeostat, at every level of recursive organisation.

A continuous analysis of KPIs allows the generation of algedonics – early alarm signals. Beer considered that such early alarms are fundamental to 'awaken' the consciousness of meta-systemic management about situations that are getting out of control, so that a support network can be accessed and the required resources to address crises can be allocated to operational units before problems escalate. A final reflection at this stage of the STM is to assess if there are mechanisms in place to generate algedonics and to quickly respond to them when they happen.

A v&s project is a learning project and should be conducted as such. Each of the previous stages of analysing an organisation, identifying required transformations, and implementing them, should be part of an in-depth, self-critical, and reflective organisational learning process. Each of the agreed self-transformation projects, while being designed and implemented, would need to develop its own learning loop. This requires continuously observing and reflecting how the implemented changes impact the organisational and processes' performance (which should result from addressing or dissolving identified pathological patterns of interaction). To close the v&s project's learning loop, we should continuously monitor those KPIs which allow us to trace the self-transformation project's development and impact.

Team Syntegrity

Beer's other major invention was the 'team syntegrity' (TS) methodology, to facilitate shared agreements among varied and sometimes conflicting interests, in large groups, inspired by Buckminster Fuller's principle of tensegrity (tensile integrity). He suggested it as a useful tool to manage the complexity of decisions in the S3/S4 homeostat, in a complex organisation or network (Beer (1994).

TS structures a 2.5-day event, following a protocol based in the geometric figure of an icosahedron. It allows a group of around 30 people to get together to address a complex issue that interest them all and to reach agreements on ways to deal with it, in a highly participatory way. Malik on Management, a Swiss consultancy company owns the copyrights of the TS protocol and has continued and expanded his work through hundreds of successful applications worldwide, during the last two decades. Espinosa and Harnden (2007) offer a briefing on the methodology and a detailed example of application. In the last decade, there has been a growing interest for experimenting the power of combining the VSM with TS to support self-transformation projects. In the following chapters, we will mention a few examples that demonstrate the usefulness of combining them.

Summary

This chapter has introduced the self-transformation methodology, as a framework to facilitate organisational and team learning as an approach to managing complexity, which has evolved over decades of practice, by adapting it to different contexts like businesses, non for profit organisations , governmental organisations, and communities.

The strength of the STM is its inclusive nature and its focus in facilitating user's learning on the VSM; however, there are still challenging issues to ensure full implementation. There are situations where the client can't (or doesn't want to afford) the time and resources to have his people trained, and in these situations the v&s may not be the best approach. Other approaches with smaller teams and faster results might be necessary.

If the client is interested, one of the implementation challenges is the feasibility of involving the right type and numbers of stakeholders and to ensure they get a deep enough understanding of the theory over the time of a project. The other challenge is to ensure they can grasp the core ideas, notwithstanding the technical language and representations. As the many case studies presented in the next chapters demonstrate, if these two conditions can be satisfied, there is a high possibility of having a positive impact in implementation.

The following case studies will offer examples of using the VSM's apparently complex language and tools in multi-cultural and diverse contexts: by carefully including multi-stakeholders in facilitated workshops; by using alternative languages (e.g., cartoons, or drama) to collectively represent the participants' perceptions; by fully involving participants in the learning process; and by building up in the collective consciousness which emerged from the process to effectively design and implement agreed self-transformation projects. They demonstrate ways forward to overcome the criticisms of the difficulty of VSM language to guide organisational transformations (Lowe et al., 2016). They also reflect on situations which could had been improved, in cases where an agreed v&s self-transformation was only partly completed, often due to political or leadership changes.

Notes

1 https://orcid.org/my-orcid?orcid=0000–0002–5200–7613
2 Permission to include it from Metaphorum.
3 Given that the VSM mapping may require of a lot of details, we normally do it first by hand, using wallpaper. Once agreements are made with the participants we can produce an electronic version of the figure, if required.
4 This is symptomatic of organisational pathology 2.24 (see Espinosa and Walker (2017), p. 490).
5 Dyson et al. (2007) offer a more systemic approach to strategic development process formation. Mingers and White (2010) offer an in-depth review of systemic approaches to strategy.
6 An initial assessment of KPIs should take place earlier in the analysis, when analysing S1's operational performance. At this stage, a more detailed assessment of the broad performance management system should take place.

References

Achterbergh, J., & Vriens, D. (2002). 'Managing viable knowledge', *Systems Research and Behavioural Sciences*, 19(3), pp. 223–241.

Atkinson, H. (2006). 'Strategy implementation: A role for the balanced scorecard?', *Management Decision*, 44, pp. 1441–1460.

Argyris, C., & Schon, D. A. (1996). *Organisational learning II. Theory, method, and practice.* Reading, MA: Addison-Wesley.

Barile, S., Saviano, M., Iandolo, F., & Calabrese, M. (2014). 'The viable systems approach and its contribution to the analysis of sustainable business behaviours', *Systems Research and Behavioural Science*, 31(6), pp. 683–695.

Beer, S. (1979). *The Heart of the Enterprise.* Chichester: John Wiley & Sons.

Beer, S. (1985). *Diagnosing the System for Organisations.* Chichester: John Wiley & Sons.

Beer, S. (1994). *Beyond Dispute: The Invention of Team Syntegrity.* Chichester: John Wiley & Sons.

Cardoso-Castro, P. P., & Espinosa, A. (2019), 'Identification of organisational pathologies: Exploration of social network analysis to support the viable system model diagnostic', *Kybernetes*, 49(2), pp. 285–312.

Cervone, H. F. (2011), 'Understanding agile project management methods using Scrum', *OCLC Systems & Services: International digital library perspectives*, 27(1), pp. 18–22.

Checkland, P. B., & Poulter, J. (2006). *Learning For Action: A Short Definitive Account of Soft Systems Methodology, and its use Practitioners, Teachers and Students.* Chichester: Wiley.

Christopher, W. (2007). *Holistic Management: Managing what Matters for Company Success.* New York: John Wiley & Sons.

Dominici, G., & Roblek, V. (2016). 'Complexity theory for a new managerial paradigm: A research framework' in *Neostrategic Management.* Cham: Springer, pp. 223–241.

Dominici, G., & Palumbo, F. (2013). 'Decoding the Japanese lean production system according to a viable systems perspective', *Systemic Practice and Action Research,* 26(2), pp. 153–171.

Dyson, R. G., Bryant, J., Morecroft, J., & O'Brien, F. (2007). 'The strategic development process' in O'Brien, F. & Dyson, R. G. (Eds.), *Supporting strategy: Frameworks, methods and models.* 1st edition. Chichester: John Wiley & Sons, pp. 3–24.

Espejo, R., Bowling, D., & Hoverstadt, P. (1999). 'The viable system model and the viplan software', *Kybernetes,* 28 (6/7), pp. 661–678.

Espejo, R. (2009). 'Performance management, the nature of regulation and the CyberSyn project', *Kybernetes,* 38(1/2), pp. 65–82.

Espejo, R., & Reyes, A. (2011). *Organizational Systems: Managing Complexity with the Viable System Model.* London: Springer.

Espinosa, A. (1995). 'Strategic Information Systems at the Colombian President's Office: A Managerial Cybernetic Perspective'. *Doctoral Thesis, Aston Business School.* Birmingham: Aston University.

Espinosa, A., & Harnden, R. (2007). 'Team syntegrity and democratic group decision making: Theory and practice', *Journal of Operational Research,* 58(8), pp. 1056–1064.

Espinosa, A., Harnden, R., & Walker, J. (2008). 'A complexity approach to sustainability – Stafford beer revisited', *European Journal of Operational Research,* 187(2), pp. 636–651.

Espinosa, A., & Walker, J. (2017). *A Complexity Approach to Sustainability: Theory and application.* 2nd edition Singapore: World Scientific Press

Flood, R. L., & Jackson, M. (1991). *Critical Systems Thinking: Directed Readings.* Chichester: John Wiley & Sons.

Gharajedaghi, J. (2007). 'Systems thinking: A case for second order-learning', *The Learning Organization,* 14(6), pp. 473–479.

Golinelli, G. M. (2010). *Viable Systems Approach – Governing Business Dynamics.* Padova: Kluwer/CEDAM.

Hoverstadt, P. (2008). *The Fractal Organization. Creating sustainable organization with the Viable Systems Model.* Chichester: John Wiley & Sons.

Jackson, M. (2003). *Systems Thinking: Creative Holism for Managers.* Chichester: John Wiley & Sons.

Jackson, M. C. (2019). *Critical Systems Thinking and the Management of Complexity: Responsible Leadership for a Complex World.* Chichester: John Wiley & Sons.

Laloux, F. (2014). *Reinventing organisations: a guide to creating organisations inspired by the next stage of human consciousness.* Nelson Parker.

Lambertz, M. (2018). *Die Intelligente Organisation. Das Playbook fur organisatorische Komplexitat,* Gottinghen: Business Village.

Lassl, W. (2019). *The viability of organisations: Diagnosing and governing organizations.* Vol 2. Vienna: Springer

Lowe, D., Martingale, L., & Yearworth, M. (2016). 'Guiding interventions in a multi-organisational context: Combining the viable system model and hierarchical process modelling for use as a problem structuring method', *Journal of the Operational Research Society,* 67(12), pp. 1481–1495.

Lowe, D., Espinosa, A., & Yearworth, M. (2020). 'Constitutive rules for guiding the use of the viable system model: Reflections on practice', *European Journal of Operational Research,* 287(3), pp. 1014–1035.

Maturana, H., & Varela, F. (1988). *The Tree of Knowledge: The Biological Roots of Human Understanding*. Boston: Shambala.

Miller, G. A. (1956). 'The Magical Number seven plus or minus two: Some limits on our capacity of processing information', *Psychological Review*, 63, pp. 81–97.

Mingers, J., & White, L. (2010). 'A review of the recent contribution of systems thinking to operational research and management science', *European Journal of Operational Research*, 207, pp. 1147–1161.

Morlidge, S. (2007). 'The Application of Organisational Cybernetics to the Design and Diagnosis of Financial Performance Management Systems'. *PhD Dissertation, Hull University Business School*, Hull: Hull University.

Pérez-Ríos, J. (2012). *Design and Diagnosis for Sustainable Organizations: The Viable System Method*. London: Springer.

Pfiffner, M. (2010), 'Five experiences with the viable system model', *Kybernetes*, 39(9/10), pp. 1615–1626.

Pfiffner, M. (2020). *Die dritte Dimension des Organisierens. Steuerung und Kommunikation*. St Gallen: Springer.

Rau, T. J., & Koch-Gonzalez, J. (2018). *Many Voices One Song: Shared Power with Sociocracy*. Amherst, MA, US: OCLC.

Robertson, B. (2015). *Holacracy: The Revolutionary Management System that Abolishes Hierarchy*, London: Penguin.

Sherehiy, B., Karwowski, W., & Layer, J. K. (2007). 'A review of enterprise agility: Concepts, frameworks, and attributes', *International Journal of Industrial Ergonomics*, 37(5), pp. 445–460.

Schwaninger, M. (2009). *Intelligent Organisations: Powerful Models for Systemic Management*. St Gallen: Springer.

Schwaninger, M., Ramage, M., & Espejo, R. (2015). 'Organizing for Sustainability: A cybernetic concept for sustainable renewal', *Kybernetes*, 44(6/7), pp. 935–954.

Snowden, D., & Boone, M. (2007). 'A Leaders Framework for decision making', *Harvard Business Review*, November. pp. 1–8.

Teece, D. J. (2012). 'Dynamic capabilities: Routines versus entrepreneurial action', *Journal of Management Studies*, 49(8), pp. 1395–1401.

Vahidi, A., Aliahmadi, A., & Teimoury, E. (2019), 'Researches status and trends of management cybernetics and viable system model', *Kybernetes*, 48(5), pp. 1011–1044.

Yolles, M. (1999). *Management Systems: A Viable Approach*. London: Financial Times Pitman.

Zahra, S. A., Sapienza, H. J., & Davidson, P. (2006). 'Entrepreneurship and dynamic capabilities: a review, model, and research agenda', *Journal of Management Studies*, 43(4), pp. 917–955.

Chapter 4

Towards More Resilient and Healthier Organisations and Societies

Undoubtedly, our current sustainability crisis has become more evident in 2020–2021 as a consequence of the COVID-19 pandemic and its devastating effect on individuals, businesses, and societies. Millions of people around the world have died; millions have lost their jobs, their houses, are starving; or are suffering from mental health problems, due to loneliness, isolation, and lack of a clear future, while a large number of businesses are going into liquidation. The impact of the COVID-19 pandemic has been devastating for too many individuals, economic sectors, and nations in the world. It has radically shifted business and research priorities.

The pandemic has been most challenging for the health sector which has been pushed to its limits, and sometimes beyond, in many nations. The next sections summarise different experiences on the need for resilience and adaptation before and during the pandemic, ending up with recent case studies in the NHS in England. Hopefully these examples demonstrate how the v&s approach may help us to collectively identify effective policies and strategies to improve individual and organisational resilience, even in situations of chaos and emergency.

Organisational Health, Resilience, and Self-Governance

In a v&s organisation, each embodied viable system is self-organised and self-governed, makes agile, real-time decisions on critical issues for its sustainability, shares knowledge and good practice among operational units, and is adaptive and resilient. Sustainability is an emerging phenomenon, resulting from conscious choices of more sustainable ways of living and working, from the individual to the household, business, region, nation, and global levels. Following Ashby (1962), the way to develop (capabilities for) self-organisation is by learning to recognise a bad organisation (in our case, unsustainable),

DOI: 10.4324/9780429490835-5

realise what is a good (more sustainable) organisation, and acting (in our case self-transforming) towards a more sustainable organisation.

In any purposeful organisation, while developing a task, people continuously learn how to self-organise to do it, how to better use their resources and capabilities, and how to improve the quality of products or services they develop. A v&s organisation is robust and resilient; it critically reviews its learning on *what* it does well and *when*, *why* it does it, and *how* to do it in a sustainable way. These are always the guiding questions for us in self-governing ourselves and our organisations. As a result of experience, a v&s organisation continuously co-evolves with its niche and co-produces new understanding and knowledge from practice, resulting when required in new process design and the promotion of new values and social behaviours.

We learn by reflecting if we achieved our goals (effectiveness), if we used appropriately the available resources (efficacy), and if we did it to the expected standards (performance). Feedback is one of the fundamental cybernetic principles and it constitutes the basis for learning, self-reference, and self-regulation. To assess our performance, we compare our organisational results with what we planned to do, notice the differences, and provide feedback to the organisation to reorient decisions and resources. On this basis, we then decide what needs to be done to improve our capabilities, skills, and performance.

One of the manager's core roles is facilitating organisational self-governance, which implies managing the learning loops involved in organisational performance. The more changeable and fluid is the environment in which we operate, the higher the demands on us for learning and co-evolving with it. Learning is the basis for resilience, adaptation, and for developing collective intelligence. Adaptation is the basis for viability and sustainability.

Beer explained in some detail the idea of 'algedonic signals' as 'early alarms' on situations that may risk organisational viability. A fundamental skill that managers need to develop is the ability to quickly recognise algedonic signals – early alarms – revealing serious threats to their organisational v&s. Self-governance results if organisations react in real time to early alarms by (sometimes dramatically) readjusting their strategies and processes to match the variety of their niches. Managing an organisation in a chaotic environment requires the best of managerial instinct and common sense, as well as the best of teamwork and the capability of continuously rebalancing the pace and direction it takes.

Early Alarms from the COVID-19 Pandemic

As explained before, a v&s organisation is organised in clusters of self-organising viable systems co-evolving with their niches, with no severance from their niches. Each embodied viable system is self-organised and self-governed; makes agile, real-time decisions on critical issues for its sustainability; shares knowledge and good practice among operational units; and is adaptive and resilient.

The COVID-19 pandemic is revealing key vulnerabilities of our globalised society and its widespread neo-liberal development model. The way that governments have dealt with this public health crisis has raised early alarms in several countries, regarding governments' capabilities for guaranteeing quality and coverage of health services. In the next sections, we explore some of the early alarms we were sensing before and during the recent pandemic, at different levels of organisation, from an individual to business and regional levels.

We will then focus on a few case studies at National Health Service (NHS) in England during the first year of the COVID-19 pandemic. These analyses will hopefully illustrate how the v&s approach and the STM may be useful to support organisations to strategically develop their sensing and adapting capabilities and to develop more resilience to cope with emergency situations.

Towards More Resilient Individuals

In most countries, individuals develop both personal and working activities, including different types of interactions with their socio-economic and environmental niches. Personal activities include being at home with the family, cooking, gardening, and producing their own food, exercising (e.g., biking, walking), reading books, connecting to topics and people through the internet, managing ones' finances (i.e., banking); shopping, participating in social or civic events (e.g., music, pub, movies) or taking holidays. Working activities include travelling to work and developing our jobs while interacting with different stakeholders from our business ecosystem.

Each one of these activities is part of our individual project to survive and develop as individuals, as members of our households, our community, our nation, and ultimately as world citizens. We self-organise for doing each one of them, and over time we develop awareness of what results in good (more sustainable) or bad (less sustainable) self-organisation. By developing criteria to make our choices towards more sustainable ways of living and interacting we can hopefully thrive and become more resilient.

Undoubtedly the long periods of recent lockdowns severely disrupted the 'normal' way of living our lives. Suddenly, we were forced into isolating ourselves in our household, avoiding social contact, and (for the lucky ones keeping their jobs) working from home. Figure 4.1 highlights those types of interactions with our niches that were challenged throughout the pandemic. The ones that most people have continued to develop 'normally' are in bold (e.g., staying with family, gardening); those disrupted and/or those we managed to keep through the internet are shown in italics (e.g., banking, traveling socialising, shopping).

On one side, the pandemic has brought some positive changes to those privileged enough to keep their jobs, while living in a home with a garden, or in

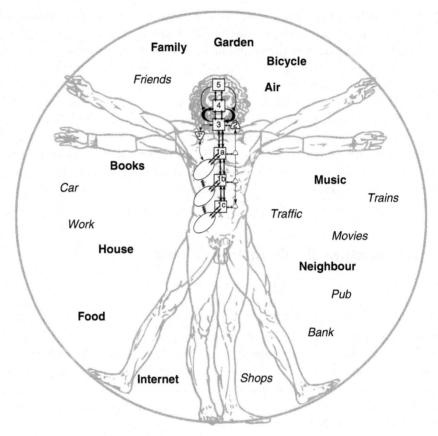

Figure 4.1 Individual in its niche

(Illustration by Jon Walker)

the countryside: for instance, enjoying clearer skies, experiencing wildlife re-appearing, having extra time from not travelling to work. But it also brought unprecedented uncertainty and fear for millions of less fortunate people, particularly in the global south, that had to remain isolated without enough income, enough space to keep themselves active and healthy, or enough government support to survive the crisis. For most of us, we experienced the lack of social contact, feelings of isolation, loneliness, and even depression.

In underdeveloped and emerging economies, the pandemic and lockdowns resulted in growing social and political unrest and massive public protests. In whatever the context we live, too many of us have faced a dramatic reduction of available choices to fight for our individual viability and sustainability. In the next section, we reflect on how by mapping ourselves as a v&s system we can develop consciousness of our different activities and priorities and make informed choices to improve our personal wellbeing and resilience.

Representing an Individual as a Viable (and Sustainable) System

Figure 4.2 represents a VSM of an individual, further developing previous work from Allena Leonard[2] and Johnson & Liber (2008). Systems 1 represent recurrent activities in an individual's life that produce something that our niche recognizes and rewards. These include all the activities identified in Figure 4.1, clustered as seven types of 'primary activities': work, learning, family, fun, personal care and health, spiritual and nature, and community engagement (taking community in a broader sense, from local to global).

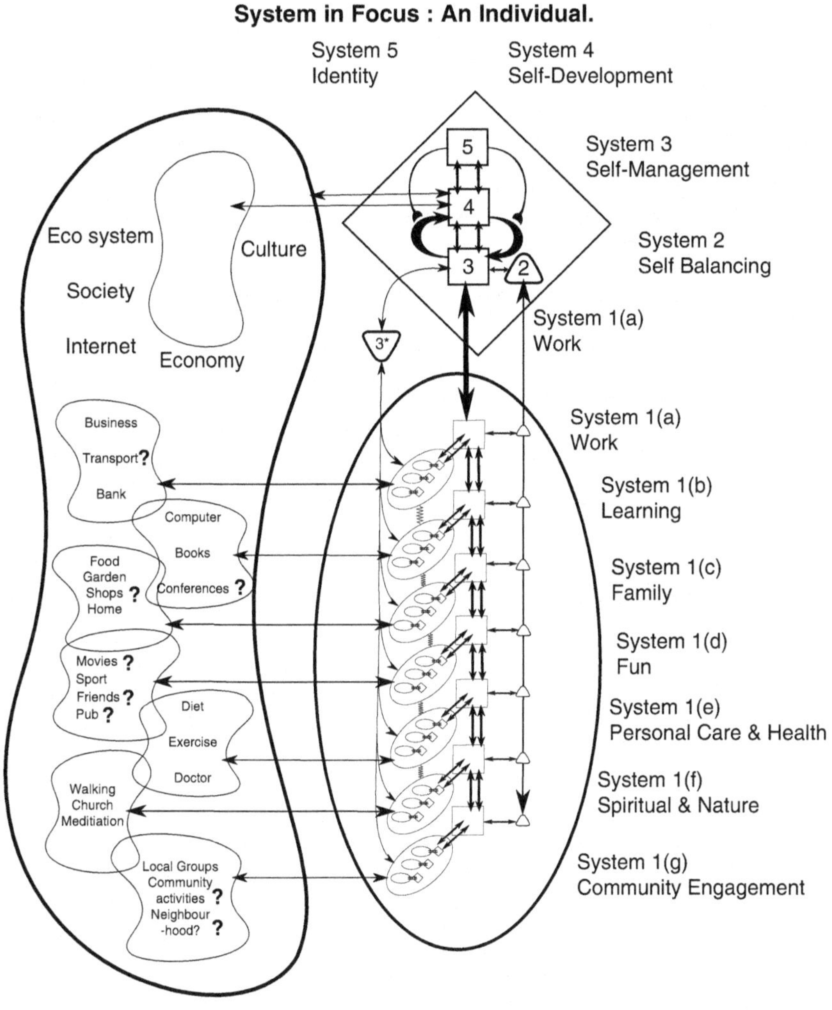

System in Focus : An Individual.

Figure 4.2 VSM mapping of an individual

(Illustration by Jon Walker)

As illustrated in Figure 4.2, System 2 roles include managing our daily agenda, managing information, and managing our communications with our niche's stakeholders. It includes all activities for coordinating our personal, work, family, social and community commitments, and most importantly for managing our work-life balance. System 3 roles include managing our physical (household, energy, water, gas), technological (computers, cars), and financial resources; learning from and synergising our different roles and activities; and self-regulating our performance in our relationships with work, family, community, and the government.

System 4 roles include planning our educational development (e.g., obtaining a university degree, re-training or developing new skills), sharing knowledge (e.g., participating in zoom conferences and events), planning investments and holidays, and keeping up to date with community, national, and global developments (e.g., by watching the news). System 5 roles include developing our ethos and values, expanding our consciousness (e.g., by learning from nature), developing critical thinking (e.g., by developing our political views). Also, we can continuously revisit and assess our different roles and identities (as individuals, members of our family, our community, and our nation).

Towards More Viable and Sustainable Individuals

While there have been some positive changes, the pandemic has challenged our ways of interacting with others, both at work and at our social and community lives. Those not having access to basic 'satisfiers' to remain physically and mentally balanced have had a much more dramatic experience and are the most affected victims of the pandemic. In many emerging economies, poor people's vulnerabilities have increased significantly, and their v&s indicators are showing early alarms continuously, while some governments manage to do very little about them.

However, the pandemic has also revealed new opportunities. It has forced us to quickly develop new skills for self-organising: i.e., for reprogramming our decisions to migrate from old habits (bad organisation) to a more sustainable way of organising our own lives (good organisation). This includes awareness of the need to live more simply (e.g., less shopping, less travelling, eating healthier food, doing regular exercise, and enjoying more relaxing time at home). It also brought us an opportunity to improve our skills in using online technology for working, shopping, banking, sharing knowledge, and even socialising. And for re-balancing our individual and social life, with more emphasis on our physical and spiritual balance, and on qualitative social relationships. In short, doing everything we can to keep ourselves healthy, resilient, and robust, both physically and emotionally.

Figure 4.3 offers an illustration of a sustainable household, where the family members are working from home, cycling to work, producing their own food, reforesting, recycling, and using renewable energy. It seems clear that one of the most positive lessons from the pandemic has been the realisation of many citizens in the world that – if possible – moving towards a more sustainable household and pattern of living would be a highly desirable choice, to better deal with the current (and even maybe other forthcoming) pandemic. Hopefully that lesson will stay with (some of) us and will contribute our conscious decision to continue progressing towards a more sustainable and resilient human societies and to more generative rather than extractive socio-economic systems.

In the following sections, we will continue exploring the same question: What have we learnt about our patterns of interactions with different social agencies that could and should be quickly transformed for us to become more resilient in the new post–COVID-19 society? And what can we do to progress towards more regenerative organisations and societies, and to reinvent our current (unsustainable) economic and development models?

Early Alarms to Businesses v&s

The pandemic has taught us that in a massive social crisis, priorities revert to those aspects that are essential for individual and social life. We all need to eat; to have a home; to work (and hopefully also to have social security); to keep healthy and in contact with nature; to have access to basic services (e.g., water, energy, gas, oil); and to keep safe. With less money to spend, less travelling, less access to shops, and less social life, we have also less exposure to social archetypes (being successful, dressing up smartly, etc.). Forcefully, we have had to re-focus on the essential aspects of our individual and social lives.

Figure 4.3 A sustainable household

(Illustration by Thom Igwe-Walker)

During 2020, we witnessed several businesses facing bankruptcy as a result of the recurrent lockdowns, in particular from non-primary sectors. For example, this affected the entertainment sector (e.g., cinemas, theatres, music halls); the tourism sector (e.g., hotels, holiday resorts, airlines); the vanity sector (e.g., hairdressers, accessories, tattoos); and even the manufacturing sector (e.g., non-essential clothing). Businesses have suffered more than in normal times from different organisational pathologies or archetypes (Espinosa & Walker, 2017, pp. 485–492). For example, we could say that the identity of non-primary businesses became ill-defined due to unexpected lack of demand – Archetype 1.1. Also, many businesses have experienced Trauma – Archetype 2.3 – ceasing activity due to their inability to respond to unpredictable circumstances; and some may even collapse or lose viability.

Other businesses operating in non-primary sectors may have experienced other types of organisational pathologies:

- They needed to develop or (redevelop) emerging services that become attractive to the transformed environment – Archetype 1.6. For example, in some supermarkets, home deliveries and online food shopping have become a major operational activity, while face-to-face shopping becomes secondary. This leads to reconsidering existing business models, like renting expensive high-street locations and paying an expensive payroll to attend to customers face to face. In some cases, it leads to website development, the rapid development of call centres, and reorganisation of their logistics for online buying and deliveries.

- Most schools and universities have shifted to online delivery of their educational services and have re-organised themselves for minimising face-to-face contact, until the lockdown measures are eased (or finally released).

- A swift change in purpose and identity may result (at least temporarily) in institutional schizophrenia (Archetype 1.10), while the old and the new way of doing things co-exist over time, and staff find their way to effectively deliver the new services and move to the new identity. The health sector in every country had, in a relatively short period, to reorganise dramatically as the number of patients increased exponentially while the primary health service providers (i.e., hospitals) were not at all prepared for the emergency. In most cases, they had to stop any elective, non-urgent treatment to privilege only COVID-19 patients, to cope with the increased demand. This sometimes resulted in a temporal shift in identity and long queues for patients awaiting an elective surgery or treatment.

- In the middle of chaos, too many people in the organisation become overworked (Archetype 2.1.). In developing countries, many employers are expecting people to continue doing the same amount of work for half the income, which means basically expecting them to overwork for less money. In many hospitals, doctors and nurses have been overworking as it has been difficult to recruit enough staff to manage the crisis effectively.

• Some organisations may be experiencing a state of shock – Archetype 2.2 – resulting in a temporal operational paralysis due to difficulties in responding to unpredictable disturbances. The tourism and massive transport industries (aviation, trains) in countries where the pandemic has gone out of control, like the United Kingdom, were examples of this archetypical behaviour in 2020 and early 2021. Also, the vanity sector has experienced a massive negative effect, as well as most luxury clothing and accessories, which are no longer needed while most of our activity and work happens inside our homes. The cultural, sports, and entertainment sectors have also been struggling in many countries, which is having a negative effect on people's mental health and overall wellbeing.

While the above examples refer to extreme situations where businesses may lose their direction or risk losing their niches in the market, due to un-predictable changes, there are ways to prevent or reduce the impact of such dramatic changes. The v&s approach recommends the design and im-plementation of systemic roles and mechanisms to continuously sense and learn about emerging trends and needs in the environment; and to become more attentive and responsive to early alarms while actively researching new opportunities that may also be emerging from the changing environment.

Towards More Resilient Businesses

To remain viable and sustainable in the long term, a business needs to improve its capability to rapidly sensing changes in its niche which may affect its via-bility and sustainability. It needs to improve its capabilities for adapting its strategic positioning, organisation, and processes to allow long-term, sus-tainable self-governance. Even during 'normal' times (as opposed to chaotic times), adaptation is always challenging as it requires a business to refocus strategy, redesign processes, develop new skills and capabilities, or improve its technostructure. This gets even harder in times of chaos when self-governance is a more challenging objective. This requires that the organisation reacts in real time when early alarms appear by (sometimes dramatically) readjusting their strategies and processes to cope with the variety of their niches.

The following case studies illustrate how the v&s approach and the STM may be useful to help a business to become more resilient and to strategically develop its capabilities in a more sustainable way. The first case – before the pandemic – and the second one – during the pandemic – demonstrate the power of the approach to support businesses facing treats to their long-term v&s.

Case Study – M*Clean (with A.C. Martinez)[3]

According to Ioannou & Serafeim (2019, p. 1), 93% of the largest 250 companies in the world produce a corporate sustainability report. While this shows an increase understanding of the importance to progress towards sustainability, there are still big gaps between the formulation and implementation of corporate sustainability strategies. The transition towards cleaner production and more responsible corporations is slower than expected – see (Engert & Baumgartner, 2016) and (Bansal & Song, 2017).

During a six-month v&s project in M*Clean,[4] a Mexican corporation, which offers cleaning services to different types of businesses, A. Martinez followed the STM methodology. She demonstrated it was very useful for supporting implementation of the company corporate sustainability (CS) strategies through participatory design of self-transformation processes and by monitoring their implementation in real time (Martinez & Espinosa, 2022).

While doing the VSM diagnosis, it first became evident that the different levels of recursive organisation had an unbalanced way of dealing with complexity (see Figure 4.4 with the agreed recursive analysis of M*Clean). There were six regional offices, each dealing with a mix of large service units (attending big corporations) and small service units (attending small and medium enterprises). Decisions were highly centralised at the national and regional levels, although the big service units (attending corporate clients) had enough autonomy, worked relatively well, and had begun to implement the agreed CS strategies. Meanwhile, the small service units were very centralised at the regional level and only managed to attend to day-to-day work issues, leaving most of the agreed long-term CS strategies unattended.

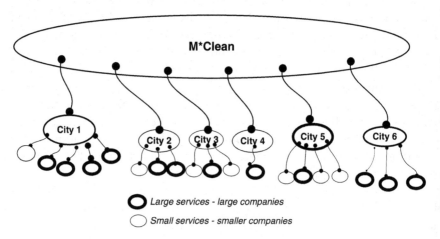

Figure 4.4 Recursive analysis M*Clean

(Illustration by Jon Walker)

Figure 4.5 shows an example of the VSM diagnosis at a small service unit (SSU). The diagnostic pointers are coded as D_1 to D_8. The diagnosis revealed that regional managers were responsible for most operational decisions for SSUs, and that they also acted as operational managers for the service units (D_1), leaving operational staff with very limited autonomy to make appropriate decisions (D_2). There were ongoing conflicts among operational staff, and they had continuous breakdowns due to lack of resources for implementing their tasks (D_3). Systems 4 and 5 were very weak and sometimes not performed at all.

Most of the manager's time was used on sorting out chaotic situations, which left them with little time for addressing their CS strategy implementation (D_6). This also resulted in limited communication with suppliers and customers and inability to respond to their requests (D_7). As a result, adaptation and innovation capabilities were underdeveloped at this level (D_5). They were very slow in developing awareness of the need to move towards greener technologies or supplies, or to attend the local community's requests (D_8).

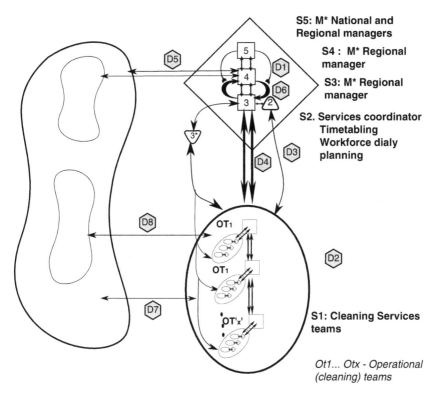

Figure 4.5 VSM diagnosis of a small service unit

(Illustration by Jon Walker)

As a result of this preliminary diagnosis, the project's participants redefined their main processes and roles. They realised they had failed to structure a proper S4 role, and thus created a strategy committee, responsible for developing organisational policies, innovation, and strategy (including CS strategy), a more comprehensible balanced score card, and a more effective way to monitor their implementation. The national managers agreed to devolve power to regional and service level managers. They soon felt the beneficial effect of their autonomy in terms of improved performance, and in having more time to address and implement their CS strategies. Also, the national managers began to have more time to address policy and strategic issues, which had previously been left unattended due to their involvement in operational issues.

At the regional level, they agreed to make efforts to improve S3 and S3*, by improving managerial capabilities for self-regulation; i.e., for monitoring operational performance and environmental negative environmental impacts. They also started to promote knowledge and information exchange between different types of operational units (i.e., large and small service units) to generate synergies. And they managed to clarify the medium- and long-term CS strategies, including the introduction of greener energy and water management and to implement projects to care for employee and local community wellbeing.

The main change at the service level was to improve self-management of the small services units by: a) giving more 'responsible autonomy' to regional managers (S1 vs S3) (e.g., the ability to make decisions autonomously and to make themselves accountable for their results); b) creating a conflict resolution role (S2); c) implementing an effective process to ensure local accountability (S1 to S3); d) creating clearer S2 mechanisms, like a weekly meeting to agree on joint action lines and responsibilities and to improve small services' coordination and communication. They also created monthly meetings to coordinate actions and share knowledge between large and small units.

They designed and implemented a real-time monitoring system. They first agreed on key operational indicators (e.g., state of the machinery, employee management's effectiveness, client satisfaction) and key sustainability indicators (e.g., percentage of educational support programs for employees' families and volume of cleaning chemicals used above standard levels). They started monitoring and reviewing their performance every two weeks, instead of annually, which led to continuous and rapid improvements in operational and sustainability performance.

The final analysis of the participants' responses showed that the participants' perception of the original conflicts changed positively on almost all the diagnostic points identified, at each level of recursive organisation. Analysis of KPIs at the end of the project showed real improvements: they implemented a program to educate 220 employees' family members; and significantly improved their environmental footprint. From 1,850 litres of chemicals that the company was using monthly, they reduced to 1,300 litres monthly. They also began to use eco-friendly cleaning products; for more details see Martinez & Espinosa (2022).

This case study demonstrates how by aligning CS strategy and structure following the STM, and by monitoring in real time the implementation of changes, an organisation may develop a more resilient and flexible structure, more capable of fully and effectively implementing CS strategies. It demonstrates the power of facilitating a self-transformation process to address structural breakdowns, which may impede effective CS implementation. The SCM supported the participants self-reflection about their operational processes and conflicts. This enabled them to identify their learning constraints and bottlenecks which were impediments for successfully implementing their agreed CS strategies.

By introducing more operational autonomy, people learned better ways of managing operational variety, and meta-systemic managers found more time to focus on designing and facilitating implementation of core CS strategies. All together this resulted in improvements in operational, social, and environmental performance for M*Clean. The case study demonstrates how the STM helps employees to more effectively integrate their capabilities, resources, and dynamic capabilities to achieve their organisational and sustainability goals.

Towards More Resilient Health Providers

As mentioned earlier, the health sector in every country has been massively affected by the COVID-19 pandemic in 2020–2022 has had to absorb its consequences more directly by very quickly getting ready to cope with a rapidly increasing number of COVID-19 patients, while delaying the provision of many other health services. Not surprisingly, it has become central to health management research agendas to find effective ways to support hospitals and other health service providers to manage public health emergencies and to develop organisational resilience.

This clearly applies to the National Health Service (NHS) in the United Kingdom, which is one of the most complex health organisations in the world. It has a budget of more than 100 billion in a year and employs more than a million employees. It is, without doubt, the most beloved British institution – as it has been offering free health services to all the residents in the United Kingdom since its creation after the second World War – and it is a world model for effective public health care. Nevertheless, due to government policies, well before 2020 it was facing a huge challenge to achieve financial efficiencies of circa £20 billion/year while improving quality of care and health outcomes.

During the last decade the NHS has been going through a process of continuous reform, aimed at improving its operational performance and the quality of its health services. It has opened the opportunity to pioneer several consulting and research projects to suggest ways of improving health organisations' performance. In the next sections, we illustrate the way the STM has been applied to support health organisations to become more resilient, capable of self-organisation and more adaptive, when dealing with the current COVID-19 pandemic.

The huge complexity of the NHS and each of its subsidiaries makes it particularly attractive to choose systemic approaches to study and analyse its current performance. They have proved useful to identify ways the NHS could be improved in terms of resilience to maintain and improve its overall quality of services and its customer and staff satisfaction and wellbeing (e.g., Seddon (2008), Ellis (2008), (Copper, 2018), (Johnson & Liber, 2008), (Walsh et al, 2018), (Espejo, 2021)).

The deeply hierarchical nature of the NHS hasn't been unnoticed by systemic and health researchers and investigative journalists. For example, Devane[5] remarks that even though successive attempts for decentralisation and empowerment of NHS staff have been made, still red tape and the desire to maintain the status quo has limited the impact of ongoing organisational reforms. Many of them have resulted in a dichotomy between the desired approach to organisation and the actual day-to-day reality most NHS staff experience. Most healthcare reforms in the last decade have focused on standardisation and process optimisation, by following a top-down model following the blueprints developed by central government. This needs to be challenged in the forthcoming institutional reforms; otherwise, we can forecast that any new NHS reorganisation will fail if the trust and primary health providers continue to work with hierarchical and bureaucratic structures.

Thankfully, some trusts have raised their awareness of the need to reconsider hierarchy, bureaucracy, and short-termism and to work more consciously at empowering staff. A few have even asked for systemic expert advice on how to progress in this direction. Operational autonomy is particularly relevant for health care, where it has been shown that empowering staff leads to enhanced creativity, motivation, and improved outcomes. As Lambertz[6] puts it:

Wartime Emergency Medical Services provide a historical lesson in how

and why decentralisation and the development of an intermediate, organisational

tier at the regional level within health services matters in creating resilience. For

decentralisation and regions to be effective in the current NHS,

they require a statutory footing, autonomy, and resources.

Through the following sections, we will first reflect on how pre-existing organisational settings before the COVID-19 pandemic in the NHS in England confirm the above broad picture. Then we will explore an in-depth VSM analysis of one specialist surgical unit (**SPU**[7]) in a Local English NHS Trust (**LEHT**[8]), aimed at suggesting adjustments to its structure to improve its operational performance. We will then reflect about the possibilities that this SPU has for improving its own resilience, while operating in the hierarchical context of this English Local Health Trust (ELHT) and dealing with the long queues resulting from the recent pandemic in the offering of specialised health services.

The learning from these v&s projects give us food for thought regarding desirable and feasible improvements for this ELHT, which may be scalable to other trusts in the United Kingdom. Later, in Chapter 8, we will reflect on how a whole British Trust recently used the VSM to assess its performance during the COVID-19, the learning and improvements achieved as a result, and the challenges it raised to future regional or national reforms to the NHS.

Preliminary VSM Analysis of the NHS in England

The National Health Service aims to improve health and to secure high-quality health care for the whole population, now and for future generations. It operates in every region, city, town, and village in the United Kingdom. It offers services to all the population in England, Scotland, Wales, and Northern Ireland, and employs more than a million people. It coordinates services from its own providers (GP practices, hospitals, social care, etc.) as well as numerous private and NGOs offering services.

In each of the four nations, the NHS is organised regionally to provide different types of health services, through a combination of own health providers (e.g., hospitals) and private providers (e.g., some specialised services). Figure 4.6 provides an example of a recursive analysis of England's NHS. Even if the NHS is undoubtedly an extremely complex organisational system and we are aware of the many the limitations it may have, it is still considered one of the top public health systems in the world in terms of quality and coverage.

The NHS in England manages to remain an excellent public health provider by continuously trying to improve itself and become more sustainable and resilient. As mentioned earlier, there have been several studies in the last decade, recommending ways for improving the patients' pathway, the way of dealing with patients and medical information, and in general, decentralising the organisational structure and providing more autonomy and flexibility to frontline health service providers.

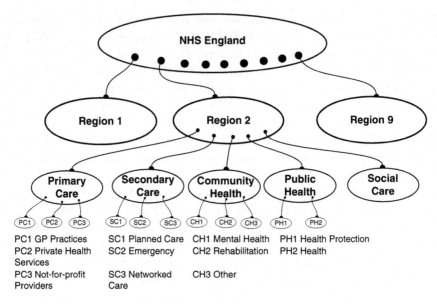

Figure 4.6 Recursive analysis of NHS England

(Illustration by Jon Walker)

During the recent COVID-19 pandemic, the NHS in England had its biggest ever challenge of effectively performing with a budget of more than £100 billion a year, by providing social and primary care with the expected level of quality and response time while attending thousands of COVID-19 patients. Most of the policies and strategies on how to deal with the pandemic are designed at the national level by NHS and national health authorities (e.g., National Health Service England, Public Health England -PHE, Health Education England -HEE), and implemented locally, in each of the four nations. As the following case studies will reveal, many underlying structural constraints have an important effect in health service organisations' resilience and their capability to respond effectively to a public health emergency.

Copper (2018) provided a VSM analysis of a regional NHS Trust, which revealed the organisational context in which it was operating – before the start of the pandemic. Figure 4.7 provides a summary of the main diagnostic issues he identified, complemented with other issues reported on NHS performance studies, at the beginning of the COVID-19 pandemic. According to these sources, the studied regional NHS operated with a highly centralized governance structure for policy, strategy, and financial decision making (D1), leaving local and regional offices suffering from uncertainty, ambiguity, and delays regarding their own strategy/policy decision making (D2). This created a paradox of conflicting discourses. While apparently promoting humanitarian and democratic management, the current practice conflicted with these narratives, which results in a culture where trust was lacking (D3).

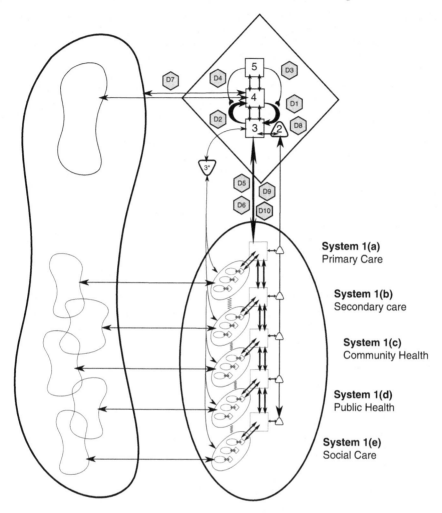

Figure 4.7 VSM diagnosis of a regional health system

(Illustration by Jon Walker)

A strong command and control approach in the allocation of financial resources resulted in top-down decisions focused on financial control and on saving money (D4). Resource allocation was not shaped by local or regional needs (D5) and there was underfunding for primary and emergency health services (D6). Strategic decisions relied too much on external consultants – who did not have the requisite variety to understand local or regional complexity (D7). The level of bureaucracy was high. For example, the executive team reported spending 70% of their time in meeting legal and regulatory demands, rather than in promoting quality services (D8). There was evidence of lack of coordination between public and private care providers (D9) and of the need for more quality health indicators and for a more evolutionary approach to adaptation (i.e., from listening to patients and clinicians) (D10).

Considering that most NHS regional and local institutions share similar structural pathologies, it is likely that other regional health systems in England begun to face the COVID-19 early in 2020 in similar situations. They were operating in a highly centralized NHS, continuously underfunded by the past governments since the 2012 act, which promoted the concept of the internal market, competition, and encouraged privatisation (Pollock & Roderick, 2015). This is important to realise, as any assessment of NHS performance during the COVID-19 pandemic needs to understand the baseline for Health Trusts, who were underequipped to deal with a massive public health crisis like COVID-19.

This may also be reflected in United Kingdom's very poor performance in the first waves of the pandemic compared to other countries worldwide. Also, comparing the United Kingdom's management of the pandemic during the first pandemic wave in 2020 with other countries globally, it looks like the U.K. government did not manage to develop timely enough consistent and robust strategies for local trusts for effectively managing it. Thankfully, this was partly compensated for later by a very effective vaccination program staring in the autumn of 2020 and still ongoing in 2022.

As the pandemic has resulted in a huge increase in the demand for (emergency) health services and long queues for elective services, it seems that the need for addressing existing performance gaps and structural constraints is more urgent than ever, as a well-performing NHS could save many lives. Espejo (2021) for example, suggests that diagnostic tests were originally out of balance with the operational capacity from hospitals and other health providers. More than ever, the imbalance between the health services capabilities and the demands for emergency and elective health care is required to be rapidly addressed. Edwards (2020)[9] considers that, instead, the government continues to progress towards an even more centralised hierarchical structure for the NHS.

A snapshot on recent reports on NHS performance during the COVID-19 pandemic confirms this broad diagnosis as well as the urgency for addressing it. For example, Butler[10] (2020) suggests that long delays for answers from the government were hindering effectiveness of local responses. According to Freeland,[11] a centralised control of emergency supplies during the first wave of the pandemic (e.g., PPE and Test & Track systems' adoption) opened space for corruption and left local providers unable to respond in a timely and effective manner. Boseley[12] says that inconsistent responses from the government demolished the public trust in the need to follow lockdown rules. Kauffman[13] also criticized the government's high reliance on chosen scientific modelling systems (big data analytics) to map social behaviours without providing specific ways to encourage self-organised responses from people.

Ideally, a timely VSM analysis of NHS Trusts may contribute to the identification of the main vulnerabilities and structural gaps, and the quick identification of core changes required to develop a more robust and resilient organisation. This would help it to better prepare to face the challenges of this and future pandemics. As we still don't know when or how new waves of this (or a new) pandemic will arise, improving NHS's resilience and adaptability is still core to its long-term v&s. There follows another example of how a v&s study may contribute to this purpose.

VSM Diagnosis of a Surgery Unit in a Local English Health Trust (with Jon Walker and Kartikae Grover)

In 2021, the author, jointly with Dr Jon Walker, conducted a systemic organisational assessment of two specialist units (SPU$_1$ and SPU$_2$) in a Local English Health Trust (LEHT) using the v&s approach and following the stages of the STM. Before we started the SPUs project, we presented its objectives, approach, and methodology to the LEHT's executive team, who welcomed and approved it. Beginning in April 2021, we held two weekly (two-hour) meetings on Zoom with Kartikae Grover,[14] the project leader at SPU$_1$, to coordinate the project development and to develop the organisational analysis. We supported him to develop a VSM survey, which he distributed to 80 employees and received feedback from around 50 people.

We developed 15 interviews with varied roles from the SPU's Health Group (HG$_2$) and with some executive roles from the trust. We also ran four workshops with an average of 12 participants representing the different roles of the SPU, aimed at:

- mapping the units' organisational complexity.
- understanding the roles responsible for the different functions and
- discussing the identified diagnostic issues and deciding collectively on the most relevant ones that needed to be actioned.

There follows a briefing on this project and reflections on how it may contribute to improving the resilience of the SPU, and of the LEHT.

Understanding the Organisational Identity

In the initial stage of the STM, we studied LEHT, HG$_2$, and SPU$_1$ and SPU$_2$ structures, their main services, the profile of their customers and staff, their historical performance, and the challenges they faced to offer quality services. The first workshop took place at the end of May 2021 via Zoom and included representatives from medical and administrative staff from LEHT, HG$_2$, SPU$_1$, and SPU$_2$. It aimed to introduce the v&s approach and the STM methodology and to develop jointly the first two stages of the methodology. We wanted to pave the way to do a preliminary mapping of LEHT and of SPU$_1$ and SPU$_2$ as v&s organisations and to clarify the SPU levels of autonomy internally and in relation to HG$_2$ and the LEHT.

During the first workshop, we discussed with the participants the vision and values of the SPUs. There was an agreement that people in the SPUs were aware of the NHS values (*working together for patients; respect and dignity; commitment to quality of care; compassion; improving lives; and everyone counts*). Also, the participants agreed to the following values from LEHT: *Great staff, great care, great future, remarkable people, and extraordinary place.* During the following months interacting with the SPUs, we verified the strength of these values in the feeling of belonging of staff, and the way they are committed to their work and interact with each other. This was later confirmed by the survey results.

Recursive Analysis – The System in Focus

Figure 4.8 presents the recursive analysis of LEHT, with the System 1s as the five health groups. During the preliminary meetings with the SPU$_1$ project leader, we discussed different versions of recursive analysis of the HG$_2$ and identified the system in focus – (highlighted in the lower circle in Figure 4.8). The system in focus for this project includes two System 1s, SPU$_1$ and SPU$_2$, which are part of the HG$_2$ (which decides on their yearly budgets and to which they are accountable). Even if they operate as in-dependent System 1s, they are represented together as the 'SPU' because they continuously coordinate their work, as all surgery patients require complementary radiology services. Each one of them has sub-systems, as illustrated in Figure 4.8.

Neither the HG$_2$ nor the SPUs had a direct involvement in responding to the pandemic, but they were indirectly affected by it, mainly due to reallocation of staff. Following the NHS guidelines, during the first wave of the pandemic the whole of elective and most of urgent medical services were stopped, to provide ample space to focus all the trust's medical staff and resources to effectively respond to the challenges posed by the pandemic. This resulted in the SPUs focused on urgent cases and delayed all elective works; they are now working hard now to catch up with delayed work. This will impact their performance for the next several years.

The detailed diagnosis began by looking at Health Group 2 as the system in focus. A full diagnosis of this viable system was not undertaken as the primary objective was a study of the SPUs. However, even a preliminary overview was instructive. A first broad question emerging from this recursive analysis was to what extent having nine System 1s in on one area (HG₂) was challenging in terms of guaranteeing synergies and spending enough time with each one of the System 1s? Most of the people responsible reported a severe lack of time to perform their jobs adequately. In extreme cases, System 3 staff were working as surgeons for three days a week, leaving only two days to manage nine extremely complex surgical units. Later, we would reconfirm the existing tensions inherent in this organisational design. Very likely because of this unmanaged complexity, the HG₂ has decided to create two 'meta-systemic management' units: Division 1 (supporting six S1s), and Division 2 (supporting three S1s).

However, from the participants' interviews, we learned that the main criteria for making this decision may had been administrative rather than by the type of service provided or by the complexity of these differing health services. We learned that there was an unexplored opportunity for further improving the synergies between the S1s, partly due to the lack of time from meta-systemic management, but also that it wasn't easy to develop given the lack of natural coherence between some of the specialities grouped in the two divisions.

With the workshops' participants, we agreed on the recursive analysis of HG₂ and identified the system in focus (highlighted in the grey circle in Figure 4.8). It includes two System 1s, SPU₁ and SPU₂, which are part of the HG₂ (which decides on its yearly budget and to which it is accountable).

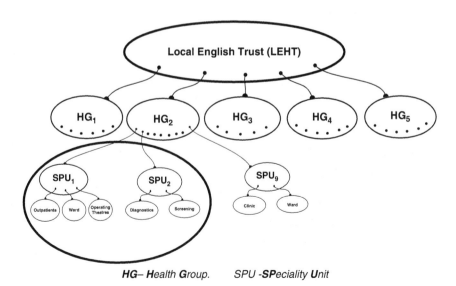

HG– Health Group.   *SPU -SPeciality Unit*

Figure 4.8 Recursive analysis of LEHT

(Illustration by Jon Walker)

Preliminary VSM Diagnosis of the LEHT

Figure 4.9 provides a generic mapping of the LEHT as a viable system and illustrates some examples of Systems 2 to 5 roles for the whole LEHT. In the LEHT the System 1s (for the whole organisation) are the Health Groups (HG_1 to HG_5). The meta-system is a service to the operational units (System 1s) and includes:

- S2 which offers a harmonising function – avoiding and managing conflicts and oscillations among Systems 1 – includes managing shared resources (e.g., scheduling wards, equipment, theatres, ward, and staff); sticking to the NHS's rules, standards and protocols (e.g., COVID guidelines, trust's values, standard processes); providing transparent information for all (e.g., the dashboard) and multidisciplinary team meetings.

- S3 which guarantees cohesion and synergetic interactions among System 1s by generating synergies and maintaining cohesion between health groups, negotiating the allocation of financial resources (budgets), physical resources (i.e., clinical wards, offices), staff (i.e., doctors, nurses, technical staff), and technological resources (medical equipment, ICT tools and computers), and by monitoring performance in real time and responding accordingly.

- S4, which continuously explores the organisational niche and provides robust knowledge to support innovation, strategy, and policy formulation and to manage interactions with external stakeholders. It is responsible for developing new/improved services, management, and technological innovations; informing policy and strategy decisions; and facilitating strategy implementation.

- S5 which defines organisational identity and policy and guarantees closure which includes defining and developing the LEHT's core vision and mission, 'ethos,' policies, and identity; ensuring these values and policies are understood throughout LEHT; and monitoring and intervening if values and policies are ignored.

Analysing LEHT with the v&s approach proved to be very valuable at that moment, as all NHS staff have suffered extreme and radical changes in the way they worked during the first years of the COVID-19 pandemic. Traditional ways of making decisions had to be quickly replaced by more flexible ones, management procedures needed to be made more flexible, and staff had to take responsibility for many operational decisions to manage the complexity of the situation experienced nationally (and globally). In such an uncertain working landscape, the more autonomous and creative the staff, the better the possibilities for effective operational and organisational performance. There follows a reflective description on the way we followed the next STM's stages in the SPUs project and the learning gained.

Full Diagnosis for SPU₁ and SPU₂

The main diagnosis involved a study of the SPU$_1$ which then became the system in focus. The SPU$_2$ diagnosis developed in parallel, as many of the issues were similar. We were, however, careful to check all conclusions with staff from this unit.

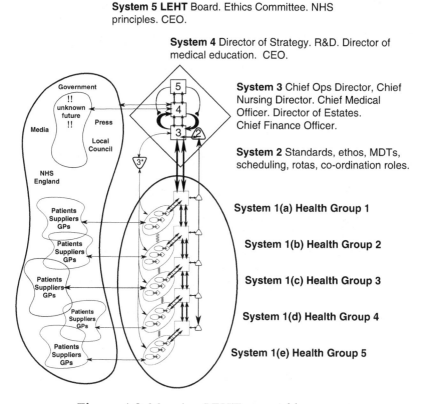

System 5 LEHT Board. Ethics Committee. NHS principles. CEO.

System 4 Director of Strategy. R&D. Director of medical education. CEO.

System 3 Chief Ops Director, Chief Nursing Director. Chief Medical Officer. Director of Estates. Chief Finance Officer.

System 2 Standards, ethos, MDTs, scheduling, rotas, co-ordination roles.

System 1(a) Health Group 1

System 1(b) Health Group 2

System 1(c) Health Group 3

System 1(d) Health Group 4

System 1(e) Health Group 5

Figure 4.9 Mapping LEHT as a viable system

(Illustration by Jon Walker)

As the STM unfolded, we developed a preliminary and a full diagnosis of the system in focus (SPU$_1$ and SPU$_2$) and began to assess their performance. Each one of the SPUs in the system in focus has an average of 30–40 staff members, including doctors, nurses, and clinical support staff. They have similar meta-systemic roles (some of them shared by the two SPUs) but there were a few minor differences (e.g., SPU$_2$ had dedicated staff and more administrative control over them). S3, S4, and S5 are developed by the respective units' clinical leads, associate directors, and senior consultants. All of them report to the HG$_2$ Triumvirate (which includes the medical director, operations management director, and director of nursing of HG$_2$).

A summary of the main issues raised by the participants from SPU$_1$ and SPU2 in the second and third workshops include an increasing number of GP referrals was putting pressure on the service; inability to respond in an agile manner to changes in the environment; not enough autonomy – permission needed for everything; tightly controlled finances; delays created due to a hierarchical structure; and complicated protocols and procedures which caused serious delays. It should be noted that many of these issues refer to the interactions between the system in focus i.e., SPU$_1$ and the larger organisation i.e., HG$_2$ and the corporate structure. We made these issues more precise in the full VSM diagnosis, as explained below.

The preliminary diagnosis pointed to some weaknesses in the organisational design of both SPU$_1$ and SPU$_2$, and more generally of the SPU. There follow more details of the full VSM diagnosis of SPU, and of its relationships to its parent organisational unit – the HG$_2$. See Figures 4.10 and 4.11.

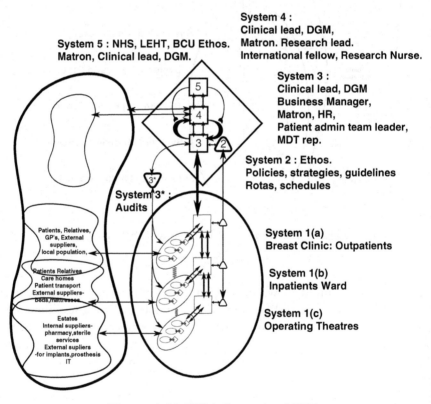

System 5 : NHS, LEHT, BCU Ethos.
Matron, Clinical lead, DGM.

System 4 :
Clinical lead, DGM,
Matron. Research lead.
International fellow, Research Nurse.

System 3 :
Clinical lead, DGM
Business Manager,
Matron, HR,
Patient admin team leader,
MDT rep.

System 2 : Ethos.
Policies, strategies, guidelines
Rotas, schedules

System 3* :
Audits

Patients, Relatives,
GP's, External
suppliers,
local population,

Patients Relatives
Care homes
Patient transport
External suppliers-
beds,mattresses

Estates
Internal suppliers-
pharmacy,sterile
services
External supliers
-for implants,prothesis
IT

System 1(a)
Breast Clinic: Outpatients

System 1(b)
Inpatients Ward

System 1(c)
Operating Theatres

Figure 4.10 VSM diagnosis of SPU$_1$

(Illustration by Jon Walker)

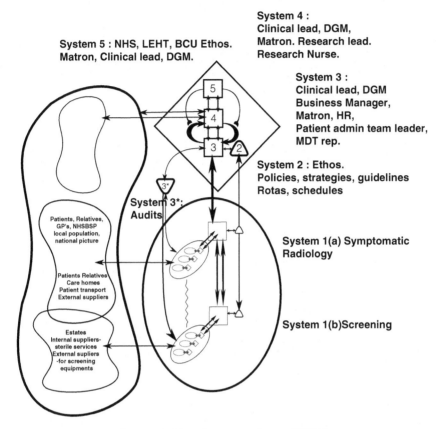

System 5 : NHS, LEHT, BCU Ethos.
Matron, Clinical lead, DGM.

System 4 :
Clinical lead, DGM,
Matron. Research lead.
Research Nurse.

System 3 :
Clinical lead, DGM
Business Manager,
Matron, HR,
Patient admin team leader,
MDT rep.

System 2 : Ethos.
Policies, strategies, guidelines
Rotas, schedules

System 3*:
Audits

Patients, Relatives,
GP's, NHSBSP
local population,
national picture

System 1(a) Symptomatic
Radiology

Patients Relatives
Care homes
Patient transport
External suppliers

Estates
Internal suppliers-
sterile services
External supliers
-for screening
equipments

System 1(b)Screening

Figure 4.11 VSM mappings of SPU$_2$

(Illustration by Jon Walker)

SYSTEM 1

From the survey, a third of people felt they didn't have enough autonomy (33%), whereas 27% felt they did. This idea of autonomy has been further explored in the workshops and interviews. An important finding was to notice that this feeling of lacking enough autonomy not only happened at the lowest levels of recursive organisation but was also expressed by managers at recursion level 1 (i.e., HG$_2$). Regarding financial control, there was a general perception that the LEHT is an organisation more driven by financial constraints than by health quality standards, which shows an entrenched schism between the ethos and values and the operational decisions. In general, the lack of autonomy is mainly when extra finances are involved. This leads to a very sluggish response to opportunities which present themselves and which would improve the quality of service offered by the SPUs.

SYSTEM 2

The interviews and the survey reveal a strong culture of teamwork, trust, collaboration, and mutual support, which provides a calming influence and has been pivotal for maintaining morale during the COVID-19 pandemic. There are well-defined clinical guidelines and most of the LEHT's policies and procedures seem to be accepted and adhered to. In 'normal' times, most staff know these policies and guidelines and the multi-disciplinary team (MDT) acts to ensure uniform policies are followed across all clinical areas. However, during the recent emergency this changed radically, as the national government was constantly suggesting many emergency policies and guidelines, which were sometimes challenging to follow and implement.

Rotas are drawn up to clearly allocate doctors and nurses effectively. Once more, in 'normal times', the surgical team staff rotas appear to function effectively within each area and a weekly timetable meeting every Friday helps to coordinate activities. The nurses in each of the operational areas manage their own rotas. Nevertheless, the triumvirate management structure of LEHT and HG_2 and the way each different role lines manages different types of operational staff leaves open the possibility of broken communications at lower levels of recursion, among the clinical, nurse, and operational managers, which may potentially result in oscillations among operational staff.

S1s have well-defined functions that tend to operate without interfering with each other. There is no reported evidence of problematic interactions among operational units from the interviews. On the contrary, the spirit of collaboration and teamwork was evident, not only inside the S1s, but also in the interaction between SPU_1 and SPU_2, which seem to be smooth and effective. Again, from the survey only a minority (21%) felt there were frequent tensions between the S1s.

Resolution of problems amongst staff is handled by the clinical lead for medical personnel. For nursing, staff issues would be dealt by the S1's lead nurse or matron. All line management for administrative issues is done at recursion levels 1 (operations management director, medical director, matron), and 2 (division general manager, business manager) rather than at the level where the service is delivered (recursion levels 3 and 4). Therefore, there are situations in which the staff supporting the clinical lead in S1s may not be capable of doing what is requested from them at a particular time, without previous approval from their line management. There is space for reviewing this scheme, to guarantee that the clinical leads directly manage their staff, rather than relying on others to line manage them on their behalf.

SYSTEM 3

According to VSM criteria, System 3 roles must have an overview of the operational units and provide real time and dynamic monitoring. Both in SPU_1 and SPU_2, the clinical leads can devote less than 10% of their time on management duties. However, they are the only ones capable of fully addressing operational breakdowns (e.g., the radiology or IT systems crash during a clinic, or no doctor turns up to do the ward round), as no one of the specialised meta-systemic management roles (finances, DGM, contracting, etc.) have an overall view of operational performance.

Different roles at recursion levels 1 (HG_2) and 2 (Division 1) take System 3 Responsibilities for the SPUs: matron, DGM (divisional general manager), BM (business managers), clinical leads (CLs), MDT team manager, HR representative, health group finance manager, performance manager. The main diagnostic issues identified were:

- There is limited capability for developing dedicated System 3 role for the SPU_1 and SPU_2 units. Instead, there is a range of System 3 roles shared at the next levels of recursion (Division 1, HG_2), which do not always manage properly the operational variety of the System 1s. Not having 'requisite variety,' some decisions are made 'blindly' without enough informed clinical criteria.

- The DGM plays significant System 3 and System 4 roles both in resource bargaining and performance monitoring across the whole of Division 1 of the HG_2, which, as said before, include six operational units, including SPU_1 and SPU_2. But it does not have enough time to spend understanding and supporting in more detail each one of the System 1s. There is an opportunity for redesigning the DGM role, to reinforce the internal System 3 and 4 capacities of both units.

- Also, the business manager, who has a role in co-ordination as well as monitoring performance, can also only devote part of his time in dealing with problems in SPU_1 and SPU_2. The matron also has a very important System 3 role, but also handles multiple specialties, so attending to the requests from each one of them results in delays and sometimes unsatisfied or delayed resource provision.

Interviewees and workshops participants revealed that there is almost no financial freedom within the system in focus. None of the operational managers in SPU or even in HG_2 have the freedom to spend their budget as they deem appropriate, nor can they change the allocation of funds between the different operations. Any significant operational change would require of the System 3 team to make a business case and put it through a lengthy approval process that goes first to HG$_2$ operational manager, then to the business review group, then to capital resources, and finally to the executive team – who makes decision supported by the finance director. Typically, this can take two years, and is a major deterrent to proposing major changes.

The SPUs from the system in focus are not involved in contracting. According to VSM criteria, for a system to be viable it needs to understand what level of service it is contracted to perform and what sort of revenues are attached. This is important because a service may be performing an activity and not realising that this is outside the contracted functions and would attract additional tariff. Also, if a service needs to manage its resources efficiently, it must have knowledge of the costs it incurs to deliver activity. That way it can identify areas where it is inefficient and work at improvements.

From the interviews there are several examples of ways in which nurses attending patients from outpatients through screening and surgery generate synergies between these operational units, by a coming-together of System 1 personnel spontaneously adopting a System 3 perspective. This is an excellent example of what (Beer, 1979, p. 207) calls a 'synergy task force,' comprised primarily of System 1 operating in a System 3 role. It would draw on the knowledge of the intersect of the System 1 which those people share, and on the positive psychology entailed in constructing synergy. However, this is unacknowledged and depends upon the goodwill of staff. Recognition and formalisation these kinds of activities could improve service delivery significantly.

SYSTEM 4

Several people within and outside the SPUs are doing S4 kinds of work, which is recognised in the workload. The business manager, matron, and clinical lead will all get information about their external environment through various sources, either directly from external agencies or through information filtered down through the health group. Other roles contributing to S4 are the representatives from drug and equipment companies; the research lead, an international fellow, and a research nurse are involved in clinical trials which are run in the SPU. Also, many medical staff are involved with national and international networks of medical practitioners who are undertaking cutting-edge research.

Generally, there is a very supportive ethos for gathering new ideas, and acceptance that continuous change and innovation is valuable in providing the best patient treatment and care. While innovation is recognised as an important element of the SPU, there are three significant issues that need to be overcome. There are no resources available for even relatively inexpensive innovations, there is little allocated time to turn an interesting piece of research into a well-researched proposal, and even if this proposal is produced, the process of obtaining approval is long and complicated.

SYSTEM 5

NHS, LEHT, and SPU vision and values are deeply embedded throughout. They are *'in the organisational DNA.'* The SPU units would not be allowed to introduce any new policies, so this sort of activity would be performed by the operations management director from the higher recursion (HG_2), dipping into a System 5 role for the SPUs. S5 also balances the capabilities of S3 and S4. In this case, both are very short of time to discharge their responsibilities and monitoring the flow of information between S3 and S4. All of this is done by the same people. Within these limitations, the System 5 ethos successfully informs all decisions made within the SPU.

Monitoring and Assessment

Central to S3's ability to function effectively is its knowledge of the performance of System 1. Its model of the operation must be thorough and up to date. The LEHT has an exemplary business intelligence system which seems to be designed to report to central government on their required performance measurements (i.e., key performance indicators or KPIs). It will collect and analyse information through various computer systems which are fed into the HG_2 or trust committees. The KPIs originating from SPU cover a variety of issues – e.g., theatre utilisation: how much of the actual theatre time is utilised in operating on patients? All KPI behaviours are scrutinised (in a top-down approach) by the triumvirate of HG_2 at monthly performance management meetings, that the clinical lead is not expected to attend and by the DGM once a week.

Generally, the people working in the SPU units are unaware of the KPIs that are generated concerning their performance and the financial implications. Most of this information is reviewed by managers in the heath group, who only pass it on to staff within the SPUs when there is a problem.

Some KPIs that would dynamically reflect real-time operational results have yet to be identified (e.g., staff to patient ratio). To improve performance management for the SPU, the recommendation is to design a dashboard specifically for the clinical leads that shows the information, which is most relevant for their operational unit, in a form which is easily accessible. If it is properly done, it should be a constant source of useful information for day-to-day decision making. It is suggested to undertake an exercise to ask staff to design their own KPIs (with the technical support of the LEHT Performance Management unit) and to focus on KPIs which will be useful for them to assess and improve their performance. Also, to organise periodic meetings to articulate the 'synergy task force' and to design new ways in which the three System 1s within SPU_1 can collaborate for their mutual benefit.

Self-Transformation Projects

Through the interviews, working meetings with the SPU leaders, and workshops, we have been developing basic proposals with the participants of what could be self-transformation projects or initiatives to address the main diagnostic issues. The aim is to generate improvements in the working environment, staff motivation, and ultimately, organisational performance. There follow some examples of the ones identified and agreed on as highly desirable and feasible.

SYSTEM 1

Measures are needed to ensure adequate 'responsible autonomy' for the three operational units. This will involve the promotion of a culture of trust to progress towards devolved responsibilities to clinical staff. Also, the development of bottom up KPIs and responsibilities for self-regulation from the operational units, and consideration of constantly available dashboards for each S1 based on 'local' KPIs. Hopefully, this may involve availability of modest amounts of money for small changes, and a procedure for agreeing to extra expenditure within a reasonable time frame.

SYSTEM 2

As every S1 has its own agendas and priorities, it is important that the metasystem makes sure they have access to their required staff, technology (e.g., medical equipment, computers), physical space (e.g., wards, theatres), and financial resources on time. It seems evident that the lack of line management over operational staff (e.g., nurses) may create conflicts of interests, which can't always be resolved in a timely and effective manner at the level where they occur. It would be desirable to explore ways of better articulating the requests for operational staff at each System 1 with the decision-making authority to provide resources to them.

SYSTEM 3

People in System 3 roles, either in the system in focus or acting in that capacity from a higher recursion, are spread thin over multiple areas of responsibility. This makes it difficult for them to have the capacity and variety to act effectively. It is important to more clearly allocate such meta-systemic support services (like financial management, DGM, BMs, etc.) under the responsibility of the clinical leads rather than expecting to manage them from above. This is the only way a proper variety balance could be achieved. This will require of a larger allocation of time for clinical leads to undertake more meta-systemic responsibilities and thus articulate an effective System 3.

Development of managerial skills for operational managers – such as basic training in performance management, staff management and financial management – would allow the clinical leads to take more responsibilities and develop 'responsible autonomy.'

It is recommended to redesign the performance management meetings to make sure clinical leads are an integral part of decision making. The information can be prepared and shared in advance from the management support roles. The meetings can then be held, effectively optimising time management and focusing on reviewing issues that need attention (managing by exception) rather than analysing all KPI behaviours. Also, it would be desirable to prototype a way of providing more operational autonomy i.e., by putting the SPU budget under the control of S3.

SYSTEM 4

Clearly, collaboration is the "glue" that holds an organisation together. In a fully systemic health care context, this would mean that staff would be invited to co-create projects and the role of management would be to facilitate staff's learning processes, respecting their own autonomy, preferences, and rhythms. There is wide space for improvement in this field. While the spirit of innovation and research exists in both S1s in the SPU, a more nurturing context for research and development could be instigated by the LEHT in general, and the HG_2. This may involve issues like negotiating a small amount of money per year to the SPU for small experiments with new ideas; simplification of the approval of business proposals and agreement on a limited time to approve or refuse them; creation of an annual (online) conference with colleagues from other SPUs in the NHS, to share best practice and exchange innovation; and development of a local stimulus for innovation with some form of recognition.

SYSTEM 5

While currently the same meta-systemic roles take responsibility for S3 and S4 issues, there is still an opportunity for designing annual meetings for reviewing developmental needs for the SPU and agreeing on main strategies and adjustments to operational policies if required. Such meetings should invite a balanced representation of S4 and S5 roles from SPU_1 and SPU_2, Division 1 and HG_2 and should result in agreeing developmental strategies for the SPU, as well as any required adjustments to operational policies and processes.

This case study illustrates how, by using VSM criteria in a SPU in a LEHT, we can contribute to creating a more decentralised, autonomous structure from the bottom up, which has the potential to become a pilot case that is then progressively replicated within the organisation. We will revisit the findings from this case study in Chapter 8, where we will report on another (ongoing) v&s project & exploring the resilience of a whole trust and assessing its capabilities to deal with the COVID-19 pandemic. We are finding similar structural pathologies in this trust in the specialist groups directly involved with attending COVID-19 patients (e.g., need for clearer clinical criteria informing decision making). Also, we are finding further confirmation of the benefits of enhancing local autonomy, which proved very useful for managing last year's pandemic emergency.

Another crucial lesson which is being confirmed in these studies is the need for developing more adequate metrics to assess operational performance, based on the quality of the health service provided, rather than on the cost of providing such services. More quality of health KPIs (e.g., listening to patients and clinicians, as the basis for assessing health performance) would be highly desirable. Devolving control to the level where decisions need to be made and simplifying some of the complicated decision-making processes will improve operational performance. It would allow staff also at the operational levels to close the loops within them in real time – and to quickly incorporate this feedback in decisions to continuously adjust and improve the quality of the health services offered. In terms of innovation and adaptation, there is room for improvement in promoting more decentralised innovation and strategy making at the local level to contribute to solutions by trusting local expertise.

In summary, the process of jointly analysing underlying structural issues in a SPU (and the LEHT) has raised awareness between the v&s project's participants of the need for urgently addressing some of the issues that proved to affect the LEHT's performance. Those that are in their hands (that they can address autonomously) are being acted upon. Those that depend on national strategies and structural changes will be feedback to the national authorities for later discussion at these levels. Hopefully these ongoing projects will also reconfirm and make more precise an effective systemic methodology, which could be expanded and replicated in other regional and national NHS Trusts, and in other private or public health services in the United Kingdom and abroad (see Chapter 8).

There follows the trust's project leader Kartikae Grover's testimony on his learning from the project:

'Participating in the v&s project has had a transformative effect on my perspective and management capabilities. The project's action learning feedback loops have resulted in improvements to our organisation, made as the project evolved. The STM approach demonstrated its effectiveness even within the rigidity of the NHS. Because solutions were co-developed with participants, they showed a willingness to help. For example, having regular meetings with the finance manager; attending health group meetings; facilitating regular innovation meetings; and the Head of Performance volunteering to design a bespoke BI dashboard for the service, have all started having a positive effect. The involvement of the Trust' Executives from the beginning provided legitimacy to the

v&s project and to my role as leader of the action research project. Not only I learned about the VSM as a practitioner, but also gained critical insights into finance, contacting, performance and other activities. Acquiring 'knowledge power' this way helped me to tackle some of the rigid hierarchical barriers in the NHS. It also helped me to help the Trust to overcome some of the expected resistance to change as our proposals would alter to some extent the balance of power and style of functioning of our unit. We have managed to successfully implement the self-transformation projects in our unit, with full support from the Trust's Executive ad it has produced important improvements in our operational and managerial performance.'

Conclusions

Beer's idea of adaptive and resilient organisations is now more relevant than ever to reinvent organisations in the context of the coronavirus pandemic worldwide. The world as we knew it has ceased to exist, and we are facing the biggest challenge our civilisation has had in recent times. Dealing with this challenge requires us to reorganise ourselves, at the individual, business, community, and regional levels, to cope with these turbulent and unprecedented times. The need for survival, adaptation, and sustainability is no longer limited to theory and academia, but is now clearly the major challenge for all businesses, communities, and governments. We are only beginning to grasp how urgently we need to address these issues.

This chapter has shown how the v&s approach and the STM can contribute to highlight desirable and feasible organisational improvements in individual, in businesses, and in particular, in health organisations. In the current context this is a research direction that is urgently needed to improve individual, businesses, and in particular, public health organisations' resilience and preparedness for future public health emergencies.

The VSM analyses reviewed in this chapter all point to generic recommendations regarding issues that are core for improving v&s in individuals and businesses.

- Decisions on how to better self-organise (more sustainably) are essential at all levels of organisations, from the individual and household to national and global levels.

- Awareness of the impact of specific decisions in the sustainability of our long-term interactions with our niches are vital for future educational and sustainability strategies.

- The COVID-19 pandemic forced us to rethink our priorities at each level, by focusing on essential issues for our v&s, which also means learning to live a simpler life, and to take more care of ours and others' health.

- We are learning that focusing on critical issues for sustainability will improve our capabilities for individual, social, and businesses v&s.
- Learning to collaborate in attending to the 'essential variables for sustainability' helps to create a more resilient social infrastructure for self-organisation and self-governance.
- Developing capabilities for sensing 'early alarms' in our niches improves our resilience, self-governance skills, and in the long term our viability and sustainability.
- An unexpected consequence of the dramatic changes we have experienced with the COVID-19 pandemic in our social and professional lives is that it has opened new opportunities for intentionally implementing systemic changes in many organisations and businesses worldwide, as demonstrated in the NHS case studies.

One of the novel research directions emerging from the v&s understanding of organisations is the analysis of very complex social systems like communities, bio-regions, or even nations, as systems urgently needed to improve resilience. This approach helps us to focus our analysis on their capabilities for self-organisation and sustainable self-governance. We shall further explore these ideas through several applications in the following chapters.

Notes

1 https://orcid.org/my-orcid?orcid=0000-0002-5200-7613
2 See more on A. Leonard – Individual VSM at Robinson, D.T. (2013), "Introducing managers to the VSM using a personal VSM", Kybernetes, Vol. 42 No. 1, pp. 125-139. https://doi.org/10.1108/03684921311295529
3 Andrea C. Martinez is a former PhD student I supervised from Los Andes University in Colombia. She led this v&s intervention as field work in her PhD research.
4 The company's real name is disguised for confidentiality reasons.
5 Leading in a matrix.
6 The virtues of decentralisation for health services in crisis.
7 We will refer to it as SPU, for confidentiality reasons.
8 We will refer to it as ELHT, for confidentiality reasons.
9 'Plans to shake-up the NHS have a central flaw'. Available online August 10th 2022 at https://blogs.bmj.com/bmj/2020/07/28/nigel-edwards-plans-to-shake-up-the-nhs-have-a-central-flaw/
10 'Emergency teams condemn government's 'controlling' approach to crisis'. Available online August 22nd 2022, at: https://www.theguardian.com/world/2020/may/15/disaster-planners-condemn-government-controlling-approach-coronavirus-crisis
11 It's taken just 12 months for Boris Johnson to create a government of sleaze'. Available online at: https://www.theguardian.com/commentisfree/2020/aug/07/its-taken-just-12-months-for-boris-johnson-to-create-a-government-of-sleaze

12 Cummings' actions show government cannot be trusted, says adviser'. Available online at: https://www.theguardian.com/politics/2020/may/25/cummings-row-risks-breach-of-public-trust-says-psychology-expert
13 COVID-19: A Study in Complexity Science and Prediction. Available online at https://www.youtube.com/watch?v=yZhOTsoNOUc
14 Dr Kartikae Grover is also a former MBA student, who learned the v&s approach during his degree. He is the clinical lead at the SPU$_1$.

References

Ashby, W. R. (1962). 'Principles of the self-organizing system' in Von Foerster, H. & Zopf, G. W. Jr. (eds.), *Principles of Self-Organization: Transactions of the University of Illinois Symposium*. London: Pergamon Press, pp. 255–278.

Beer, S. (1979). *Heart of the enterprise*. London: John Wiley & Sons.

Bansal, P., & Song, H. C. (2017). 'Similar but not the same: Differentiating corporate sustainability from corporate responsibility', *Academy of Management Annals*, 11(1), pp. 105–149.

Copper, D. (2018). 'Systems thinking and organisational change in the NHS: From heroic to system leadership' in Barile, S., Espejo, R., Perko, I., & Saviano, M. (eds.), *Cybernetics and Systems: Social and Business Decisions*. London: Routledge, pp. 349–352.

Ellis, B. S., (2008). 'Managing governance programmes in primary care: lessons from case studies on the implementation of clinical governance in two primary care Trusts'. *PhD Dissertation*. Preston: University of Central Lancashire.

Engert, S., & Baumgartner, R. J. (2016). 'Corporate sustainability strategy–bridging the gap between formulation and implementation', *Journal of Cleaner Production*, 113, pp. 822–834.

Espejo, R. (2021). 'COVID-19. Research Note', *Systems Research and Behavioural Sciences*, 38(1), pp. 184–186.

Espinosa, A., & Walker, J. (2017). *A complexity approach to sustainability: Theory and Application*. 2nd edition. Singapore: World Scientific Press.

Ioannou, I., & Serafeim, G. (2019). 'Corporate sustainability: A strategy?', *Harvard Business School Accounting & Management Unit, Working Paper No 19–065*.

Johnson, M., & Liber, O. (2008). 'The Personal Learning *Environment and the human condition: from theory to teaching practice'*, *Interactive* Learning Environments, 16(1), pp. 3–15.

Martinez, A. C., & Espinosa, A. (2022). 'Corporate viability and sustainability: A case study in a mexican corporation', *Systems Research and Behavioural Sciences*, 39(1), pp. 143–158.

Pollock,A. M., & Roderick, P. (2015). 'Why the Queen's Speech on 19 May should include a bill to reinstate the NHS in England'. *BMJ, p* 350. h2257. doi: 10.1136/bmj.h2257.

Seddon, J. W. (2008). *Systems Thinking in the Public Sector*. London: Triarchy Press.

Walsh, M., Kittler, M. G., & Mahal, D. (2018). 'Towards a new paradigm of healthcare: Addressing challenges to professional identities through Community Operational Research', *European Journal of Operational Research*, 268, pp. 1125–1133.

Chapter 5

'Fits Like a Glove': The VSM for Supporting More Systemic Educational Organisations

From Non-Systemic to Systemic Education and Educational Institutions

Acknowledgement of pitfalls of traditional approaches to education in Western countries has been growing over the last few decades. Some of the pioneer systems and cybernetic thinkers recognised such limitations long ago and paved the way for suggesting and developing what we will call in this chapter a more systemic approach to education. If fully implemented, this approach would also require a complete transformation of the current way of managing such institutions.

The education system is one of the most precious institutions for societal viability and sustainability, as it creates a learning context for providing children with varied skills to be able to survive as productive, autonomous, and responsible adults in their society. One would think that it should be there that all innovations in every field of knowledge would be absorbed most quickly and transferred into new curricula, educational methods, or content. But many of us experienced educators share the same frustrating experience on how difficult it is to transform our approach to education and even more, to radically transform a school, a university, or even an entire educational sector in a country.

It comes as a surprise how paradoxically resistant schools and universities are when it is time to re-learn or rethink traditional ideas about education or to rethink their organisations. More than ever, long-term viability and sustainability of our human societies relies heavily on finding effective ways to rethink education. Only then we can raise a new generation of more autonomous, creative, adaptive, and critical children, well prepared to reinvent our institutions and societies, to make them work in a more sustainable, equitable, and humane way.

DOI: 10.4324/9780429490835-6

What Is a Non-Systemic Approach to Education?

The autocratic mindset that has dominated organisations and in particular schools from the pre-industrial era results in an educational system in which the teacher is seen as the knower, and the students as the passive recipients of knowledge transmission, expected to obey and respect numerous rules and behavioural codes. The teacher is expected to have detailed knowledge of every aspect of an established syllabus, and to teach it in such a way that every student progresses through the expected stages of learning in a satisfactorily way.

However, teachers do not always have the requisite variety to facilitate effective learning from the students of the skills the syllabus expects them to develop. Not always does the school's curriculum (as set up by local or national educational authorities) have requisite variety to address the evolving knowledge in every disciplinary field. Many times, both the standard syllabus and the traditional ways of delivering it can erode creativity and the desire to learn from students.

A non-systemic school focuses on developing cognitive skills for children, and sees learning as a rational process, where knowledge is divided into separate unconnected subjects. It privileges quantitative over qualitative skills development, provides little or no flexibility and expects students to obey instructions without question.[2] This traditional school *too effectively attenuate* environmental variety, which may result in making teachers' lives more manageable, but does not necessarily open rich enough learning opportunities for students or make their learning process engaging or enjoyable.

Towards More Systemic Educational Institutions

According to Reyes (2019), pioneers in systemic education include Dewey (1938), who suggested to shift education towards providing meaningful experiences for students; Tagore (1929), designing learning spaces for children based on a playful environment to develop a natural learning atmosphere in schools; Illich (1971), promoting a de-schooling society, where every aspect of the student's life becomes a learning experience that will help them become active citizens; and Freire (2007), considering learners as co-creators of knowledge and offering an approach to develop critical learners and active citizens, through education.

Pask (1988) introduced conversation theory and clarified the way conversations support different ways of 'understanding,' learning styles and strategies, and highlighted the relevance of 'learning to learn.' Von Foerster (1995, pp. 298–299) explained learning as *'those situations where an organism behaves differently before and after an exposure to the environment.'* He argued that *'the prevalence of education in the balance of learning paralyzes man's poetic ability, his power to endow the world with his personal meaning.'* Von Foerster Voss 1996) explained how by taking a wider, more humane, and systemic understanding of learning, we can transform education in the classroom and even reinvent schools. Also, Maturana (1990, pp. 26–32) explained what he called the *'biology of education,'* explaining education as the process through which individuals co-exist with others, by accepting themselves and others, and making their beings more congruent with other beings.

Systemic learning is seen as both a cognitive and an emotional process. To manage complex problems we need curiosity, creativity, openness to varying viewpoints, and critical thinking. A systemic school should provide a rich context for students to explore the world through learning projects to address complex problems, and to *'learn to learn.'* A learning project seeks to hone the learner's adaptive capacity in her relationships: with herself; with others in her family, community, and society; and with her environment – see Figure 5.1 – showing systemic tools to support learning in each domain. Systemic education is naturally based on humanism, ecological thinking, ethics, and multi-culturalism.

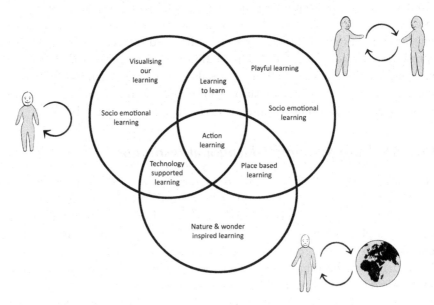

Figure 5.1 Systemic learning

(Illustration by Thom Igwe-Walker)

Systemic education is student centred. It sees the teacher as a facilitator of the students' learning rather than a provider of information. Students learn 'by doing,' through transdisciplinary action learning projects, and develop cognitive, social, and communicative skills. Learning is also context, nature, and place based. We will enjoy much more the learning when there is a strong motivation to learn. Learning to relate to others has a huge socio-emotional component. A rich interaction with someone allows us to exchange more information and to share more knowledge than a cold, distant, or hostile one.

Technology can provide an effective context for systemic learning as it offers access to an immense repository of knowledge sources; it is the most effective variety amplifier we can imagine! It allows visualisation, recording, managing, and sharing our knowledge; and it even allows relational learning when the face-to-face interaction is not possible or desirable (as during the COVID-19 pandemic when we were all learning online). Nowadays, the wide availability of information and educational resources on the internet open very interesting and innovative opportunities for self-organised individual and collective learning. A cybernetic approach to education[3] amplifies students' variety by allowing them to self-organise their learning space in the classroom, co-learn with their classmates, and by closing their learning loop through critically self-assessing their learning outputs and experience.

In the old times, the boundaries for the knowledge acquired by exploring your niche may have coincided with how far you could travel. Nowadays, the boundary for learning diffuses across the extensive knowledge repositories that learners can access through the web. The variety of information available in the external environment has increased exponentially and the possibilities of accessing it continue to expand. But this context of 'explosive variety' has also reduced dramatically our capability for closing our learning loops.

It is now feasible to create proper informational and communicational filters to amplify the variety of educational content, by coaching students to explore the core questions they may have at a particular stage of their own development through self-research. Combining a systemic approach to education with state-of-the-art communication and information technologies opens a gateway for dramatic transformation of the classroom and of educational institutions, as the following case studies will demonstrate.

A systemic educational institution promotes what we describe here as systemic education and systemic learning. To be viable and sustainable, an educational institution should also be socially and environmentally responsible, embed sustainability values at the core of its programs, and apply these principles in its way of managing resources and its relationships with its community and ecological niche. Systemic educational approaches in Europe, like the Regio Emilia approach and the Finish educational approach, have shown very good outcomes, compared with more traditional educational approaches, and have become increasingly popular in pioneering schools, which are now implementing them progressively at different levels (starting at kindergarten and primary schools). The case studies presented below will offer examples of ongoing self-transformations towards more systemic and sustainable educational institutions supported by the v&s approach and the STM.

As would be confirmed later, there are growing number of examples on how the VSM and Team Syntegrity can inspire alternative ways of delivering education and/or transforming an educational institution towards a more viable and sustainable organisation. It seems clearer now that schools and higher education institutions worldwide are more aware every day of the imminent need for developing new skills and capabilities in students to deal with the increasing volatility and complexity of the 21st century. And that a more systemic and cybernetic approach to learning and to manage educational institutions would be central to progress in this direction.

Self-Transformation of ELF – The Whole Story (with Jon Walker and Vladimir Pop)

Chapter 2 introduced the v&s project at the ELF school in Cluj, Romania, and Chapter 3 offered several examples of VSM diagnosis from the project. As mentioned previously, we visited ELF five times during 2019 to coach the project team in identifying, designing, and implementing their required self-transformations. Through four-hour daily workshops, during a week – in each visit –we developed the VSM diagnosis at each level of organisation, from the school to the grade level and agreed on feasible and desirable changes. In each workshop, we worked in teams with representatives from meta-systemic and operational roles and, when relevant, also invited students and parents.

When we started the ELF project early in 2019, it was operating successfully: children, parents, and teachers' assessments demonstrated a very good average satisfaction; the educational authorities were satisfied with the annual school's assessment; and finances were healthy. As the school's reputation had been growing steadily over the years, demand for places at the schools was also growing and the owners decided to invest in a new development site to expand the educational offer. Aware of shortages in the existing structure, the owners wanted our advice to improve it in preparation for the new developments. There follows an overview of the whole project and a final reflection on the learning achieved by the ELF schools.

Clarifying the School's Identity

During the first one-week v&s workshop in March 2019, we introduced the v&s approach and the self-transformation methodology. We created the steering committee for the project (with representatives from academic and administrative roles from each school) and started the first two stages of the methodology. We began to discuss with them our understanding of systemic education and how we would expect to progress first in the direction of rethinking the way of delivering education in the classroom; and secondly, in transforming the existing structure towards a more 'cybernetically sound' self-organised, resilient, and adaptive structure. We then ran a creative session, drawing cartoons about the current schools' challenges and para-doxes.

The cartoon from the first group of participants in the workshop (Figure 3.2) described a very positive working environment and the major challenge in the immediate future: to prepare the current structure for the planned expansion, including the design of new high and primary schools, and the building of new premises. A second cartoon (not presented here) re-presented the headmasters and teachers as hard-working bees, facing big survival challenges, and potential threats (e.g., losing unity and cohesion of the schools); getting through the cobwebs (from educational authorities' bu-reaucracy); being ready to offer secondary education to all children finishing their primary education (they were only running up to 9th grade in 2019, and intending to deliver 10th grade in 2020); and being capable of producing a sensible and feasible development plan for the schools.

During the workshop, the participants agreed on the following identity statement:

> ELF is a private school in Cluj which offers education (from kindergarten to grade 10) by creating a friendly creative and safe educational environment to motivate children to learn and grow, resulting in the overall and harmonious development of children's skills and inclinations resulting in autonomous, adaptive, and responsible individuals and citizens.

It was clear that a driving force of the school's continued success was the very humanistic, creative, and holistic view of education that the founder had embedded in the culture of ELF from the very beginning. Even if not calling it a 'systemic' school originally, their values resonated strongly with systemic values, which unsurprisingly resulted in us discovering that the expected systemic transformation was already in progress, especially at some levels in the school, as will be evidenced later.

We clarified the purpose of the self-transformation process: to support ELF to continue as the best private school in Cluj's history for children from all social levels; to create its own curriculum (e.g., inspired in Cambridge cur-riculum); to get the structure ready for the school's expansion; and to continue developing the ELF brand. These challenges required ELF to promptly move towards even more innovative, systemic, and child-centred quality education while remaining in the top leagues in the country.

Recursive Analysis

As mentioned earlier, it took us more than one session to finally agree on a recursive mapping of ELF that represented most accurately the current distribution of complexity among the schools (Figure 3.4). During the first year of the project, we would need to revisit once more this mapping, when exploring possibilities for the new structure once the new schools came into existence.

VSM Diagnosis

During the first workshop, we started by mapping the KGs and the PSs/HS as viable systems. While coaching the participants into VSM mapping their different roles of the KGs and the schools, we began to identify their main organisational weaknesses and/or pathologies.

Preliminary Diagnosis

There was a general feeling that they needed to improve the management of complexity at each school level and in ELF, as the current school management was overloaded with variety, which in their words '*sometimes resulted in inefficient action, lacking coordination, and management becoming absorbed by detail.*' They also began to clarify the owners' roles in the school, which hadn't previously been clear enough to everyone. Some expected innovations and improvements in the educational services began to be outlined in this preliminary diagnosis, such as the need for developing new optional modules in the UPS and HS (e.g., biology/IT instead of chemistry/physics). Also, the need for encouraging more creativity and innovation in teaching, while preserving quality education, and the need for more use of ICT to support teachers and students in the classroom.

In the primary schools (PSs), it was agreed to explore further the possibility of providing more autonomy to each of the headmasters (HMs), regarding both administrative functions (e.g., managing budgets and expenses, fee collection), and academic issues (e.g., relationships with parents and students, discipline issues). At the KGs the preliminary diagnosis revealed very few structural problems. Each headmaster felt they had enough autonomy to respond effectively and procedures were in place to deal with conflicts of interest; and the headmasters articulated both Systems 3 and 4 through regular meetings and discussions by phone and social media. S5 involved a strong ELF ethos that everyone subscribed to. Over the following workshops, we continued to explore further the bottlenecks in the management of complexity inside each system, and in the interaction among systems.

Full Diagnosis at the Schools

At the level of the schools, the project's participants recognised that the ELF headmaster had been taking most of the responsibilities in all three schools for both academic and administrative decisions, including communications with teachers, parents, and sometimes with students having special requests. As a result, she was suffering from the 'control dilemma' (Archetype 2.23 – see Espinosa & Walker (2017, pp. 485–492)) i.e., continuously requesting detailed information from lower operational levels, resulting in being completely overloaded by variety, which was creating bottlenecks and delays in strategic decision making.

Although she had a good team providing her administrative support, this team also suffered from delays and sometimes conflictive interactions with schoolteachers and headmasters, as most managerial decisions were taken at the ELF level. As the preliminary VSM diagnosis at the level of ELF had already signalled this type of alert, when we delved into the next level of diagnosis (recursion level 1, the school, and the kindergartens), we already knew that we'd need to devolve responsibilities previously taken by ELF's headmaster for several managerial issues. Figure 3.6. offered a summary of diagnostic issues.[4]

Full Diagnosis at the Kindergartens

In general, the kindergartens were already very well organised, had a very positive working environment, and only needed a bit of extra support to allow them to be in control of their own administrative and technical improvements. The v&s workshops made visible the strengths of their ongoing process and structural improvements and provided an opportunity for them to share with the schools.

The full diagnosis of the kindergartens made evident that at this level, there had been an intuitively 'cybernetically sound' ways of managing the KGs: The three KG coordinators had regular meetings to assess ongoing problems (S3), address any alarms raised by parents or teachers (S3*), share academic innovation (S4), and support each other at all levels. While developing their S2, they had established a comprehensive set of standards and procedures, which applied to all kindergartens, including standard curricula for all kindergartens, teachers guide, caregivers guide, handbook of procedures, unified job descriptions and contracts of employment.

During the v&s workshops, it was agreed that they should and will support other schools (PS, HS) to progress in a similar direction. We identified other issues that could be improved and agreed on going forward (see Figure 3.8). Most diagnostic issues were acted upon over the project's lifetime. Some required further design and continued to be implemented by the team when we concluded the project.

The Self-Regulatory Homeostat (S1/S2/S3)

It was clear that the kindergartens were very autonomous regarding academic issues, but still could benefit from gaining more administrative autonomy in day-to-day issues, as the centralised management was creating delays in urgent decisions. It was agreed that more responsibility will be taken by the co-ordinators regarding administrative decisions (like management of fees, teachers, and communications with parents), thus enhancing their local autonomy. To take extra responsibilities they would be provided with extra secretarial and administrative support, which was agreed.

A different situation was observable in the schools (see Figure 3.6 examples of VSM diagnosis in ELF schools). ELF's headmaster (who also acted as primary school, upper primary school, and high school headmaster) was taking responsibility for most S3, S3*, and some S2 roles – with some support from central administrative roles. This created several delays and resulted in an enormous workload for her, lessening her availability for more strategic issues. Lots of her time was devoted to sorting out requests and information. It was agreed that by delegating some of these roles to the primary school headmasters, a more balanced structure would emerge. The more decentralised structure begun to show benefits very shortly after implementing them, both in terms of agility and flexibility of decision making, and in terms of each school's capabilities for self-management and self-regulation.

The Adaptation Mechanism (S3/S4/S5)

In ELF, the Board of Administration (BoA) was the formal S5. It met once a year and included a representative from the owners, all six headmasters, a teacher representing each of the schools, a representative from the city council, and three parents. Except for the city council and the parent representatives, all the other participants met a few times a year at the school council, to review the school's progress and performance. The school council contributed to close the loop on issues of identity and policy (S5), innovation and development (S4), and assessing the school's performance according to educational authorities' assessment standards and procedures (S3).

We identified that headmasters needed to allocate more time to fully develop their S4/S5 roles (people's development, educational development, physical and technological development, and organisational development). Also, they decided to design more robust strategic decision-making spaces (e.g., more inclusive, and timely ways of preparing the formal annual school report were agreed). They also agreed to meet four times a year at the school council, and to clarify their agenda for each meeting. In the August meeting they would discuss managerial and educational innovations; new roles and process redesign; sharing good practice; and adjustments to internal rules.

In the November meeting they would decide on the school plan, admission, and recruitment projects. In the February meeting they would make agreements on admission and fee policy; new recruitments; educational reports; and infrastructure developments. In the final meeting (May) they would focus on reviewing the school year's performance.

To strengthen S4 strategy and innovation capabilities, it was decided to design and implement a strategic council in each school, including representatives from the metasystem and from each of the systems 1 (i.e., grades' headteachers and teachers leading innovations in each school). This council will meet several times a year to share local innovations and to decide on each school's strategic academic innovation and research projects (e.g., the Erasmus projects). They also recognised the need for a new S4 role to lead the school's sustainability strategy and appointed a former primary headmaster into this role. Finally, another governance mechanism that was reviewed and discussed was the parents council: It had become clear that each school designed and operated their parents council differently, so they made an agreement to share best practices and to collectively decide on best ways to run this council in all schools.

Aligning Strategy, Structure, and Information Systems

During the workshops, we understood that once the new upper primary and high school were operating at the new premises, there would be a need to rethink meta-systemic management, to integrate all primary schools and all upper primary and high schools. An emerging level of organisation to deal with this increased complexity would be designed – more precisely, a meta-systemic management for primaries and a meta-systemic management for the UPS/HSs. This understanding helped us later to focus on some of the self-transformation projects to further develop autonomy and leadership for the headmasters in primary, upper primary, and high schools. To improve strategic information management in all schools, responsibilities for ICT innovations in the classroom were given to natural leaders who had pioneered them up to that point in each school. Other strategies for strengthening the use of online educational software were agreed on and implemented in the schools.

Self-Transformation Projects and Plan

ELF's team was a strongly oriented action learning team. Most of the issues we identified in one workshop were addressed and resolved by them by the time we came back a few months later. Devolution of 'responsible autonomy' and re-distribution of responsibilities for meta-systemic management in each of the schools were very quickly put into practice; it was implemented by providing extra administrative support for headmasters in each school so that they could spend more time in their S4/S5 roles. They clarified new roles and processes for sustainability strategies, managing infrastructure developments, managing inventories and acquisitions, and implemented them aiming to give more flexibility and autonomy to each school. These improvements quickly alleviated several bottlenecks reported during the diagnosis.

Monitoring and Assessing Performance

At the final workshop, we identified the main aspects in which the existing performance management systems should be improved. It included redesigning KPIs based on operational performance, managing them using real-time information, and developing the capability to produce algedonics, when required. They realised they needed a more effective way for assessment information to cascade from grades and classes – where such information is produced – up to the next levels of recursive organisation (the school). This required that headteachers continuously summarise and update their results to higher organisational levels, in time to collate them for the annual school performance assessment. And very importantly, they understood the need for designing democratic and participatory decision-making spaces to review operational performance (S3/S1) at each school. It was also agreed to review current student and teacher assessment systems, and to design more robust assessment systems.

Reviewing ELF's Self-Transformation

There follows a brief review from Vladimir Pop on his experience and learning through the self-transformation process in ELF in 2019:

> I first experienced the Viable System Model during the Systems and Complexity Management module of my EMBA, taught by Angela Espinosa. Having understood the basics of the VSM (i.e., synergy, autonomy, and empowerment), I realised applying this model on the organisation that I have been part of would fit like a glove. The fast-paced growth of ELF during the last five years – it doubled in size! – put a lot of pressure on both the structure and the maintenance of quality of educational services. To assure long-term survival and competitiveness, ELF school needed to embrace change. And so, our adventure started. ELF went through a series of workshops during which the V&S approach was applied to review ELF's structure and operational activity. The workshops provided a healthy, open, and informal environment for the management team to agree upon current vision, structure, roles, and issues, based on which recommendations for improvement were made. I can witness that by applying the v&s approach to our organisation resulted in ELF emerging as a much healthier organisation than before with improved flexibility, adaptability, autonomy, synergy, and finally with a well-designed and updated structure. During the pandemic in 2020–2021 ELF has managed to

demonstrate an amazingly short span for reacting and adapting to the new situation and succeeded in the required fast re-organisation of the whole school to teach online and to introduce the new lockdown rules. Having been now operating in much more flexible structures weighted heavily in dealing successfully with the changes that the pandemic implied and in enhancing the quality of our services. I would like to state that the reaction of an organisation during a crisis reveals its weaknesses and its strengths. I confirm that the improvements gained through the 'self-transformation' project were essential in the survival of the company throughout the pandemic and I would encourage to use this systemic approach to anybody who desires a healthier organisation both from structure and product/service point of view.

This is perhaps, one of the very few VSM applications in which the VSM model was understood at a deep level by the people working within the organisation. Their acceptance of this new way of working was, to some extent, the result of their approach to education, and Vladimir Pop's insight that the VSM would '*fit like a glove*' in the ELF schools.

Designing TINTA, a Systemic Education Online Provider (with G. Ramirez)

Gabriela Ramirez (GR), a former MSc student of mine from Los Andes University, Colombia, approached me in 2018 to support her in designing a start-up company to develop innovative systemic educational content for primary schools. She had pioneered project-based learning (PBL) approaches to deliver primary education in alternative schools near Bogota. She was confident that there was a niche in the evolving market of web-based educational tools for schools, for offering an innovative and fully systemic approach to support home-school and online education for the classroom, both in Latin American– and in English-speaking countries.

Her market research reconfirmed that none of the main suppliers of PBL educational content on the web, offered a comprehensive systemic package which would enable teachers and school administrators to progressively transform the classroom, and hopefully, also contribute to inspire a more systemic organisation of the school. She hired me to support her in designing the start-up company (*TINTA is the original name in Spanish*) and its initial development by following the v&s approach and using the STM.

Once her shareholders agreed on the business plan and the operational and developmental budget for the first two years of the project, she created the company as a commercial society: She got advice on the current legislation for development and commercialisation of e-resources and on intellectual property and began recruiting the operational team. After a year of designing and developing the online platform and educational resources, TINTA was launched in February 2020, just before COVID-19 started to spread world-wide, when this type of offering became more relevant than ever. There follows a summary of the VSM design of the company, and the self-assessment of the company during its first year. Also, a reflection on the learning from this start-up design and the way it contributes to progressing towards a more systemic view of education.

TINTA's Approach to Systemic Education

Building on GR's experience using project-based learning (PBL) in primary schools, TINTA aimed at designing systemic educational projects that would provide the opportunity for students and teachers to collectively address social and environmental complexity, through multi-disciplinary action learning projects. Rather than giving students a fixed 'recipe' (i.e., a textbook containing established disciplinary knowledge on a particular field, like mathematics, language, or science) in a PBL approach, the teacher would facilitate the learning of the students on a particular complex situation – relevant to their current stage of life.

Traditionally, curricula are based on certain content students must learn to advance in their studies. But once the consequence of having all that knowledge just one click away on any smartphone are understood, it loses relevance. Differently, PBL aims to make learning real, to solve a question that needs attention and to do so from different perspectives and areas of knowledge. This approach keeps students motivated and empowers them both to solve problems and to 'own' their learning process. Most importantly, project-based methodologies seek to teach children to solve real problems while learning how to use specific skills.

Rather than learning facts and information, the important issue is what to do with it. The learning process can then become more about the skills and less about the content. While developing the project, students will have to ask questions, organise information, take on different roles; work with one or more teams; interpret data; compare points of views; understand the relations between different phenomena; take on different perspectives; observe and analyse possible solutions; make decisions; present to an audience; and receive feedback. All these skills are useful for any career they may choose later. They are essential for *learning how to learn*.

Although project-based learning methodologies have been widely adopted, their implementation varies greatly. For some schools, it may just include a small project within a specific area, like studying the growth of a plant in biology, or writing a diary in English class, or maybe discovering the different applications of a mathematical formula. In other schools, projects are involved in all areas and therefore become transdisciplinary. They may include how to help decontaminate a river that passes close to their school, observing the perspectives of people contaminating it, measuring its pH in different locations, understanding the river's historical and social importance, researching the different species that live or lived in it, mapping it, and learning about its geography, etc. A project like this allows students to understand the river as a system: It leads them to observe connections, to model them and to seek solutions, acknowledging there may be many of them.

When the project is the main learning methodology and it includes all areas and community members, then it becomes complex enough to work on all skills. It accomplishes its true purpose of making the learning process *systemic*. In VSM language, TINTA aimed to design online educational resources to act as 'attenuators' of environmental variety or 'amplifiers' of the students' or teacher's variety, by empowering the students and teacher's collective to develop joint research projects, on issues of real interest for students, aimed at developing systemic capabilities. TINTA's online resources aimed at addressing the development of capabilities in three (interrelated) domains of relationships in a particular learning project: Students and teachers would need to interact more closely with themselves (becoming critical learners), with others (developing more skills for relational learning), and with Nature (developing skills for environmental and ecological learning) – see Figure 5.1.

To design a transdisciplinary, systemic curriculum, we began by clarifying the sort of 'systemic' capabilities that children will need to (creatively and enjoyably) develop through PBL projects. It took some time to study the standard curriculum established by educational authorities both in Latin America and North America, to summarise the standard set of skills in American schools, and to choose a robust set of transdisciplinary skills. TINTA designed projects developing such skills in the areas of language, mathematics, and physical and social sciences. The induction course for resource developers included both an introduction to systemic learning, to this transdisciplinary curriculum, as well as a collaborative practice co-designing systemic resources focused on developing the desirable skills.

Agreeing on TINTA's Identity

From the beginning of TINTA's inception phase, we developed several v&s workshops, first with the shareholders and then with the employees, to design the organisation. There follows a review of the way TINTA was born and came to life, and the learning at each stage.

At the first meetings, we agreed with the shareholders on TINTA's statement of identity, as follows:

> *TINTA is an organisation aiming to contribute to innovate on primary education practice by providing primary school teachers with educational content to support project-based learning, and using state of the art, bilingual, systemic, and*

transdisciplinary content in the main educational areas (mathematics, language, sciences, and social sciences). Also, by offering a systemic approach for documenting the educational projects, that will not only comply with educational requirements from schools and educational authorities, but will allow them to make connections, to visualize the learning cycle and to minimise the time used in repetitive tasks. And by supporting private and public schools in their own self-transformation processes, by coaching them in using systemic organisational learning approaches and methodologies

Recursive Analysis – TINTA's Primary Services

Having agreed on this organisational identity, we progressed onto representing the primary activities required to implement TINTA's purpose. We developed the first recursive mapping of the expected organisation – see Figure 5.2 – including three operational units (S1). The first one was to develop systemic educational content in the five key educational areas in a primary school: language, social and natural sciences, and mathematics. This was the operational system that was fully developed in the first year of TINTA's operation. The second and third operational systems were still in design mode when writing this review (and thus are represented by dotted lines in the diagram). We will focus on the first operational unit for the VSM analysis of TINTA.

TINTA hired more than 30 (part-time) learning resource developers; two thematic leaders; two graphic designers; a computer and systems engineer who

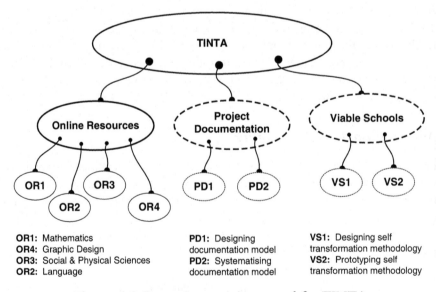

OR1: Mathematics	**PD1:** Designing	**VS1:** Designing self
OR4: Graphic Design	documentation model	transformation methodology
OR3: Social & Physical Sciences	**PD2:** Systematising	**VS2:** Prototyping self
OR2: Language	documentation model	transformation methodology

Figure 5.2 Recursive mapping agreed for TINTA

(Illustration by Jon Walker)

would develop the online platform; and a part-time accountant, administrator, and lawyer. I provided systemic coaching to all employees, through the first year of TINTA's development. During 2019 and 2020, TINTA focused on designing and developing the online platform and educational resources, organised in three thematic teams each one with their leaders (mathematics, language, and social and physical sciences). When most of the resources were ready, TINTA was officially launched early in 2020 at an international conference on systemic education TINTA held in Bogota.[5]

Designing TINTA's Organisation with VSM Criteria

Figure 5.3 represents an initial VSM modelling of TINTA, taking our system in focus as the online resources development unit, as agreed on in workshops with its members during the first year of operation.

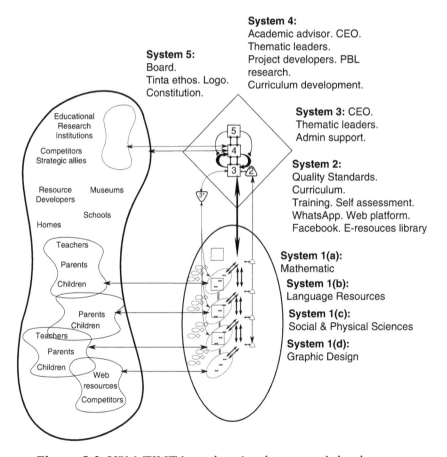

Figure 5.3 VSM TINTA – educational resources' development

(Illustration by Jon Walker)

The S1s were the resource development activities in the three thematic areas. The thematic leaders coordinated groups of developers, which included recruiting, training, and monitoring the delivered resources' quality. They also interacted with the graphic designers who received draft resources, did their graphic design, and uploaded them to the platform. There follows examples of meta-systemic roles (underlined) and *mechanisms* (highlighted in italics) in this first year of operation:

- S2: Thematic leaders prevented oscillations at the operational level, originally by leading *training workshops* for coaching developers and graphic designers, about *TINTA's educational approach, values, curriculum,* and *systemic capabilities* to be nurtured by the online resources. When recruiting personnel, they shared *application forms* and *criteria for assessing applicants*; they also coordinated *employees' operational plans* and jointly defined and reviewed *quality standards for resources development*.

  - While coordinating development of resources, they created a *WhatsApp's team* to liaise and decide on issues regarding interactions with developers.

  - They shared information in Google *Drive Folders*: *calendar and agendas* for meetings; *resource development plans and employees*; *developing resources spreadsheet*; and an *e-resources library* including all the final resources to be uploaded in the platform.

- S3: Supported by an administrative assistant and an accountant, GR negotiated resources development plans and the required developers' recruitment with the thematic leaders. The accountability channel included negotiation of *developers' contracts* and *assessment of their results* (online results quality). The academic advisor developed a S3* role in monitoring the quality of e-resources developed.

- S4: GR did the market research and developed TINTA's business plan with her shareholders. She hired an ICT expert to design the online platform and I supported the team to agree on the functionality, design and features required to implement the online services. Then she hired two graphic designers to produce final design for resources to be uploaded at the platform. GR and the thematic leaders were permanently exploring the educational environment to be attentive to related research on other online educational resources and events, identified strategic allies and contributed to TINTA's *Facebook page*.

- S5: Originally, with the support of a lawyer, GR and her shareholders decided on TINTA's *constitution, ethos, brand, and logo*. Every six months, they held an *executive committee* to reflect on the stage of development of TINTA, and to agree on necessary adjustments to the business plan and business strategies. GR and I presented there a review of the emerging organisation and any identified need for improvements in ongoing interactions.

TINTA Coming to Life: First Self-Assessment

After the first six months of developing TINTA resources with the 30 developers, we agreed on a *preliminary VSM diagnosis* of the start-up company, after asking every member of TINTA to respond to an *electronic VSM survey*. Afterwards, we ran a *self-evaluation workshop* with all employees, to discuss the diagnosis and to get their feedback on desirable improvements. People perceived TINTA's operational performance very positively (56.5% strongly agreed and 39.1% agreed that TINTA showed high performance in developing online, systemic educational resources). Most of them also agreed TINTA promoted autonomy, creativity, and innovation.

They felt the developer vs management interactions were very effective, (S1/S2/S3 – clear values, products requested, procedures, and criteria for quality control). They saw some room for improvement in terms of the speed for providing feedback about improvements in the products delivered and in managing conflict when disagreements arose between developers and thematic leaders.

TINTA's effectiveness in developing products and the e-business platform, and in preparing for the next stages of development (S3/S4/S5) were also well assessed. Some people found room for improvements in encouraging more of their contributions to research and networking, further developing sustainability awareness in TINTA's products and services and improving benchmarking. People had in general, a very good perception of TINTA's self-governance, but some saw room for improvement in assessing what has been learned and challenges to improve performance.

In the *self-assessment workshop*, these issues were further clarified, and other more precise issues raised, like developing a space for reviewing the curriculum and products design with developers. They also suggested developing a Google drive to visualise each developer's past, current, and forthcoming products, and assessments to encourage self-management. It was interesting in terms of meta-cognition to see the summary of new skills that developers felt they have acquired, while working for TINTA: enjoying myths; creating fictional stories; learning to make more effective decisions; learning in unexpected and more didactic ways; multi-culturally learning; and in having fun while learning.

With this learning from the VSM survey and the self-assessment workshop, TINTA's team felt well equipped to improve their organisation. The last months of 2020 TINTA saw a continuous increase in the number of visitors to the web platform. TINTA still continues learning, developing, and self-assessing the start-up organisation.[6] There follows a testimony from GR on the way the VSM helped structuring the company and the learning they got from it.

> Organizing and leading TINTA with the VSM structure seemed very natural from the start. Everything simply made sense and came together with coherence and flexibility, especially since it took all the educational concepts and mindsets. I had already worked with to the management area making it much easier to envision and put into practice. It became a very clear fractal organisation in which the composition of the teams, the decision-making processes, the meetings, the methodology, the supporting pedagogy, and the actual product work under the same framework. This became especially evident as the team met. Most of the work has always been done online even before the pandemic, having very few actual meetings with the resource creative team. Once we did the feedback meeting the whole team was aligned and full of creative ideas for TINTA. Our difficulty has been to understand that most of our potential clients don't work in this same way. So, although teachers may understand and appreciate what we do it must reach management teams that seem to have different agendas. What happens in the classroom in most schools is not implied in the work of the rest of the school staff nor its headmaster in some cases.

Systemic Education in Higher Education Institutions

Systemic Management in Universities around the World

According to Atwater, Kannan, and Stephens (2008), the need for a more systemic education in higher education institutions has been increasingly discussed in the systemic-cybernetic communities. Olaya (2019) argues that most public universities still operate in centralised, controlled structures, inspired by the 'new public management' approach. Recent research demonstrates that it results in less academic freedom, administrative vs academic tensions regarding academic planning, growth of administrative staff and centralisation of decision-making. Even more, that the governance processes not always result in enhanced quality of learning and teaching, but commodifies and monetises education.

There had been several universities pioneering systemic programmes and approaches to management education. In Europe, the University of St. Gallen in Switzerland and the Universities of Hull and Lancaster in the United Kingdom have developed their own systemic approaches to management education since the 1980s (Schwaninger, 2019, Jackson, 2019, pp. xvii–xxiii) and continue to do so, with very good results. Hull University Business School had not only led systemic education in England, but its Centre of Systems Studies is considered a world centre of excellence in systems studies.[7]

Malik Management Zentrum in St. Gallen also has delivered an accredited master program in managerial cybernetics and system management for about 10 years. In the Americas, several universities (e.g., Los Andes in Colombia and the Technological Institute of Monterrey in Mexico) have pioneered systems and cybernetics postgraduate programs since the 1990s. There are now several universities in America developing new systemic education programs, including Portland University and the Sloan School of Management in MIT.

Schwaninger (2019) supports the claim that systemic approaches to education improve the content and method for delivering education, as they offer more holistic perspectives, combine analysis and synthesis, and support transdisciplinary research. He demonstrates the impact the St. Gallen Management approach has had in many German speaking countries, i.e., in awakening innovation and environmental responsibility, as the underlying model (the VSM) explicitly includes the ecological dimension as a matter of concern.

Saeed & Gamal (2019) demonstrate through multiple examples the power of the VSM approach to deal with the increasing complexity of universities. They quote Yolles's (1999) VSM study at the City of Liverpool Community College and Hart and Paucar-Caceres (2017) assessment – with stakeholders' participation – of the educational process in a northern English university. Lopez-Garay & Reyes (2020) describes a systemic-cybernetic model used recently in a regional university in Colombia for more effectively preparing students for the transdisciplinary challenges of the 21st century.

Several examples illustrate how to use the VSM to design an educational module by supporting students to think more holistically and by designing robust attenuators and amplifiers in student assessment, students support, curriculum and teaching (e.g., Millwood and Powell (2011), Gregory and Miller (2014); Parra, Sarmiento, and Fatta (2017)). Liber (2004) and Johnson & Liber (2008) provide a toolkit to support teachers to manage the students' variety based on VSM principles. Also, Britain et al. (2007) designed a virtual learning environment to support variety management in a U.K. university. Pérez-Ríos et al. (2012) used the VSM to support the physical design of a university campus in Spain.

Štrukelj et al. 2019, from the University of Maribor, argue that the way of designing pedagogical work significantly affects development of competences. And that a more systemic design of modules will improve autonomy, creativity, and communications among the students. Murga-Menoyo, Espinosa, and Novo (2017) demonstrate how the *transition initiatives* and their universities share a common vision of sustainability and the potential for further progressing into a bottom-up organisational model for university management, promoting continuous innovation and fostering its transformation toward sustainability.

An interesting development in using the VSM to guide self-transformation in a university comes from a former PhD student, Pour Mohammad (2019).

She used the VSM approach to support (Foundation Year) students' self-organisation and networking for improved group learning. Her results corroborated relevant improvements in students' skill level and performance, and the development of an effective knowledge network. She concluded that 'guided self-organisation' is a more effective approach for skill development than traditional methods. She also demonstrates that it created an effective context in which a knowledge network was able to reproduce itself (i.e., the students self-organised to replicate the experiment later in other modules).

Magdalena University (v&s) Case Study

The following (ongoing) case study in a Colombian university illustrates how the v&s approach can inspire a better way of strategically managing a university, by combining the VSM and Team Syntegrity to invite participation to effectively align the university strategy and structure.

Between March 2018 and March 2020, my partner (Jon Walker) and I were invited by Magdalena University (MU) to support their ongoing strategic and organisational development processes. This university was seriously committed to develop as a more systemic and sustainable organisation and a third-generation university, by using the v&s and Team Syntegrity – among other systemic approaches. The chancellor (Dr. Pablo Vera), and two of the vice chancellors (Dr Ernesto A. Galvis and Dr John Taborda (JT) – at that point head of the planning office and leader of the project), have PhDs in complex systems approaches, so the design of their whole organisation and strategy has been inspired in systemic principles.

After learning about the university's organisation and strategy, we led five workshops with participation from academics and administrators from all faculty and research centres to support their effort to align their current structure and their ongoing strategy. During our first visit, we introduced the v&s approach to a select group of participants and discussed with them the project's design: It included representatives from academic and administrative roles from every faculty and a group of graduated students supporting the v&s project.

During the second visit, we developed a Syntegration type of event, based on S. Beer's book, 'Beyond Dispute,' and on the previous experiences we had in participating in and in leading syntegrations. JT – with a team of more than 10 people[8] – supported us in the design and running of the event, which had a very good participation. For the previous two years the planning office has developed participatory planning events during which they have agreed with all faculties on the university, their vision, and research strategy for the next decade: 'to develop the biocultural campus of the university as a regional innovation hub in sustainability.' That is why the university leaders agreed on the opening question as: 'The biocultural campus of the University of Magdalena as a regional innovation hub in sustainability: Progress and challenges.'

The event took place at the university campus, between the 22nd and 24th of March 2018. The 12 topics to discuss during the event – regarding the university vision and strategic positioning – were agreed on in advance, following several workshops and extensive participation:

- Managing water resources and adopting indigenous values- water as a sacred resource.
- Promotion of healthy living habits and lifestyles (exercise, nutrition, etc.).
- Developing an art culture with expression of knowledge and recognition of biodiversity.
- Moving towards a circular economy (e.g., recycling, organic agriculture).
- Inclusion – respect for diversity, acceptance, and protection of communities with differential capacities, ethnic, religious, and sexual minorities.
- Open Knowledge Dialogue, open-source education.
- Adoption of agile methodologies under the premise of #People First.
- Entrepreneurial Culture – Innovation Hubs: improvement of processes and infrastructure from technological solutions.
- Culture of Saving and Taking Advantage of Renewable Energy Sources (solar, wind, marine, etc.).
- Multicultural and Plurilingual Campus.
- Cultural Global and Glocal – Internationalization at home.
- Solidarity Culture: creation of social value and impact on communities.

The event ran successfully and created a robust context for reaching agreements about specific projects and initiatives to develop the agreed strategic direction. The event also contributed to identify integrating (systemic) themes, shared by all faculties and research centres – what S. Beer designed as the 'kernel' for strategic directions – innovation and entrepreneurship; technology and education; local development; rural development; sustainability and biocultural diversity.

JT and his team continued during 2019 leading strategic development workshops where participants learned more about the v&s approach and begun to do preliminary VSM mapping of some units. They first agreed on strategic clusters which will be responsible for implementing the CS strategy, based on the results of the syntegration type of event: CO: Governance and Cooperation; CU: Culture, Learning and Well-Being; CI: Research, Development, and Innovation; CS: Inclusion and Social Responsibility; CE: Campus and Ecosystem Management. As shown in Figure 5.4, this structure of clusters is closely connected with the main ecosystems of the Magdalena department such as the Sierra Nevada de Santa Marta, Ciénaga Grande de Santa Marta, the Caribbean Sea, and the Magdalena River.

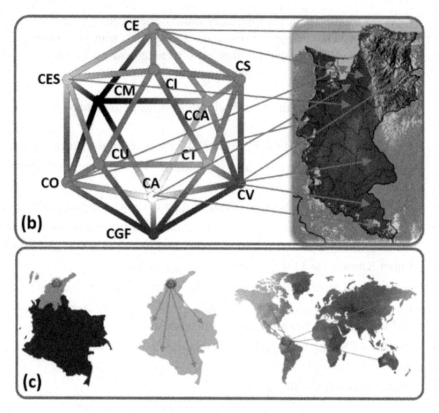

Figure 5.4 Team Syntegrity – agreed research strategies vs. regional ecosystems

(Illustration by John Taborda)

During our visit in March 2019, we introduced the project team to the v&s approach, and jointly with varied participants from all units, produced preliminary VSM mappings of the strategic business units. After our last visit in 2020, the project team has continued progressing on VSM mapping of the different units, aiming at creating a robust context to facilitate implementation of the agreed strategic directions for each unit and for the university. They have found it useful to organise internal and external networks implementing the agreements from the syntegration type of event: by developing the agreed strategic clusters – CI to CE as core nodes in UM's network – each one operating with sufficient autonomy, but all maintaining cohesion with UM sustainability strategy.

UM considers that these icosahedral networks design for the university campus will allow it to develop as a regional innovation hub more effectively. During 2020, the project team continued mapping the S1s and meta-systemic units of the university for progressing in implementing their agreed sustainability strategy. The intention of the VSM mapping has been to develop an organisational architecture to support self-governance with a focus on sustainability, which must provide self-control and monitoring mechanisms that encourage an environment of mutual trust and local autonomy supported by schemes that allow the sharing of information and knowledge on relevant issues.

There has been enormous amount of creativity in the implementation of projects within the broad strategies and structures agreed at the v&s project. Currently there is an emerging funded project led by Katherine Farrell, who also started the v&s project as an invited professor in the university, including several participants in the v&s project that will replicate the v&s approach to support one of the poorest communities to improve their resilience, by improving their physical infrastructure and capabilities to provide eco-tourism services. There follows a testimony from Dr. Eduardo Forero, an anthropologist academic from the university who actively participated in the v&s project – and in designing this new project – about its impact:

> *The effects of the v&s project have been very important since it has been reflected in the positive impact of the university on the community and the environment. Despite the incidents of the pandemic, the level of innovation, the creation of new programs, collaborative strategies, working networks and exchanges of scientific and traditional knowledge have contributed importantly to making the missionary exercise of the university more adaptable and balanced.*

Self-Transformation of Educational Institutions – Post-COVID-19

Undoubtedly the COVID-19 pandemic imposed a dramatic structural change to thousands of educational institutions around the globe in 2020–2021, which needed to be implemented in weeks, and may have long-term consequences. This seems to be the right time to reconsider promoting a more in-depth and permanent change in schools and higher education systems in many countries, towards a more systemic, humanistic, and creative way of providing education. The pandemic has shown that it can be done, using the best of the current web infrastructure. We have shown several examples on how the v&s approach is useful to design more systemic educational transformations, aiming to prepare more autonomous, innovative, and adaptive individuals, better suited to co-evolve in our current chaotic and highly complex environment.

The ELF case study demonstrates that a v&s self-transformation at the school level is not only possible but highly desirable. It helps a school to become better organised, to reduce the tensions between teachers and managers that end up limiting their options for providing quality education.

And it also helps a school to develop adaptive capabilities and become more resilient, which is precisely the issue most urgently needed in the current pandemic.

TINTA's case study also demonstrates that the v&s approach can be highly productive and creative, regarding the design of a systemic online educational resource's provider. The VSM design not only guaranteed a lean, well balanced, and effective organisational structure, but was also highly compatible with TINTA's values of providing human and nature centred systemic education. The structure and the processes designed to implement TINTA allowed collaborators to learn to interact in a way that promoted horizontal, equalitarian, and creative relationships, and this influenced the company's performance. As an innovative start-up, it may still need a few years more to get established and become financially viable. But the first steps of development indicated good possibilities for a promising future.

The examples from many universities introducing systemic approaches to education and systemic modules in their curriculum, can be followed by other universities that are only beginning their journey towards more systemic and sustainability-oriented curriculums and organisations. Magdalena university's case study demonstrates a way in which a sustainability strategy may be embedded in the organisational structure and therefore can be more effectively implemented. It illustrates the power of combining VSM with Team Syntegrity, to clarify strategic direction, and to agree on structural adjustments required for strategy implementation. This complements previous research combining the VSM and Team Syntegrity to support development and implementation of a sustainability strategy in a university, by promoting self-organisation and networking (Knowles 2009). It also complements Mejia & Espinosa's (2007) experiment for using Team Syntegrity to facilitate systemic learning in a university module.

Hopefully, these case studies demonstrate that progressing towards more systemic education and towards creating educational institutions that are more resilient, adaptive, and better prepared to deal with chaotic and complex environments and that educate more autonomous and resilient students is not only possible, but highly desirable. And that we have systemic approaches and tools to make it happen, if we decide to do so, that have proved to work in this context. We will revisit the topic in Chapter 8, when reflecting about the possibility of designing a massive systemic change in the education sector of a country, an experience from the 1990s in Colombia (Espinosa & Jackson, 2002). This massive change is currently on its way, as institutions like the United Nations are already suggesting progressing into a more systemic approach for education globally.[9]

Notes

1 https://www.hull.ac.uk/work-with-us/research/groups/centre-for-systems-studies
2 See Robinson's video illustrating the characteristics of non-systemic education 'RSA ANIMATE: Changing Education Paradigms,' available online October 11th, 2021, at Changing Education.
3 See the International Bateson Institute at https://batesoninstitute.org/
4 Diagnostic issues are colour coded: those in grey represent topics we agreed in the workshops and were in the process of being actioned; and those in italics were topics which required of additional design of new roles or mechanisms but were agreed for later implementation.
5 See TINTA's online platform at: www.tinta.org
6 Even if the project has been in stand up the last year, due to GR's maternity leave.
7 https://www.hull.ac.uk/work-with-us/research/groups/centre-for-systems-studies
8 Facilitators: Dr. David Guzman, Maria Alejandra Rueda, Jairo Abello were supporting us in the organisers' team; as well as graduated students from UM: Luis Correa, Maria José Castillo, Carlos Pardo, and Angela Rueda. Logisticians: Silvia Guerrero, Milagros Carrillo, Margarita Sierra, Yanira Martinez.
9 Chief Executives Board for Coordination (2017), The United Nations System Leadership Framework, United Nations System, Genève/New York, NY. Available at: https://unsceb.org/united-nations-system-leadership-framework

References

Atwater, J. B., Kannan, V. R., & Stephens, A. A. (2008). 'Cultivating systemic thinking in the next generation of business leaders', *Academy of Management Learning and Education*, 7(1), pp. 9–25.

Britain, S., Perry, S., Liber, O., & Rees, W. (2007). 'Modelling organisational factors affecting the development of e-learning in a university using a cybernetics approach', *Journal of SocioCybernetics*, 5(1/2), pp. 6–22.

Dewey, J. (1938). *Experience and Education*. New York: Kappa Delta Pi.

Espinosa, A., & Jackson, M. C. (2002). 'A systemic look at educational development programs: Two perspectives on a recent Colombian experience', *Kybernetes*, 31(9/10), pp. 1324–1335.

Espinosa, A. & Walker, J. (2017). A Complexity Approach to Sustainability. Theory and Application. 2nd edn. Singapore: World Scientific Press. pp. 1–544.

Freire, P. (2007). *Pedagogy of the Oppressed*. New York: Continuum.

Gregory, A., & Miller, S. (2014), 'Using systems thinking to educate for sustainability in a business school', *Systems*, 2(3), pp. 313–327.

Hart, D., & Paucar-Caceres, A. (2017), 'A utilisation focussed and viable systems approach for evaluating technology supported learning', *European Journal of Operational Research*, 259(2), pp. 626–641.

Illich, I. (1971). *Deschooling Society*. New York: Harper Row.

Jackson, M. C. (2019), *Critical Systems Thinking and the Management of Complexity: Responsible Leadership for a Complex World*. Chichester: Wiley.

Johnson, M., & Liber, O. (2008). 'The personal learning environment and the human condition: From theory to teaching practice', *Interactive Learning Environments*, 16(1), pp. 3–15.

Knowles, K., & Espinosa, A. (2009). 'Towards a holistic framework for environmental change: The role of normative behaviour and informal networking to enhance sustainable business practices', *Systemic Practice and Action Research*, 22(4), pp. 275–291.

Liber, O. (2004), 'Cybernetics, e-learning and the education system', *International Journal of Learning Technology*, 1(1), pp. 127–140.

Lopez-Garay, H., & Reyes, A. (2020). 'Learning the "systems language": The current challenge for engineering education', *Kybernetes*, 48(7), pp. 1418–1436

Maturana, H. (1990). *Emociones y lenguaje en educación y política*. Santiago: Hachette Communication CED.

Mejia, A., & Espinosa, A. (2007). 'Team syntegrity as a learning tool: Some considerations about its capacity to promote critical learning', *Systems Research and Behavioural Science*, 24(1), pp. 27–35.

Millwood, R., & Powell, S. (2011), 'A cybernetic analysis of a university-wide curriculum innovation', *Campus-Wide Information Systems*, 28(4), pp. 258–274.

Murga-Menoyo, M.Á., Espinosa Á., & Novo M. (2017). 'What do we imagine the campuses of tomorrow will be like? Universities' transition toward sustainability in the light of the transition initiatives' in Leal Filho W., Azeiteiro U., Alves F., & Molthan-Hill P. (eds.), *Handbook of Theory and Practice of Sustainable Development in Higher Education*. World Sustainability Series. Cham: Springer.

Olaya, C. (2019). 'The experimenting university', *Kybernetes*, 48(7), pp. 1398–1416.

Parra, C. A. T., Sarmiento, S. C. G., & Fatta, D. (2017), 'Studying university as social systems using the viable system model: MApp and semantic web technologies at the industrial university of Santander', *Journal of Organisational Transformation and Social Change*, 14(1), pp. 56–77.

Pask, G. (1988). 'Learning strategies, teaching strategies, and conceptual or learning style' in Schmeck, R. (ed.), *Learning Strategies and Learning Styles*. New York: Plenum Publishing Corp, pp. 83–100.

Pérez-Ríos, J. (2012). *Design and Diagnosis for Sustainable Organizations: The Viable System Method*. Berlin: Springer-Verlag.

Pour Mohammad, S. (2019). 'A Systemic Study of Learners' Knowledge Sharing and Collaborative Skills Development: A Case Study in a British Business School', *PhD Dissertation, Faculty of Business, Law and Politics*. Hull: Hull University.

Reyes, A. (2019). 'Introduction to the special issue: Rethinking higher education for the 21st century: A cyber-systemic contribution', *Kybernetes*, 48(7), pp. 1373–1375.

Saeed, S., & Gamal, S. (2019). 'The viable system model and its applications in higher education: An overview', *Kybernetes*, 48(3), pp. 438–450.

Schwaninger, M. (2019). 'Cybersystemic education: Enabling society for a better future', *Kybernetes*, 48(7), pp. 1376–1397.

Štrukelj, T., Zlatanovic, D., & Nikolic, H. (2019). 'A cyber-systemic learning action approach towards selected students', *Kybernetes*, 48(7), pp. 1516–1533.

Tagore, R. (1929). 'Ideals of education', *The Visva-Bharati Quarterly*, April-July, 73(4), pp. 73–74.

Von Foerster (1995). *Cybernetics of Cybernetics. Or, the control of control and the communication of communication*. Minneapolis: Future Systems, Inc.

Von Foerster (1996). 'Reinventing school: Lethology, a theory of learning and knowing in the face of the unknowable, indefinable, undecidable' in Voss, R. (ed.), *Reinventing the school*. 2nd edition. Berlin: Illuminated hand, pp. 14–32.

Yolles, M. (1999). *Management Systems: A Viable Approach*. London: London: Financial Times Pitman.

Chapter 6

v&s in Organisational Networks

Complex Organisational Systems as Social Networks

When developing his theory of organisational viability (VSM) Beer was inspired by Warren McCulloch's understanding of the physiological organisation of the body and brain functions as a neural network. Contrary to the beliefs in the last century that the brain was the organ of intelligence managing the operation of the body, this understanding of the brain/body relationship as a flat, self-organised neural network represented a complete shift in paradigm. Intelligence is distributed throughout all organs: Each organ operates autonomously using its own dedicated brain while the central nervous system coordinates and harmonises the different body functions.

Using this analogy to explain human organisations was perhaps too much of a challenge in the 20th century, when most businesses and public organisations around the world were still organised following traditional models of pyramidal, hierarchical organisations. Instead, the VSM described a viable (organisational) system as a network of autonomous and still cohesive teams of people, jointly implementing a shared organisational purpose and distributing labour in a way that maximised local effectiveness and minimised the need for central control.

The idea of the internet was born from the same pioneering cybernetic theories that gave birth to the VSM. Following McCulloch (1965) and Bavelas's (1952) seminal works, Beer aimed to shed light on the connectivity of organisational teams, while performing joint tasks, and the efficiency of particular network configurations to communicate and/or to interact within nodes. Beer (1994, pp. 75–95) described core issues in these interactions: team performance, group dispersion, relative centrality, and peripherality; and explained their impact on team morale. He suggested the idea of organisational pathologies and illustrated it with five pathologies: management opacity (low morale); overwork, shock, trauma, and neurosis. It was precisely by combining an in-depth understanding of social networks, with pioneering cybernetic ideas of self-regulation and homeostasis, that he developed the VSM as a theory of organisational viability.

DOI: 10.4324/9780429490835-7

Beer didn't live to witness the rise of the 21st century, when the wide availability of informatics and telecommunication technologies (ICT) now allow his organisational model to become fully operational and widespread in the business and economic world. The new web infrastructure has changed the patterns of interaction of individuals and organisations by releasing geographical barriers and even providing worldwide real-time access to information, as he dreamt.

Contemporary organisations are more innovative, effective, and well connected locally and globally, and better in marketing their products and services. The speed of change of the markets and the neoliberal approach to the global economy have created a new context where organisations need to be smarter and faster in developing their products and services; understanding their political, economic, and environmental niches; and developing capabilities to adapt to the emerging socio-environmental landscapes. Organisations worldwide are now more willing to experiment with innovative network designs, and some are doing so, intuitively, with promising results (e.g., *teal organisations* – Laloux (2014)). Others are doing it also, supported by sound theories and tools like the next sections will illustrate.

The Rise of Social Networks (21st Century)

Since McCulloch (1965), there have been important developments in network theory, which studies generic networks, including physical (e.g., electronic networks), technological, and biological networks. Complex adaptive systems (CAS) theories, inspired by the original cybernetic theories of self-organisation, study self-organised networks that exhibit coherent – yet unpredictable – global behaviours, which result from dynamic and nonlinear interactions among the nodes (Gell-Mann, 1994), (Holland, 1998). Each node is an autonomous agent, follows simple rules, is affected by positive and negative feedback loops, and co-evolves with its changing environment.

A CAS has a history (exhibits path-dependence), co-evolves through a fitness' landscape, and produces emergent structures resulting from self-organisation. After periods of apparent stability, it can go through abrupt changes, allowing the emergence of new behaviours. Kauffman (2000) explains that the most complex states in a network emerge at the 'edge of chaos' – equivalent to the transition phase of non-equilibrium thermodynamics – which is the state where innovation and creativity emerge at their best. According to Prigogine (1961), new order emerges by continuous production of entropy, when there are high levels of interaction with the environment.

The theory of CAS has proven useful for understanding and modelling natural systems as networks and studying their emergent behaviours (e.g., a particular virus develops into an epidemic like COVID-19 (Kossinets & Watts, 2006). It has also inspired new approaches to organisational design and organisational behaviour (Stacey, 2003; Lissack & Letiche, 2002; Richardson, 2008; Allen et al., 2011). Nevertheless, many of these new complexity approaches remain to be used as interesting metaphors to inspire new ways of leadership or innovative strategies (Palmberg, 2009), but do not provide full methodological guidance on how to radically transform complex organisations towards more self-organised neural-like networks.

On the other hand, the development of new social media and its associated platforms (e.g., Facebook, Instagram, WhatsApp, YouTube, etc.), has enabled substantial changes in the patterns of communication among individuals and organisations, and the way they manage their reputations. Complexity inspired tools like social network analysis (SNA) and big data analytics have been increasingly used to support organisational strategy and political marketing. SNA is a popular method that allows mapping complex social networks and studying emerging patterns of interaction among agents. The availability of super-computers and the surge of 'big data analytics' that allows analysis of massive data bases are having a big influence both in industrial and political marketing.

For example, the study of social networks has recently become widely used to analyse emerging narratives which explains (and can even direct) specific individual and/or organisational behaviours (e.g., Snowden (2000). These new tools have massively influenced political marketing and are changing the world of politics worldwide (not always in very positive ways, unfortunately). It's now well established how specialised consultancies (i.e., Cambridge Analytics) have misused private information from massive personal data bases (e.g., Facebook) to analyse commonly followed narratives, identify emotional triggers for specific clusters of users, and trigger their buying (or voting!) decisions in particular directions in the interests of those hiring the services (Swann (2020, pp. 156–157).

Some of the most popular online platforms which have massively changed social and economic behaviours, like Facebook and Twitter, have failed to respect privacy of data, created doubtful new ways of managing the political economy, and haven't provided more useful user-centred mechanisms for self-organisation and self-determination as Beer (1975) has suggested – see a more detailed critique in Swann (2020, pp. 140, 141). The power of these tools to analyse massive amounts of data and provide powerful diagnosis of existing narratives, is not to be underestimated. But even if they offer valuable insights on the nature and meaning of people's narratives, they do not always offer clear insights on what to do to transform organisations in a direction self-determined by its people.

Paradoxically, it has been precisely in the context of the COVID-19, that new Information and Communication Technology's tools inspired in SNA have proven to be highly beneficial to societies for developing testing and tracking systems worldwide. The trace and track applications are also based on social network theory to identify who a COVID-19 patient has been in contact with and alert these people to self-isolate to avoid the risk of infection. It has had a positive impact in countries who used it early enough during the pandemic to control its spread.

Clearly, CAS theories and related tools are no guarantee that the organisational system or society adopting them will be more resilient, more viable, or more sustainable. As argued in the past chapters, it is only when there is a robust context for self-regulation and self-governance and a strong ethos of sustainability that viability and sustainability will emerge. The following sections are selected case studies I have led or supervised, exploring, and clarifying the complementarity between VSM, CAS, and SNA approaches and tools.

What Is a v&s Network?

In our current global environment, many organisations have engaged in inter-organisational collaborations through alliances, contracts, and agreements, to enable them to share resources and capabilities, and therefore to be able to gain from specific market opportunities. However, by taking this approach they also face a paradox, which is that the more complex their inter-organisational networks, the more challenging it is to keep self-regulated internal agents, as these internal systems also will be dynamically co-evolving with their allies and competitors in their niches (Ritala et al., 2012).

The VSM explains in detail how the nodes of an *organisational network* are connected in non-linear ways and how each of them follows the same principles of self-organisation and distributed management to achieve a collective purpose (Bohorquez & Espinosa, 2015). It is only now that the mobile and web technologies provide individuals instant access to people and institutions around the world, that it is finally feasible to fully implement Beer's dream of self-regulated, distributed networks operating with real-time management.

It is not surprising that more and more people are interested in re-discovering and exploring Beer's original theory or suggesting closely related theories and tools that are attracting increasing numbers of practitioners, like holacracy (Robertson, 2015) and sociocracy (Cumps, 2019). Both of them – regularly used in community and not-for-profit organisations – offer pragmatic and relatively simple recipes for implementing networked organisations, which coincide with the original VSM principles.

A viable and sustainable (v&s) network is a coherent, fluid, and adaptive network of subsidiary organisations that shares a particular purpose and self-organise and self-govern themselves to cooperate effectively to achieve their share purpose. Figure 6.1 depicts an example of a v&s organisational network, including 10 autonomous sub-organisational networks, cohesively linked by a meta-system ('M'). Each one of the embedded networks is v&s.

that is, behave autonomously, learn continuously, and adjust its own internal organisation to co-evolve with its niche, without severance from it. The more these nodes must address increasing environmental pressures the more they need to quickly reconfigure their own resources and organisation (self-organise and self-govern).

They may decide, reflexively, to become a v&s network to be better placed for managing complexity, by sharing a global sustainability and re-generative ethos and values, cooperating in producing greener products and services, developing adaptive capabilities, and sharing meta-systemic man-agement roles and mechanisms. An organisation will develop such cap-abilities, if and only if, each of the networked sub-organisations 'learns to learn' how to produce their own products or services and how to do it while maintaining the network's cohesion – working towards a similar ethos, e.g., sustainable development goals.

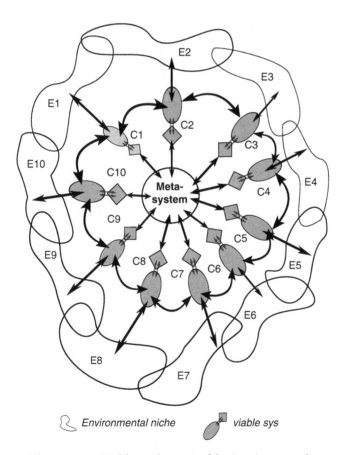

Figure 6.1 Viable and sustainable (v&s) networks

(Illustration by Jon Walker)

Learning to learn results from reflexive learning about how to develop primary tasks with good performance; how to adjust the internal organisation to match the niche's variety; and how to achieve closure by continuously reviewing organisational identity, ethos, values, and policies. VSM criterion supports a resilient network design, which guarantees increased opportunities for cooperation and collaboration to emerge, rather than expecting cooperation to result from central control and imposition. The rest of this chapter will offer examples of v&s network's design and reflect upon the learning from implementing it (or failing to do so).

Designing self-governed networks is particularly relevant in the context of sustainability. It is not good enough to make a particular organisation more sustainable if its suppliers and customers do not adopt the same values and ethos to become more sustainable. As discussed before, sustainability would only emerge as a networked effort from individuals to households, to businesses, communities, and regions. The following sections explain in more detail how the v&s approach can be useful to support more viable and sustainable organisational networks.

Background Research on VSM and Social Networks

Aiming to clarify the complementarities between VSM and CAS, the author has led several research projects over the last decade. There follows a summary of the main conclusions from a sample of them.

Watts (2010) wanted to understand the challenges and paradoxes of implementing the governmental strategy of strategic partnerships in North Yorkshire, UK, in the cultural and tourism sectors. She used the VSM for mapping the regional tourism and cultural networks and then undertook a SNA analysis of the interactions between the nodes. The VSM analysis allowed her to understand the limitations of existing strategic partnerships, as for instance, the lack of proper meta-systemic management roles and mechanisms at the regional level, which were not covered by the strategic allies. The SNA analysis of the network made clearer the disparities in power among the strategic allies, as those bigger and more central in the network were more capable of leading strategic collaboration initiatives. Watts's findings were an exciting start to continue to deepen our understanding in this type of study.

Knowles and Espinosa (2009) were aiming to develop and implement a participatory, bottom-up environmental strategy for a university campus. We wanted to design a methodology to raise sustainability awareness and invite staff and students to lead the formulation and implementation of greening strategies for the campus. We believed that the best path to a sustainable organisation (and more broadly a society), would be to instigate adoption of individual choices, based more on social and environmental values than individual concerns. Change can only occur when most members in an organisation massively change their awareness and make choices towards more sustainable actions.

We used a combination of the VSM (to analyse the existing organisational structure), SNA (to identify natural eco-leaders and their connections), and a version of a syntegration workshop[2] to democratically and creatively co-design the environmental strategy for the campus. Once we had agreed on such a strategy, the final stages of the project were to adjust the existing structure with the required new roles and responsibilities for implementing the agreed strategy, and to develop the required communication, learning and peer control mechanisms to support the learning process. The project had a positive impact in the way the campus managed its sustainability strategy and demonstrated the effectiveness of a bottom-up approach to co-design and implement sustainability strategies, led by a network of natural eco-leaders.

From 2007–2010, Jon Walker and I supported the self-organisation process of the eco-village in Cloughjordan, Ireland. We used the VSM to map the community organisation – when they were still building the houses and developing the community projects – and to mentor them to learn the v&s approach and theory in such a way that they could continue operating in the cooperative and sustainable community organisation they designed and made happen (Espinosa & Walker, 2013). At the end of the project P. P. Cardoso developed a SNA analysis of the emerging networks of relationships between the members of the eco-village (Espinosa et al., 2011).

He demonstrated that the v&s project resulted in more effective meta-systemic management; improved communications among members; more effective self-regulatory skills; a better working environment; clearer roles and communication channels; and more effective interactions with their niche (Espinosa et al., 2011). In Cardoso and Espinosa (2020), we have clarified how these combined VSM, and SNA analyses were used in this case study to identify organisational pathologies.

Also inspired by Beer's VSM, Espejo (2015) suggests an *Enterprise Complexity Model (ECM)* as a distributed governance model of an ecology of networked enterprises guiding the enterprises' collective self-organisation towards more global values and policies. It does this by creating, regulating, and producing products and services that are deemed necessary to handle societal problems and in general of the global ecology and economy. Espejo talks about the embodiment of an ECM as a liquid enterprise, a network of enterprises.

Through this preliminary research, we learnt about the very positive complementarity between the VSM and the SNA to manage complexity in internal and external organisational networks. While the VSM provides theory and methodology to design roles and interactions which contribute to organisational viability and sustainability, SNA can support detailed analysis of the quality of interactions between key individuals in each organisational network. It helps to assess the directionality, intensity, and strength of existing links, as well as the co-evolution of groups and their connectedness over time. The following case studies present more recent research and suggest new directions to design and to manage complexity in sustainable organisational networks (or what Espejo would call a *liquid enterprise*), by combining v&s with SNA, and Team Syntegrity (TS).

Example: A v&s Industrial Network

An effective sustainability strategy implemented by some members of an industry in a particular region (e.g., fostering cleaner production processes and practices) may not have enough impact if other members of the same industry do not collaborate, by following the example and cleaning their own production. B. Van Hoof[3] led a project for 10 years in Mexico, involving a network of 189 companies from 17 sustainable supply networks – the Mexican Sustainable Supply Network (MSSN). They were organised in smaller networks of about 10 small and medium enterprises (SME), supplying products to an 'anchor' company.

The anchor company was leading implementation of a cleaner supply network with all its suppliers and invited them to join the MSSN program, which happened through regular workshops with representatives from the anchor companies and the supplier SMEs, facilitated by Van Hoof and his team. The results were a remarkable increase to 75% rate of implementation of agreed collaborative projects to clean the supply chain (Van Hoof and Thiell, 2–14). Together with Van Hoof, we did a retrospective VSM analysis of a subsidiary network – an anchor company with its suppliers – collaborating for cleaning their production.

The VSM analysis aimed at clarifying the nature of the network's design which could then be highlighted and enhanced for a second implementation of the program, this time in Colombia (Espinosa et al., 2014; Espinosa & Walker, 2017, pp. 280–299). Figure 6.2 presents a VSM mapping of the MSSN with a few examples of S1 to S5 roles and mechanisms.

The VSM analysis of the MSSN revealed that the meta-systemic roles taken by the sponsoring organisation should become embedded in the individual networks. It confirmed the effectiveness of some collaboration roles and mechanisms between the SMEs as meta-systemic roles for ensuring the network's v&s. Relevant meta-systemic roles, which contributed to the network's ethos, cohesion, and synergy, included sharing learning systems in collaborative projects, disseminating best practices among different subsystems, and their learning by doing approach.

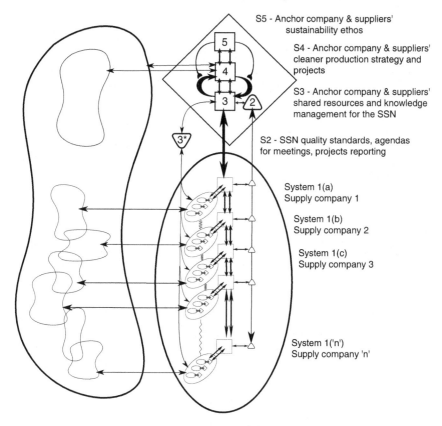

Figure 6.2 VSM of the MSSN

(Illustrated by Jon Walker)

The project demonstrated that once trust is established between the participants (System 2) the normally competitive relationship between the supply companies can be superceded by a collaborative approach which led to the dissemination of best practice. The analysis also suggested the possibility of replicating such meta-systemic management roles at regional levels of recursion. Such recommendations helped the design of the Colombian SSN (about 100 companies from the agricultural industry), which is still showing very good results. There follow other case studies analysing sustainable self-governance of communities co-existing in an SSE, from a v&s perspective.

Designing a State-Owned Enterprise on a Complex Environment (with Alfadhal Al Hinai and Jon Walker)

Designing a start-up in our complex world environment is very challenging, as from the moment of inception. A new start-up needs to develop the right type of structure and capabilities to formulate their vision, identity, structures, and strategies, and to allocate and configure their resources. To achieve these capabilities, they require specific networking and partnership functions in their inception phase. Complex systems approaches are particularly useful for designing the start-up as a self-organised network, capable of dealing with non-linear interactions, uncertainty, and unpredictability in its niche market. The following case study reflects on the learning from using the v&s approach – combined with SNA – to support the design of the Omani Broadband Company as a start-up.

Complexity Challenges to Design a National Broadband Network

Since 2000, when Oman became a full member in the World Trade Organisation (WTO), the government started implementing a neo-liberal telecom regime, by opening the market to competition and gaining access to leading-edge technology. Their 2013 National Broadband Strategy (NBS) suggested to create a new State-Owned Enterprise, the Omani Broadband Company (OBC). The OBC will be responsible for implementing and expanding the broadband networks throughout the Sultanate, and for supervising all projects implementing the Digital Oman's Strategy.

Alfadhal Al Hinai's (AAH) – as part of his PhD project[4] – was invited as a participant observer to contribute to the systemic design of this new company, as a complex organisational network. He used the VSM to analyse the evolving organisational design, and the required capabilities the OBC needed to develop for effective implementation of its purpose. And he also used SNA to understand and analyse the dynamic emergence from the interactions between key roles from the start-up's initial processes. The OBC was expected to recruit around 200 new employees in the following three years. Following an action research case study approach, and a network-centric view of organisation, he advised the government from the inception of the idea to the final decisions on organisational design.

The next sections brief on his use of the v&s approach to provide design criteria for the organisational network (both its external interactions with the government and the industry and its internal operating model) and of SNA for observing the dynamic behaviour of the start-up organisation during its first year of development (Al-Hinai, 2017).

VSM Design of the OBC

In the summer of 2014, Jon Walker, Alfadhal Al Hinai, and I ran two initial workshops with the OBC management to do a VSM analysis of the emerging organisational network. The 15 participants in the workshops (including top management, technical directors, and leading consultants) had agreed that a network design with autonomous operational nodes for the multi-agency was desirable. The OBC should be capable of developing the required internal capabilities and of managing the necessary partnerships to implement their organisational purposes. Providing autonomy to the operational units would allow them to manage their own customers and markets, while maintaining cohesion with other organisations in their industry ecosystem.

In preparation for the three-day workshop, AAH had studied the OBC strategy and its business ecosystem, and the preliminary organisational design the hired external consultants recommended. He also did a recursive analysis and a preliminary VSM mapping of the service sector. Three weeks later, AAH presented the recommendations for adjustments to the OBC's design in a management report and discussed it with senior managers. There follows details and reflections of each of the agreements obtained and the nature of the learning gained.

Agreements on Organisational Identity

The first day we agreed with the participants about the OBC's identity and asked them to develop rich pictures of the existing dilemmas of the developing OBC. The cartoons revealed OBC workers' perception of an uneven dis-tribution of power between government sponsors and the OBC; the com-petitive nature of the business environment; the challenging path still required to develop the start-up; fear of the unknown future; and acknowledgment of shadowed, unseen opportunities in the market. After this discussion, the group agreed the following statement of identity for the OBC:

> OBC provides, maintains and promotes an efficient, future-proof broadband infrastructure, enabling high-speed, reliable, affordable internet access for all residents and businesses in Oman. Its mission is to deliver economic and social benefits in alignment with the government's vision of building a sustainable, knowledge-based economy.

Recursive Analysis

We then moved on to the recursive analysis of the OBC. We worked in three groups, each of which had a facilitator. They ended up working for several hours due to the complexity of the decision to agree on the best alternative, between the several options that emerged during the workshop. A major dilemma was to choose the first level of complexity unfolding either by geography, or type of service, which would have important consequences for the final organisational structure.

There were three types of technology supporting the broadband infra-structure. The *fibre technology* will include existing operators in Muscat and other cities, which may become shareholders of OBC, and new investments in fibre infrastructure in other locations. The tower infrastructure will both manage the existing tower infrastructure in urban and rural areas used by telecom and service providers and promote new towers' construction. The satellite and wireless infrastructure will provide broadband services to the more remote rural areas, where other infrastructure was not commercially viable.

The participants analysed three alternative recursive organisational designs. The first one prioritised geography, so it focused on the three main regions in Oman: the northern, central, and southern regions. The second and third recursive mappings provided a mixture of geography and type of technology supporting the broadband services (as not all regions had the same sort of broadband infrastructure.) After intense debate and many turnarounds in examining the value proposition of each alternative configuration, the group decided on the recursive model in Figure 6.3 as the best alternative.

In the agreed model, at recursion level 0, the OBC is responsible for over-seeing the design, deployment, and maintenance of broadband infrastructure nationwide. At recursion 1, there are the three types of businesses: fibre, tower, and satellite. The final level represents the primary activities for operating each type of service: design, build, connect, and maintain, which would be sub-contracted to private companies overseen by OBC. This recursive mapping provided an effective structure for each type of service, allowed streamlining operational processes, was cost-effective to accelerate broadband infrastructure development across the country, and provided autonomy to each operational unit (Al-Hinai, 2017).

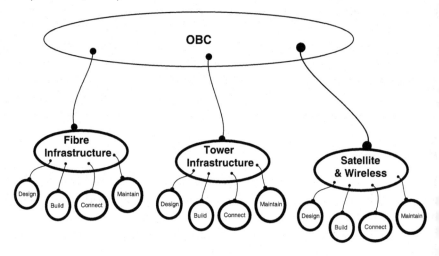

Figure 6.3 OBC – recursive analysis

(Illustrated by Jon Walker)

VSM Design

We then focused on identifying the types of roles necessary to design the OBC as a viable system by coaching the workshop's participants in VSM theory. We agreed on the VSM mapping at recursion levels 0/1 – see Figure 6.4. It maps S1 including three business units – fibre, tower, and satellite – and provides examples of the meta-systemic roles responsible for supporting them (e.g., overall policy, strategy, commercial activities, and resources allocation).

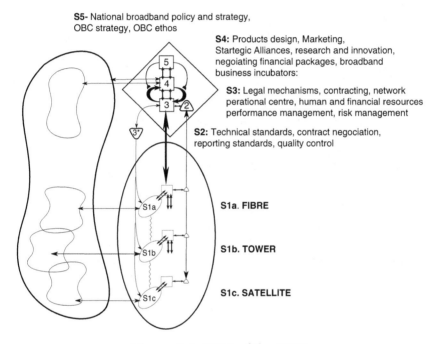

S5- National broadband policy and strategy, OBC strategy, OBC ethos

S4: Products design, Marketing, Startegic Alliances, research and innovation, negoiating financial packages, broadband business incubators:

S3: Legal mechanisms, contracting, network perational centre, human and financial resources performance management, risk management

S2: Technical standards, contract negociation, reporting standards, quality control

S1a. FIBRE

S1b. TOWER

S1c. SATELLITE

Figure 6.4 VSM of the OBC

(Illustrated by Jon Walker)

Taking as an example the fibre unit, we then agreed on a VSM mapping for each operational unit (recursion level 1/2). Each unit will receive a periodic work schedule on requested broadband infrastructure installations in different locations, develop a master plan on specific work schedules and projects, engage in the bidding process until a particular contractor gets the job, and start delivering the services. It will also attend to residential and commercial requests for broadband infrastructure connections and/or maintenance.

Each project will follow four stages: design the project, build, and implement the work activities, connect/roll out the broadband connection to the customer, and maintain the quality of the installed service. These stages were mapped as the S1s in the VSM at the next level of recursion. Identifying the roles and mechanisms required to develop S2 to S5 functions helped to verify the robustness and gaps of the organisational design of the start-up and suggest detailed improvements.

AAH prepared a management report specifying suggested roles and responsibilities for the operational and management units inspired in this VSM design. For example, there would be a Quality Control Call Centre responsible for System 2 functions like contract management, tendering, evaluation and awarding criteria, work schedule and time frames, technical standards, and quality control. System 3 roles include negotiating resources, operational plans, and performance assessment and would be led by the technical, planning, and project management units, and the 'Network Monitoring Centre'. System 4 roles include researching connectivity opportunities, technological innovations, and strategic planning and would be the responsibility of the technical planning, business support, commercial, and product design units. The System 5 roles of policy making, code of practice's formulation, and master plans would be the responsibility of the head of each operating unit and the Board of Directors.

A month later, AAH met the OBC managers at an executive meeting to discuss the management report. They considered the systemic structure was more balanced, less bureaucratic, and very likely less expensive to implement than the original one suggested by the consultants. It provided a more inclusive identity statement; a more streamlined and light management structure; more autonomous operational units; clearer and more powerful strategic and policy roles; and a structure better prepared to encourage sustainable development of the local economy. Nevertheless, the OBC managers first tried to implement the structure suggested by the hired consultants, which only captured a few elements of the VSM structure.

Social Network Analysis

AAH's research was also aimed at studying the dynamic behaviour of the OBC start-up during its first year of operation to gain an in depth understanding of how the internal and external networks were co-evolving, and to provide insights into the social behaviour behind these network structures. He used SNA to assess the directionality, intensity, and strength of existing links among the emerging roles in the OBC; and to analyse their co-evolution and connectedness over time.

He got permission to access nearly 57,000 email logs of the OBC from the company's email servers, from October 2014 to October 2016, assuming these would be representative of internal and external social interactions and classified the main nature of the roles exchanging emails using VSM distinctions. The emails recorded exchanges between a network of 2,089 visible nodes (31 internal members of OBC, and 2,058 outsiders). The analysis recorded 4,877 visible edges, all actual relationships or interactions across these nodes. Figure 6.5 exemplifies an SNA mapping of interactions among the nodes identified on the network. The original figures were colour coded, distinguishing each node by its type (S1 to S5) to allow visualisation of the density and relevance of communications among VSM types of roles.

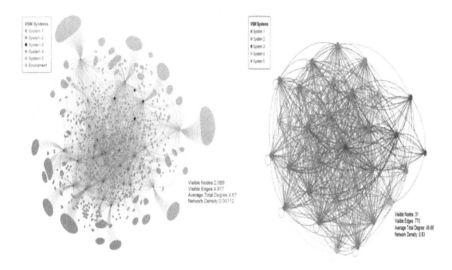

Figure 6.5 SNA of the external and internal networks vs VSM roles (OBC)

(Adapted from Al-Hinai, 2017, pp. 36, 202; Fig. 38, p. 205)

From several comparative SNA analysis, he demonstrated several features of the emerging dynamics of interaction between roles inside and outside the OBC. For example, he found out that during the first stages of the start-up, all VSM systems had strong links with the outside environment. The computed density of external interactions between the VSM subsystems and the environment was: S1 − 7%; S2 − 6%; S3 − 6%; S4 − 3%; S5 − 9%. S5 had the highest network density to the environment at 9%; which could reflect S5's need to communicate with many organisations at the ICT industry level as well as at the level of the national economy. In this start-up, all members tend to communicate with external members to facilitate the acquisition of new opportunities that dynamically emerge in the environment. S1 has the highest communication with environment, followed by S4 and S5. This may explain ongoing conflicts of power between S3, S4, and S5 during these preliminary stages of organisational development.

Five Years Later

In 2019, the government announced the establishment of Omani Information Technology and Communications Group, an entity owned by State General Reserve Fund. It included a number of operational companies: Oman Broadband Company, Oman Towers Company, Space Communication Technologies Company, and other new IT companies established in partnership with the private sector. The v&s project conducted in 2014 had predicted these opportunities and had suggested a robust organisational structure to build capacities from each operational company to operate under the holding company or group, even if at the time they were not fully implemented. It also had recommended design of the meta-systemic functions at different recursive levels, based on the concept of viability and system identity.

Building on these recommendations, it was easier for the new group in 2019 to develop a shared service centre providing corporate business support (i.e., HR, finance, project management) to the operational companies. Also, they were keener to provide autonomy for these companies to self-manage their own technical and operational functions. There follow a few scripts from the participants in the v&s project, which confirmed the nature of the v&s learning.

> ... this model offered a holistic view for positioning the company within the more macro contexts of the wider broadband industry as well as the Omani economy as a whole ...

> ... VSM is powerful for engaging individuals when designing their organisation and challenging their previous design notions ...

> ... the use of VSM is effective for understanding the organisation from an integrated perspective, understanding its vision and its key objectives, though maintaining this understanding does require regularly revisiting the model and evaluating according to new challenges and contexts ...

Redesigning a Latin-American 2nd Generation Broadband Network (with Martha Giraldo and Jon Walker)

In the last decade, there has been a fast development of a second-generation internet broadband transnational networks with a much bigger bandwidth, which enables many innovative second-generation broadband services (2^g-BS). In 2012, there were 13 countries already connected to such a network, providing 2^g-BS to academic and research institutions in Europe and the Americas. We will review the organisational design of one of these networks created in 2008, as a not-for-profit corporation, as part of the 'Latin American

2nd Generation Broadband Network' (LA^{2}BN). We will call it the *National 2nd generation Broadband Network* (N^{2}BN). It was originally financed by the national government, which hoped it will soon produce enough revenue to support itself. There were eight regional nodes, connecting around 140 organisations, mostly universities and research institutes.

All nodes were originally selling 2^g-BS and aimed also at collaborating in innovative research projects supported by this powerful broadband infrastructure. The national node coordinated the N^{2}BN and sold second-generation broadband services to regional nodes and organisations. The main dilemma they had at that time was that each node was handling its own services and tariffs, but the network as a whole was not working effectively enough. The N^{2}BN had a loose identity, and there were conflicts of interest among nodes competing in the same markets, with differing fees. Martha Giraldo, N^{2}BN director at the time, hired me and Jon Walker'I, (February – June 2012) to lead a self-transformation process to support the network's reorganisation.

After preliminary research on the N^{2}BN services, culture, and structure, we decided to test a methodology combining the strengths of Team Syntegrity (TS) and the VSM. As mentioned earlier, Beer invented Team Syntegrity, which very importantly complements and completes the VSM theory and practice, as a method to manage complex group decisions by facilitating effective and highly interactive team dynamics.

We first ran a two-day workshop inspired by Team Syntegrity principles to develop a shared vision of the desired organisation for N^{2}BN, with 34 participants representing the national and regional nodes, customers, and users, to respond to the following opening question:[5]

> *What does N2BN need to do, and how should it self-organise to become a continuously learning, effective, and innovative collaborative network, and a leader in Latin America in offering 2^{g}BS services for supporting science, innovation, education, and culture?*

While we were running the workshop, a few of the facilitators interviewed the different actors to grasp preliminary insights for the VSM diagnosis simultaneously. The result of this workshop was the discussion of 12 topics based on 'statements of importance' that outlined the criteria for redesigning N^{2}BN's organisation. The broad topics agreed on were technologic infrastructure, state policy, education visibility, networks of the future, regional networks, organisational strengthening, focus on content, university vs. industry articulation, innovation virtual space, future vision, unified negotiation, and sustainability. Each of the thematic teams produced a 'consolidated statement of importance' as the result of their discussions – see below an example for the theme 'education visibility.'

N2BN must position itself as a legitimate speaker for the knowledge society, by aligning its policies with the ICT sector's policies. It also must contribute actively to the international network's building up and development, by becoming a platform that permits innovation and development through projects that demonstrate the social power of this new technology.

The consolidated statements of importance provided an overview of the desired organisational features: strong autonomous regions; a robust, fast, secure network; collaborative regional organisations; unified service levels; strong links with the outside world; capacity to plan, adapt, and co-evolve with the external environment; pro-active development of new services; and projects to demonstrate the network's potential use and power. The survey with participants resulted in an 87% satisfaction with the workshop. Most participants felt they had reached very clear agreements on the required features for a new network's structure. This proved to be a very valuable starting point and direction for the self-transformation project to come.

N^2BN *Identity*

The final day of the workshop, we offered an introduction to VSM theory, and reviewed each one of their desired organisation agreements through the VSM theoretical lens. The participants agreed on the following statement of *desired* identity for the N^2BN:

N^2BN is a civil, not-for-profit private corporation responsible for the provision and continuous development of a new-generation network to:

- *Increase the quality of educational processes.*
- *Enable, encourage, and promote the exchange of knowledge as collaborative research between universities, research-institutes, and other institutions.*
- *Connect Colombian educational and research institutions with their peers throughout the world.*
- *Create and promote links between academic, governmental, and private research institutions working on research and innovation.*

They agreed on the need to progress from mostly providing fibre-optic broadband connectivity into leading and providing visibility of advanced 2^g-B–related research. While some networks were still in the first stage of mainly providing connectivity services, only the national nodes and a few others were beginning to work also in collaborative 2^g-B research projects.

Recursive Analysis

Figure 6.6 presents a recursive analysis of N^2BN: It had eight regions, each one providing (broadly speaking) connectivity services and only a few also providing other value-adding services (i.e., projects development, video conferences, grid computing, virtual laboratories, etc.).

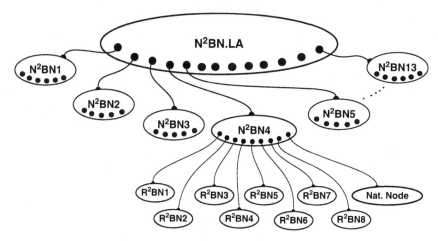

Figure 6.6 N^2BN recursive analysis

(Illustration by Jon Walker)

VSM Diagnosis

Over the next three months after the workshop, we did a full diagnosis of the N^2BN and generated agreements with its members on core self-transformation projects. Through interviews with representatives from the regional and national nodes, we identified and assessed System 1 to 5 roles and interactions – see Figure 6.7 with the VSM diagram. The regional nodes were doing an excellent work, the infrastructure was robust, and the new broad-band services were excellent. The N^2BN was one of the top four networks in Latin America, and much innovative work was being undertaken at all levels in N^2BN. However, there were several issues deterring the overall network's performance.

For example, ambiguous boundaries for service provision between the nodes (D1); no accountability to the national node (D2); unclear communication, technical, and academic responsibilities (D3); disparity of regional fees and service standards (D4); absence of mechanisms for sharing best-practice, economies of scale, or collaborative projects (D5); poor academic profiles of some regional members and associates (D6); scarce scientific and technical presence in international scenes (D7); not enough incentives or mechanisms to enhance collaborative projects (D8); an unbalanced board's composition (heavily weighted in favour of the regions) (D9); unclear intervention rules to enforce network's policies (D10); and poor governance due to lack of accountability from the regions (D11).

Very centrally, there was a clear tension between the mission of N^2BN as a new generation network available to much of Colombian educational and research institutions and its current identity as a broadband connectivity provider – which generates income to the regions (Archetype 1.5 in Espinosa and Walker (2017, pp. 485–492)). It was also clear that N^2BN should become more innovative and pro-active in research, and that the new structure should contribute to making it a more responsive, innovative organisational network.

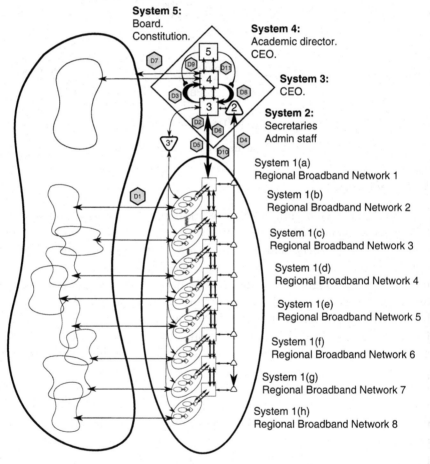

Figure 6.7 VSM diagnosis of the N^2BN

(Illustration by Jon Walker)

Aligning Strategy and Structure

Based on the agreements from the workshop and the VSM diagnosis, we suggested a clearer identity statement for N^2BN, as a state-of-the-art, new generation academic network offering high-quality services with guaranteed levels of reliability offering integral connectivity services (including video-conferencing, streaming, open access repositories, grid computing and virtual laboratories, among others) to educational and research institutions; promoting development of collaborative projects with partner institutions nationally and internationally in alignment with government and industries innovation strategies; and linking education and culture at all levels, as an evolving social and technological learning network.

The 'desired identity' required N^2BN shifting from a technological service provider, into more of a social innovation network. Based on that, we then progressed to develop a VSM mapping of the 'desired organisation'. The main difference between it and the existing identity, was that the national node would have more explicit connectivity service responsibilities and the regions would have a more explicit task of coordinating regional social innovation networks. The regional nodes would continue taking responsibility for the process of bidding for connectivity services in the region, but they would operate through a cooperative bidding scheme, aiming for national standards and savings. Several meta-systemic functions that were very weak needed redesign.

The final stage at the v&s project was to recommend desirable self-transformations, which included:

- Designing new contracts between the national and regional nodes (S3); producing performance indicators for services sold and ongoing collaborative projects; ensuring the nodes were legally bounded and accountable to the whole network; clarifying the director's role to create a more effective context for self-governance.

- Designing anti-oscillatory roles and mechanisms (S2): introducing standard fees and services for all nodes; clarifying quality and evaluation criteria for N^2BN projects; sharing information between all nodes about fees; introducing assessment standards.

- Clarifying S4 roles and mechanisms including responsibilities of executive and academic directors, for forging strong links with key actors in the external environment; for bringing in and summarising trends and innovations of interest to the nodes; for sharing innovations and successful case studies from users; creating a panel of experts to advise on 2g-BS innovations; developing periodic strategy and holding innovation meetings among the nodes.

- Re-designing the N^2BN and R^2BN boards (S5) to include a more balanced representation from the stakeholders and define policies for formulation and assessment of projects and services, content generation and sharing, and fees standardization.

At the final stage of the project, we presented and discussed the diagnosis and recommendations with the N^2BN and R^2BNs. After several iterations – some face to face, some virtual – agreements were reached regarding the suggested self-transformations, and the N^2BN and R^2BNs decided on plans for implementation. However, not all the recommendations were implemented, and the director resigned after failing to progress in the agreed directions. After a few years of unresolved tensions, some of the regional networks withdrew from the N^2BN.

This case study illustrated another v&s paradox: that even in a highly amenable network development strategy (developed in a highly participatory way through a Syntegration type of workshop) when it comes to implementation, we can't avoid a few agents co-opting the final decisions and following individual interests. While the nodes that rebelled to the suggested new structure retained their power in the short term, they affected negatively in the medium term the network's viability and sustainability. Nevertheless, recent testimonies from key actors who actively participated in the VSM project in 2012 (Martha Ines Giraldo, then N^2BN director) and witnessed its later development (Camilo Jaimes, communications director from 2008–2018) confirm the value of the v&s project, and confirm that the N^2BN is still now, eight years later, trying to, but still struggling, to develop in the v&s project agreed direction.

Martha Ines Giraldo (ex-Director N^2BN)

> *Although service-level agreements had been envisaged, rate structures and service offerings for customers varied substantially from one region to another, resulting not in a single national service but in eight different service offerings. This generated discomfort among the clients and a great wear and tear on the national coordination, which was unable to advance in the implementation of the purpose of the network to develop collaborative and research projects. Although this dual purpose of the network was clarified in the v&s project, once it concluded, the regional managers did not adjust their positions, since they wanted to preserve their privileges and autonomy in generating income. For this reason, I ended up resigning my position by losing interest in continuing to navigate in the midst of this deep dichotomy. I consider that from the beginning, profiles of directors in research topics should have been foreseen in the structure of the regional nodes, which was the purpose for which the network was created. Even now, eight years later, the network has not managed to consolidate itself as a leader in research but only as a provider of connectivity services, but it still nowadays continues to aspire to advance in that direction.*

Camilo Jaimes (ex–Communications Director N²BN)

> *While the v&s project was excellent to provide the network with an agreed vision of the desired organisation, once the project concluded, some of the regional directors refused to implement the main directions for change: to regulate fees for the 2BN connectivity, to re-structure the governance system, to enhance regional account-ability, and to develop research products and services. They feared they may lose power by going in that direction. Their refusal to progress as agreed, resulted in the resignation of the N²BN director. Unfortunately, the new director did not progress enough in the agreed changes and the network began to lose credibility with the national government and academic institutions. In 2016, they tried again to re-structure the Board of Directors, this time giving more power to the national government institutions and less to the regional nodes. Very little has progressed regarding academic and research services offered by the network, which has diminished its national and international reputation.*

Designing Strategies for Supply Chain Integration at the UK Offshore Wind Industry *(with Julija Danilova)*

With ever-increasing concerns over climate change, more attention has been placed on reducing carbon emissions in the energy sector, which drives the development of renewable energy across the globe. In the United Kingdom, a renewable energy sector that plays a key role in the national carbon emission reduction targets is the offshore wind (OSW). The United Kingdom is the largest OSW market in the world in terms of installed OSW farms since 2008. The OSW industry has become an important national asset contributing to decarbonisation of the energy sector and to the development of local economic value (Whitmarsh, 2019).

The key success factors in this nascent industry are to build a more integrated supply chain and a more collaborative approach in building future OSW projects. Nevertheless, there is still little research explaining what supply chain integration means in the context of the OSW and how it can be achieved in practice. Julija Danilova (JD)[6] focused her exploratory PhD research in filling this gap and chose to use the v&s and the STM to analyse supply chain integration (SCI) at the United Kingdom's OSW industry (Danilova, 2021).

Her research focused on fixed bottom OSW farms (those whose wind turbine foundations are fixed to the seabed), as opposed to floating OSW farms. The OSW industry distinguishes four phases of a wind farm's life cycle: a) development and consenting, b) construction and commissioning, c) operations and maintenance, and d) decommissioning (Poulsen & Lema, 2017). JD's research focused on phases a) and b), as they relate to project-based supply chain processes. The OSW industry presents an interesting context to study SCI because it relates to a project-based environment, as

OSW farms can be characterised as temporary in nature. JD provides a very interesting example of how to design collaboration strategies for a complex organisational network at the developing and building stages of an offshore wind farm.

A review of SCI literature revealed that even though systems thinking has been recognised by many as a valuable perspective for a holistic understanding of supply chains, systemic methodologies have hardly been applied in SCI (Grant, 2012; Koh et al., 2017); and only a few VSM articles relate to SCI (Puche et al. (2016); Chan (2011)). In this context, JD framed her exploratory case study research as:

> How can a system thinking approach, the VSM, help to understand the current state of SCI in the OSW industry and reveal potential areas for improvement to facilitate greater performance of the whole supply chain?

Together with participants from 16 organisations in the UK Northeast OSW industry and using VSM criteria and STM tools to map and analyse the information, they identified the main obstacles to integration, and decided on feasible and creative strategies to enhance SCI in this industry. The following sections provide a brief review of JD's analyses and findings.

Analysing SCI with the STM

As usual in the STM, this first stage helped to refine the boundaries of the system in focus. The working identity of the system in focus was agreed on as follows, with participation from all stakeholders:

> Offshore wind supply chain is a temporary system comprising businesses that by providing their products and services are engaged in the process of developing and building OSW farms that once completed produce clean electricity that is supplied to the ultimate consumers of electricity. (Danilova, 2021)

After defining the identity of the system, JD developed a recursive analysis – see Figure 6.8. The first level of recursion includes the two main primary activities: a) development and b) construction. At the development level there are three primary tasks: securing consent for the wind farm; wind farm design and engineering; and procurement of the necessary tier one components such as wind turbines, foundations, cables, and other materials. Sub-tasks for the construction phase include supply and construction of main components installation, and commissioning of the wind farm.

Given that receiving consent to build a wind farm is one of the most important tasks determining whether OSW project would go ahead, the activity of securing consent can be further subdivided into environmental impac

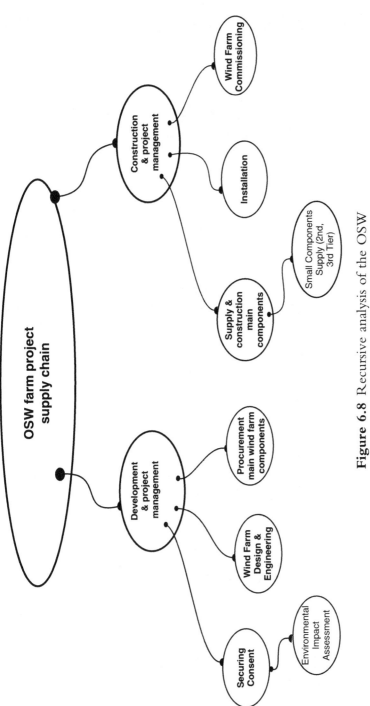

Figure 6.8 Recursive analysis of the OSW

(Illustration by Jon Walker [Inspired in Danilova (2021, p. 118)])

assessment (EIA) activities. It includes specialist consultancy work involving different environmental survey tasks to identify the potential impact of the proposed wind farm project on the physical, biological, and human environment during different stages of its life cycle. The construction of OSW projects also involves a range of different activities and second tier suppliers supplying smaller components. As the focus of this study was on exploring the current integration among different organisations in charge of primary tasks, the system in focus only included recursion levels 0/1.

A selective sample of participants was invited to contribute to the research through semi-structured interviews including 15 companies: OSW developers, wind turbine manufacturers, turbine foundation manufacturers, subsea cable manufacturers, offshore and onshore substation contractors, vessel services providers for OSW installation tasks, suppliers of smaller components such as secondary steel fabricators, EIA specialist consultancies, and other companies related to the OSW.

The questions in the semi-structured interviews explored themes related to SCI previously identified in the literature as well as themes related to the network's organisation, inspired by the VSM theory. The study aimed to analyse the extent to which all supply chain members were important to the creation of a more integrated supply chain; which formal and informal arrangements OSW supply chain members used to facilitate supply chain integration; the extent to which OSW industry players shared the same value drivers, such as time, cost, and quality when participating in an OSW project; and the extent and means of information sharing among supply chain members.

The VSM inspired questions aimed to recognise: the participants perceptions of their companies' primary tasks in relation to the OSW project (S1); any issues with customer order/tasks fulfilment procedures, day-to-day communication amongst supply chain members, conflict/issue management procedures, and the use of ISO standards or similar guidelines (S2); the nature of contractual arrangements among supply chain members, and the management of change of original customer orders (S3); existing formal and informal customer auditing procedures and inspections (S3*); the adaptability of each organisation to issues such as technological, political, social, legal, and environmental changes (S4); and the developers' roles as the ultimate decision makers within the OSW supply chain in relation to SCI (S5).

VSM findings

The VSM diagnosis was performed by analysing each individual interview in the light of VSM and SCI theories. S1 includes the suppliers that form part of the studied OSW supply chain, each of which is an independent business and operates in its own markets and is autonomous. S2 represents the supply chain coordination mechanisms, which vary among suppliers depending on their type and role (i.e., service providers or component manufacturers). There are, however, few common standards, such as ISO standards – ISO9001, ISO14001, ISO18001 – used by the OSW industry, that help to coordinate all major suppliers in terms of quality, environmental management, and health and safety. More S2 examples include vessel traffic coordination using various surveillance equipment and software programs and the rehearsal of concept room. The rehearsal of concept room is a very important S2. It is a physical space used for daily meetings, at the onshore substation contractor, open for all parties on a construction site, to allow them to raise any issues and collectively find solutions.

The management of the OSW project supply chain (S3) is performed through contractual arrangements between OSW project developers and suppliers. Common contract types used are FIDIC-based contracts (Fédération Internationale Des Ingénieurs-Conseils), LOGIC (Leading Oil and Gas Industry Competitiveness), and BIMCO (Baltic and International Maritime Council). S3* involves supplier audits, which usually happen before forming contractual arrangements. S4 tasks include R&D, front-end engineering and design (FEED), and the design of a wind farm. There are a range of external organisations that provide their industry wide R&D expertise (e.g., Offshore Renewable Energy Catapult; Offshore Wind Innovation Hub, Offshore Wind Growth Partnership, Aura Innovation Centre, and the Carbon Trust). S5 is fulfilled by the developers as the ultimate decision makers within the OSW projects; therefore, an OSW project's culture and integration would largely depend on the developers' approaches to building OSW projects.

In general, the VSM diagnosis showed that the *ad hoc* nature of OSW projects requires establishing balance between S1 and a metasystem every time a new project begins, which results from lengthy contract negotiations for new projects, which results in a lack of contract standardisation. The high degree of auditing and control of suppliers suggests a lack of developed trust between supply chain parties. The participants recognised that even if collaboration agreements could help to pre-agreed contract terms and prices between S1 and the metasystem and thus develop greater trust, such agreements have been of limited use.

The analysis also revealed that development and construction of such large projects as OSW farms are prone to delays, which impacts the overall project programme (the main S2 mechanism). Delays can be caused by external factors (e.g., bad weather conditions making offshore work difficult) or internal factors (e.g., issues at individual supplier levels). However, causes for delays are often not visible to supply chain members, which makes it difficult to keep supply chain coordination in balance.

It also found that the temporary relationships between project developers and their suppliers makes S4 at the project supply chain level almost non-existent, so there are limited joined products and services development between supply chain parties which leads to imbalances in the development of the OSW supply chain overall. Some supply chain areas can be more developed than others due to more dynamic capabilities of individual suppliers (S4). This suggests that there can be shortages in some areas of products and services and surpluses in others.

Identified imbalances between the operations and the metasystem suggest that achieving supply chain–wide integration or collaboration is a complex task. To achieve integration, there needs to be mechanisms in place to encourage collaboration and to make communication between relevant parties more open and effective. The analysis has shown that such mechanisms are largely driven by the project developers, as the ultimate decision makers and creators of project ethos. This makes it possible to suggest that OSW SCI would largely depend upon developers approaches to build OSW farms and their approaches to manage project supply chains.

Suggested Reorganisation Strategies

Following the research findings, two SCI strategies based on VSM criteria were proposed. The first one, the 'viable SCI strategy', suggests that supply chain parties of an OSW project act as one team or one cohesive network coordinated by an OSW project developer (rather than through contractors as intermediaries); participants considered it helps to achieve more 'partnership-type' relationships. It also suggests using preferred suppliers and contractors over multiple projects, to allow more alignment among supply chain parties. This would help to achieve better standardisation and commonality across supply chain and improve the dynamic balance of the supply chain as a whole system.

The second was the '*strategic cluster integration strategy*', which aims at integrating a specific part of supply chain as devolved and collaborative supply chain clusters. It involves a purposeful organisation of a cluster of business partners for collaborative working towards a common goal. This strategy can also facilitate greater standardisation and commonality in contract terms and communication among partners; and it helps to achieve efficiencies in product design and engineering contributing to efficiencies throughout the rest of the supply chain.

Learning from the Research

The VSM analyses of the supply chain as an organisational network were useful in studying integration of the supply chain as it helped to analyse effectiveness of current and potential interactions among supply chain members. The analyses helped to propose two SCI strategies outlining how supply chain partners could achieve more integration in practice. JD's research has contributed to research on SCI, which has predominantly focused on the question of 'what' can facilitate integration rather than 'how' it can be achieved in practice. However, taking this study's exploratory nature, further practical research would be desirable to explore the feasibility of implementing the proposed strategies.

Dilemmas of Self-Governance in Organisational Networks

While a network structure seems ideal and necessary to survive and thrive in our contemporary complex world environment, and having a flat, self-organising structure is undoubtedly the best possible strategy to manage complexity in networked organisations operating in turbulent environments, we have identified in previous case studies some dilemmas and paradoxes that such types of structures can still experience.

Van Hoof's case study in the Mexican Sustainable Supply Network (MSSN) confirmed the relevance of embedding collaboration in the design of a network aiming to foster a more sustainable supply network. Applying the VSM criteria to review the first Sustainable Supply Network (SSN) design revealed gaps in the structure which could be addressed when replicating the project in another region (i.e., Colombia). While the Mexican network produced excellent results, its sustainability wasn't guaranteed, so the analysis suggested designing similar roles and practices within each one of the anchor companies own networks. In other words, replicating the already successful governance structure at lower levels of recursive organisation. Also, the study showed the relevance of collaborative learning to build up social capital and clarified further the roles required to strengthen the learning and adaptation capabilities of the networks members at every level of recursive organisation.

The OBC on one side illustrated the relevance of designing a complex network structure following principles of recursiveness, focusing resources and knowledge in the nodes (System 1), and creating a light and effective meta-system at each level of organisation. The main dilemma this network faced was to minimise bureaucracy at the meta-systemic management level, and to empower the nodes to be as autonomous and self-organised as possible. The complexity of internal and external interactions of this networked organisation also needed to be tempered by good organisational design. While at the beginning the Board of Directors decided to implement the consultants design (more centralised than the VSM recommended structure and with a denser meta-systemic structure), a few years later they reverted to a network design more aligned with our original recommendations (autonomous nodes, leaner meta-systemic structure).

A key paradox was the need to centralise certain technical roles, like the monitoring centre for broadband services in each system. As these services operate online, it's possible to sum up information from all the nodes, through hardware and software at the central level, without centralising decisions. The paradox is then how to keep some meta-systemic functions operating at the network level, while fostering autonomous nodes' ability to provide local services. The new ICT infrastructure, which keeps technical cohesion while allowing nodes' operational autonomy, solves this paradox, without severance from individual nodes' autonomy or to the networks' overall performance.

In the N^2BN case, we learnt another key dilemma of v&s network's design: While self-regulated, autonomous nodes are the ideal structure according to VSM principles, too much autonomy may end up in a pathological network (see Archetype 3.3. 'Poor governance due to over empowered S1s' in Espinosa and Walker (2017, pp. 485–492). A v&s network requires both, enough autonomy for the nodes and an effective governance structure, which was rudimentary in this case study. N^2BN was suffering of lack of cohesion and missed opportunities for synergetic behaviours and learning, due to poor contract specification with individual nodes and lack of governance structures at the level of the network. The paradox is that the more autonomy you provide to the nodes, without proper governance, the less cohesion you may have in the network, which can result in risks to viability (as this case illustrated).

We also learnt, in this case, about the power of making collective agreements on a desirable structure, as part of a self-transformation process – which we achieved through the syntegration type of workshop in N^2BN. Having participation and commitment from all nodes regarding their desired development strategy, the way was paved for a more effective design of a self-transformation project, as this case study demonstrated. The paradox is that even in a highly amenable network development strategy, when it comes to implementation, we can't avoid emerging political and individual conflicts of interest to affect decisions on implementation.

In this case study, a few of the most powerful and influential regional nodes ended up co-opting the process and preventing full implementation of the new structure, as they didn't want to reduce their levels of income. The paradox is that by keeping power and control on their nodes, they negatively affected the whole network's performance and reputation and the situation resulted over time in a smaller, fragmented and less viable N^2BN network. Undoubtedly, there is much more we can learn from doing a v&s inspired self-transformation and dealing with the internal power structures. This continues to be one area where there is still lots more to explore.

This case study also illustrates the relevance of reconfiguring dynamic capabilities as a strategy to close the complexity gap between a network and its niche; only the clusters that aligned their interests to relevant institutions in the local, national, and international level survived, while those refusing collaboration and more altruistic purposes ended up over time, splitting away from the network. The dilemma that the nodes were facing was to focus on their actuality (what they did at the time), rather than their capabilities and potentialities (what they could do better by improving their structure). Preferring a short-term individual strategy rather than collaborating for a more effective network structure resulted in important losses for the network's long-term viability.

The OSW case study demonstrates the power of VSM criteria to both diagnose and strengthen an organisational network. As in most 'liquid organisations' (as Espejo (2015) will call these types of networks), designing a robust metasystem is fundamental for the networks' cohesion and performance. Nonetheless, each autonomous node will naturally push on their own direction and may relentlessly avoid committing to the network's agreed strategies and policies if they are not offered short-term gains. But this paradox, as demonstrated in this case study will only result – if not dealt with by proper network design – in a fragmented, disintegrated network, which will threaten each node's viability and sustainability. Once more, the VSM criteria proved useful to jointly identifying the networks' weakest aspects and defining clear strategies' for improving long-term viability and sustainability of the nodes and the network.

Notes

1 https://orcid.org/my-orcid?orcid=0000–0002-5200–7613
2 Allena Leonard advised us on the design of a one-day syntegration. The author led the workshop and Kathryn and Pedro Pablo Cardoso facilitated it.
3 Bernard Van Hoof is a professor in industrial ecology from Los Andes University Business School.
4 Supervised by the author and Dr Richard Vidgen.
5 We had facilitation support from David Guzman, Maria Alejandra Rueda, and Nydia Gil; and logistics support from Maria Lucia Espinosa and Sebastian Cardenas.
6 Supervised by Professor David Grant and the author.

References

Al-Hinai, A. (2017). 'A Systemic Approach to Investigating the Optimum Design of a Start-up Organisation in a Multi-Agency Environment'. *PhD Dissertation, Faculty of Business, Law and Politics*. Hull: University of Hull.

Allen, P., Maguire, S., & McKelvey, B. (2011). *The SAGE Handbook of Complexity and Management*. London: SAGE Publications Ltd.

Bavelas, A. (1950). 'Communication patterns in task-oriented groups', *Journal of the Acoustical Society of America*, 22(6), pp. 723–730.

Beer, S. (1975). *Designing Freedom*. Chichester: John Wiley & Sons.

Beer, S. (1979). *The Heart of the Enterprise*. Chichester: John Wiley & Sons.

Beer, S. (1994). 'The impact of cybernetics on the concept of industrial organisation' in Harden, R. & Leonard, A. (eds.), *How Many Grapes Went into the Wine*. Chichester: Wiley & Sons, pp. 75–95.

Bohorquez, L. E., & Espinosa, A. (2015). 'Theoretical approaches to managing complexity in organizations: A comparative analysis', *Estudios Gerenciales*, 31, pp. 20–29.

Cardoso, P. P., & Espinosa, A. (2020). 'Identification of organisational pathologies: Exploration of social network analysis to support the viable system model diagnostic', *Kybernetes*, 49(2), pp. 285–312.

Chan, J. W. K. (2011). 'Enhancing organisational resilience: application of Viable System Model and MCDA in a small Hong Kong company', *International Journal of Production Research*, 49(18), pp. 5545–5563.

Cumps, J. (2019). *Sociocracy 3.0 – The Novel. Unleash the Full Potential of People and Organizations*. Leuven: Lannoo Campus Publishers.

Danilova, J. (2021). 'Exploratory case study of the UK offshore wind supply chain integration potential using principles of the Viable System Model'. *PhD Dissertation. Faculty of Business, Law and Politics*. Hull: University of Hull.

Espejo, R. (2015). 'An enterprise complexity model: Variety engineering and dynamic capabilities', *International Journal of Systems and Society*, 2(1), pp. 1–22.

Espinosa, A., Cardoso, P. P., Arcaute, E., & Christensen, K. (2011). 'Complexity approaches to self-organisation: A case study in an Irish eco-village', *Kybernetes*, 40(3/4), pp. 536–558.

Espinosa, A., & Walker, J. (2013). 'Complexity management in practice: A VSM intervention in an Irish Eco- Community', *European Journal of Operational Research*, 225(1), pp. 118–129.

Espinosa, A., Walker, J. y, & van Hoof, B. (2014). 'Viability of industrial networks: sustainable supply networks in México' in Proceedings of the 16th Congress world Organisation of Systems and Cybernetics (WOSC) 'Our self-organising world: from disruption to reparation'. 15th–17th October. Ibague, Colombia: WOSC.

Espinosa, A., & Walker, J. (2017). *A Complexity Approach to Sustainability. Theory and Application*. 2nd ed. Imperial College Complexity Book Series, Vol (5). Singapore: World Scientific Press.

Gell-Mann, M. (1994). 'Complex adaptive systems' in G. A. Cowan, D. Pines, & D. Meltzer (eds.), *Complexity: Metaphors, Models and Reality*. México: Addison-Wesley, pp. 17–45.

Grant, D. B. (2012). *Logistics Management*. London: Pearson Education.

Holland, J. (1998). *Emergence: From chaos to order*. Oxford: Oxford University Press.

Kauffman, S. (2000). *Investigations*. Oxford: Oxford University Press.

Knowles, K., & Espinosa, A. (2009). 'Towards an holistic framework for environmental change: the role of normative behaviour and informal networking to enhance sustainable business practice', *Systemic Practice and Action Research*, 22, pp. 275–291.

Koh, L. S. C., Gunasekaran, A., Morris, J., Obayi, R., & Ebrahimi, S. M. (2017) 'Conceptualizing a circular framework of supply chain resource sustainability' *International Journal of Operations and Production Management*, 37 (10), pp. 1520–1540.

Kossinets, G., & Watts, D. J. (2006). 'Empirical analysis of an evolving social network' *Science*, 311(5757), pp. 88–90.

Laloux, F. (2014). *Reinventing Organizations: A Guide to Creating Organizations Inspired by the Next Stage of Human Consciousness*, Brussels: Nelson Parker.

Lissack, M., & Letiche, H. (2002). 'Complexity, emergence, resilience, and coherence: gaining perspective on organizations and their study', *Emergence*, 4(3), pp. 72–94.

McCulloch, W. (1965). *Embodiments of Mind*. Cambridge, MA: MIT Press.

Palmberg, K. (2009). 'Complex adaptive systems as metaphors for organizational management', *The Learning Organization*, 16(6), pp. 483–498.

Poulsen, T., & Lema, R. (2017), 'Is the supply chain ready for the green transformation? The case of offshore wind logistics', *Renewable and Sustainable Energy Reviews*, 73, pp. 758–771.

Prigogine, I. (1961). *Thermodynamics of Irreversible Processes*. 2nd edition. New York: Interscience.

Puche, J., Ponte, B., Costas, J., Pino, R., & de la Fuente, D. (2016), 'Systemic approach to supply chain management through the viable system model and the theory of constraints', *Production Planning and Control*, 27 (5), pp. 421–430

Richardson, K. A. (2008). 'Managing complex organizations: complexity thinking and the science and art of management'. *Emergence, Complexity and Organization*, 10(2), pp. 13–26.

Ritala, P., Hurmelinna-Laukkanen, P., & Nätti, S. (2012). 'Coordination in innovation-generating business networks – the case of Finnish Mobile TV development', *Journal of Business & Industrial Marketing*, 27(4), pp. 324–334.

Robertson, B. (2015). *Holacracy: The Revolutionary Management System that Abolishes Hierarchy*. London: Penguin.

Snowden, D. (2000). 'New wine in old wineskins: from organic to complex knowledge management through the use of story', *Emergence*, 2(4), pp. 50–64.

Stacey, R. D. (2003). *Complexity and Group Processes: A Radically Social Understanding of Individuals*. New York: Brunner-Routledge.

Swann, T. (2020). 'Anarchist cybernetics. Control and communication in radical politics' in King, D. & Parker, M. (eds.), *Organizations and Activism Series*. Bristol: Bristol University Press.

Van Hoof, B., & Thiell, M. (2014). 'Collaboration capacity for sustainable supply chain management: small and medium-sized enterprises in Mexico', *Journal of Cleaner Production*, 67, pp. 239–248.

Watts, M. (2009). 'Collaborative implementation network structures: cultural tourism implementation in an English Seaside context', *Systemic Practice and Action Research*, 22(4), pp. 293–311.

Whitmarsh, M. (2019). *The UK Offshore Wind Industry: Supply Chain Review*. London: Offshore Wind Industry Council – UK.

Chapter 7

Sustainable Self-Governance

The word 'cybernetics' comes from the Greek 'kybernetes,' meaning 'governance'; that is, to steer, navigate, or govern. Cybernetics has been defined as 'the science of governance.' When S. Beer developed the Viable System Model, he aimed to improve upon established management practices in those early days (1970s), which were focused on business profitability, process efficiency and effectiveness, and shareholders' satisfaction. Like other pioneering ideas it has taken a long time for the VSM to become widely adopted. Only in the 1980s did scholars and practitioners acknowledge the need to understand how organisations need to take responsibility for their stakeholders' interactions (e.g., Freeman, 1984); and only recently the idea of governance for sustainability has begun to develop (e.g., Drucker, 2003; Vester, 2007).

In those early days, people thought of *governance* more like a way of assuring that organisational structures, processes, and strategies were aligned to shareholders' expectations and therefore capable of producing their expected financial results. The idea of corporate sustainability instead of (only) corporate profitability was widely spread and lived up to by well-managed companies/organisations. But it was not attractive enough to draw the interest of many organisations – therefore, less popular than what was required. Pioneering governance theories were originally related to stakeholder's theory, and heavily influenced by management theories, like New Institutional Economics (i.e., Williamson, 1979, 1996), with a clear emphasis in economic transactions between individuals and firms, as the main engine of our socio-economic development.

More recently, governance researchers have supported the need to evolve into more systemic understanding of governance: How could complex organisations *'self-organise'* and *'self-govern,'* in non-autocratic ways? We are now witnessing a growing awareness than flatter, more flexible, and agile organisational structures are required to cope with continuously increasing environmental complexity, as Beer originally suggested. Not surprisingly, most of Beer's followers agree that the VSM is a theory of organisational

 DOI: 10.4324/9780429490835-8

governance, and currently remains one of the most robust ways to understand governance available (Malik, 2011; Espinosa & Walker, 2017, Schwaninger, 2019; Pfiffner, 2020).

Schwaninger (2019) suggests that more systemic governance approaches like the VSM focus more on viability than on profit maximisation; include more stakeholder participation rather than focusing on shareholders' interests; balance short- and long-term views; and give way to multidimensional performance measurements. In his own words (p. 18):

> The long history of applications since the invention of the VSM corroborates: this model is above the fashions and buzzwords, which supersede each other hastily in discussions about management and governance.

He offers examples of companies he has advised on governance issues, using the VSM, and demonstrates that in every case, the company has improved its governance system; in one case, by developing a weak System 4 and more robust 3/4/5 interactions; in a second case by developing a robust corporate planning and reporting system inspired in the VSM. In both cases, observations on corporate performance after a few years demonstrated important improvements in organisational and sustainability performance and in corporate responsibility. Previous chapters in this book have provided several examples of effective VSM interventions resulting in improved organisational governance and performance, and there are many other examples in the VSM literature (see for example Türke, 2008).

When comparing business governance with the governance of more complex social systems, like a community, an ecosystem, an ecoregion, or a nation, it becomes clear that a new idea of governance inspired in the understanding of complex systems is urgently needed. After a brief review of the best-known theories of governance, the next sections introduce the v&s framework for assessing sustainable governance. This is illustrated through a number of v&s case studies in community and eco-regional governance, followed by reflections on the governance lessons learned. Hopefully it will contribute to outline a path to continue developing Beer's original theory in a useful way to address sustainable governance paradoxes and dilemmas in social systems handling massive complexity and aiming to move beyond current sustainable practices into a truly regenerative economy.

Contemporary Approaches to Governance

There are two major trends in contemporary (Western) approaches to governance. The first one is focused on understanding issues of government rather than governance, with an emphasis on political aspects. The second one is focused in understanding the shareholders' rights and the formal structure of organisations. Following a briefing on these trends in studies of governance, this chapter introduces the v&s sustainable governance framework and explains how it complements such approaches.

Traditional Approaches to Governance

Rather than establishing a coherent discipline and approaches to governance, the existing governance literature offers several eclectic approaches to governance, each one exhibiting different assumptions and coming from – sometimes conflicting – theoretical postures. Tricker (2015) suggests that even if the understanding of governance has varied interpretations and approaches, most of them identify at least four dimensions as central to studies of governance: structure, process, mechanism, and strategy.

According to Levi-Faur (2012), Williamson's (1979) work on transaction costs, economics, and governance of contractual relations was highly influential in setting the agenda for governance studies. Williamson (1996) understands institutions as norms, rules, values, and beliefs. He discusses the roles of the general manager and the Board of Directors (BoD), the type of contracts that regulate social and economic interactions between agents, and other rules of interaction that get institutionalised over time. His idea of governance focuses on preventing or mitigating the costs resulting from problems of agency.

Wallis and Oates (1988) discussed another prominent approach to governance studies focused on decentralisation in public management as a strategy to improve public services' performance, accountability, and government response capability. Faguet (2012) criticizes this approach, saying that it only tries to establish linear causality correlations between measurable variables in specific sectors. He offers alternative examples in Pakistan, Colombia, Bolivia, and México, which demonstrate that recent decentralisation strategies have resulted in improved participation and governance.

A more systemic understanding of governance comes from Leach et al. 2007, p. 41), who, following Giddens structuration theory, see governance as institutional relationships and policies that regulate agents and organisational interactions. They consider that a governance system needs to recognise the multiplicity of actors and networks that potentially can have political participation, the capabilities to make political decisions – acknowledging tensions between structure and agency – the power structures dominating knowledge and speeches, and the historic and geographical contexts.

Tihanyi et al. (2014) defined corporate governance as the companies' self-regulatory system with particular emphasis in understanding relationship between top managers, shareholders, and interests' groups. In the public sector, they analyse how decentralised and democratic action network (including communities, NGOs, etc.) contribute to create public assets or values. Also, Bryson et al. (2014) analysed which organisational arrangements manage to implement collective actions more effectively. Bula and Espejo (2012) discuss governance and democracy inspired in the VSM and reflect upon it, using the historical development of democratic and inclusive governance in Colombia. They confirm there is a broad field for further applying the VSM in the political domain, like for example understanding structural constraints that inhibit citizens' participation in global issues.

However, most traditional governance approaches do not explicitly address issues of sustainability. They are more concerned with defending economic growth and the imperatives of shareholder return, in the private sector; or the short-term interests of elected politicians in the public sector. There are a few exceptions, like Kooiman (2003) who suggests that the emerging patterns of interactions between key social, political, and administrative actors in issues of sustainability may have more incidence in effecting sustainability than more traditional approaches to governance. As Farrell et al. (2005, p. 143) say, 'sustainable development is a political concept, replete with governance questions.'

Gnan et al. (2013) have also studied the relationship of corporate governance in the context of sustainability through involvement with different interest groups. Howard-Grenville et al. (2014, p. 615) argued that climate change will affect the social order, as well as the governance and power structures in governments and institutions, their resilience, work patterns, and governance systems. As suggested in previous chapters, they reconfirm the need to urgently improve the resilience and adaptive capability of organisations, to improve their self-governance for sustainability.

Collaborative Approaches to Governance

Gunderson and Holling (2002) have developed the *panarchy* approach, which offers guidelines to study governance in socio-ecological systems. They define socio-ecological systems (SES) as recurrent systems of biophysical and social interactions which develop long-term resilience and sustainability. They understand self-governance as the capability for effective collective action to address the main socio-ecological dilemmas affecting quality of life of the inhabitants in a particular SES. Sustainable self-governance results from stakeholders keeping a thermodynamic equilibrium within their socio-ecological niche.

Similarly, Waltner-Toews et al. (2008) explain a SES as a self-organised complex adaptive system and offer the SOHO model to analyse its ecosystem services, carrying capacity, and the network of interactions of its agents, complementing and expanding the panarchy approach. They offer criteria to analyse governance processes, functions, and structures and in particular the thermodynamic reality of such processes and structures.

Even if these approaches have influenced the v&s approach described here, as they both come from an understanding of SES as complex (adaptive) systems, they don't explain *how* to analyse interactions among nested agents at different levels in an SES. In Andrade et al. (2012), we compared the ecosystem, new institutional economics, and the v&s approaches to sustainable governance.

Elinor Ostrom's (1990) work on the governance of the commons is highly compatible and complementary to the v&s approach to (sustainable) governance (Espinosa and Walker 2017, pp. 411–424). She demonstrated through multiple documented case studies that bottom-up self-managed forms of governance have successfully maintained the health of land and sea and forests in many countries, for thousands of years. The v&s is a systemic and transdisciplinary approach, aiming to clarify how to produce more balanced structures, capable of more effectively fostering adaptive capabilities to improve organisational and/or societal resilience. In our view, it is by developing more sustainable self-governance that we may accelerate a transition towards more sustainable communities, businesses, and societies.

The following sections present in detail the v&s criteria for sustainable self-governance, and examples of participatory action research case studies which demonstrates the practical power of this approach. In all of them, the emphasis has been in creating a robust context for collectively addressing the main paradoxes and dilemmas for sustainable self-governance in a SES, including the different types of agents involved in (or affected by) strategic decisions for the SES's long-term sustainability.

Sustainable Self-Governance (v&s)

Organisations learn when implementing and monitoring strategy, by self-assessing the results of organisational development projects, and their impact in performance (first-order learning). But they also require second-order learning to review the direction of strategic changes, the alignment between their identity, ethos and policies, and the design of processes to implement them. To be self-governed an organisation needs to continuously adjust its performance (first-order learning) to react quickly and effectively to changes in its niche; and to continuously adapt its own organisation, and processes (second-order learning).

The v&s approach understands sustainable self-governance, as a continuous learning process organisations go through, while aiming to progress in an agreed strategic direction, by self-organising and self-governing itself. It does it by adjusting its own model of organisation processes, resources, and strategic direction. In v&s terms, an organisation develops sustainable self-governance only if it:

a) Deploys requisite variety in its multiple dimensions of interactions with the stakeholders in its socio-ecological niche.

b) Self-organises, by developing an adaptive structure to become more resilient and sustainable.

c) Learns to learn by continuously rethinking its policy and strategy under a clear sustainability ethos, firmly embedded in its culture, and daily decisions.

Sustainable self-governance is the ability of an organisational system (e.g., business, community, region) to sustainably implement its purpose, while maintaining homeostasis in its interaction with its niche. A structure inspired in v&s criteria (i.e., flatter, networked, more robust and flexible) creates optimal conditions for self-organisation and self-governance. A self-organised network has better probabilities of dealing with the complexity of its niche by keeping each node's essential variables in homeostasis. On the contrary, a hierarchical, rigid organisational structure may result in delayed strategic decisions and responses and in poorer communication between operational units.

To develop sustainable self-governance, an organisation needs to develop capabilities for self-governance in the long term by self-organising and learning to learn, and by continuously adopting more sustainable ways of co-evolving with its socio-ecological niche. In a v&s organisation, each System 1 is itself v&s. It means that it is led by a clear sustainability ethos, and is continuously improving its operational and sustainable performance, which results in more qualitative interactions with stakeholders and non-severance to its niche; recursive sustainable self-governance is then a necessary and sufficient condition for organisational v&s.

Towards Sustainable Self-Governance

Long-term dynamic equilibrium in an SSE is more likely to result from co-operative self-organised networks, peers controlling their use of ecological services, and their (symbiotic) ways of co-evolving with their niche. For each organisation in a SES, sustainable self-governance requires at least the following structural requirements (see more detail in Espinosa & Walker, 2017, pp. 117–138):

- A System 5, led by a sustainability ethos, and capable of effectively managing the variety of Systems 3/4 interactions.

- A System 4, capable of dealing with the economic, ecological, and social variety of its niche; and of continuously searching for and identifying innovative and sustainable organisational development options.

- A System 3, able to create an effective context for self-organisation for System 1 by distributing the core tasks' complexity and by generating synergies – i.e., allowing S1s to share the available resources and knowledge.

- A System 2, capable of preventing oscillations among System 1s, and of nurturing a culture of self-organisation and peer control (i.e., by providing them with effective and transparent information and communication mechanisms).

- A System 1, capable of sustainable self-governance, resilient, and adaptive to a continuously changing niche.

As mentioned in Chapter 2, to evolve as a v&s system, an organisation needs to design and maintain different types of homeostats; Figure 2.14 highlights those homeostats that are critical to sustainable self-governance:

A Between operations and the niche.
B Between the meta-systemic management and the operations.
C Between the organisation and the niche.
D Between Systems 3 and 4.
E Between Systems 3, 4, and 5.

The following v&s criteria help to identify the conditions in which these homeostats operate and what can be enhanced in them, to improve adaptive and self-governance capabilities.

A Framework to Assess Sustainable Self-Governance

Table 7.1 summarises the type of capabilities required for sustainable self-governance in complex organisations and networks (see details in Espinosa, 2015; Espinosa & Walker, 2017, p. 137).

Co-Evolution with Its Niche

As a result of a healthy co-evolution with their niche, complex organisational networks develop resilience and, in the long term, they improve their options for sustainability. This can be fostered by ensuring that at all levels of recursion an organisation is:

- *Working on what really matters:* Many times, organisations underperform because members spend too much time and resources in tasks that don' add value to their core products or services. Understanding primary task

Table 7.1 Framework for assessing sustainable governance

Core Issues	Required Capabilities
1. *Co-evolution with Its Niche*	1a Working on what really matters
	1b Monitoring essential variables for v&s
	1c Managing algedonics
	1d Agile decision-making
	1e Acting on core issues for v&s
2. *Autonomy & Cohesion*	2a Ensuring operational autonomy
	2b Dealing with conflicting interests
	2c Ensuring accountability and synergies
	2d Developing learning and adaptive capabilities
	2e Providing closure on v&s issues
3. *Recursive Governance*	3a Linking local and global governance issues and decisions
	3b Enabling conditions for sustainable governance at each level of (embedded and embedding) organisation

(attractors[2]) and continuously reviewing their organisational design, identifying wasteful tasks, and leaning their processes' design is fundamental to organisational effectiveness and to develop capability for self-governance. The tasks we choose to focus on determine our operational performance, which is how we keep balanced the environment vs. operations homeostat (homeostat A in Figure 2.14).

- *Monitoring essential variables for v&s*: Beer use to say: the purpose of the system is what it does. To find out how well we do, we need to observe and measure *what* we do and *how sustainably* we do it. For designing homeostat B (Figure 2.14), we identify the *essential variables*, measure them continuously through key performance indicators (KPIs), and make sure they are operating within their (physiological) limits. That includes not only essential variables for 'financial' viability (e.g., *market position*), but also for sustainability in the long run (e.g., *carbon footprint, resource depletion*).

- *Managing algedonics*: algedonics are 'early alarms' produced by statistical filtration of historical KPI's data. Having algedonic alarms offers the possibility of early responses to address issues that may not yet be producing a crisis, but if unmanaged, may result in a crisis affecting organisational v&s. A typical example is the algedonics produced for volcanic eruptions, which can observe and alert citizens of a town, by producing an 'orange' algedonic signal (to raise awareness of imminent eruption), or a 'red' one (to force immediate evacuation).

- *Agile decision-making:* This is enabled by a real-time performance management system (PMS) operating in decision-making spaces with requisite variety (i.e., by enabling a particular level of organisation to decide on issues that can only be managed at that level). A robust decision-making space must be:

  - Self-referent: enable participants to design the agenda by collectively working out the main issues they are concerned with.

  - Inclusive: offer a balanced opportunity to participate to those representing the outside and then (S4) and the inside and now (S3 and representatives of S1s).

  - Proactive: promote agreements to act collectively on the decisions reached.

  - Capable of managing algedonics: Beer (1979, p. 242) suggests designing an 'operations room' for crisis management, which could be designed to deal with algedonics and to coordinate emergency actions when required (more in Chapter 8).

- *Acting on core issues for v&s:* by effectively responding to the niche's changes and by closing the learning loops. System 4 continuously monitors the niche and alerts of any threats or opportunities (i.e., by managing the homeostat C in Figure 2.14). It allows development of learning and adaptive capabilities – i.e., to observe, sense, and respond to our perceptions of the environment – as in Teece (2012)). To close the loop on our developmental path, we need to assess operational results from the internal and external perspectives, as well as our capabilities for taking new opportunities for development.

Autonomy and Cohesion

- *Ensuring operational autonomy*: The most powerful strategy for managing complexity is by developing 'responsible autonomy' among embedded nested, organisations, in a context of distributed control. System 3 enhances System 1's self-regulatory capability and concentrates in managing only the 'residual variety' – the variety which hasn't been absorbed by System 1. This allows S3 to concentrate on issues of strategic rather than operational management.

- *Dealing with conflicting interests:* A v&s organisation develops a sustainability ethos, as part of its S2, i.e., a culture of embedded values like respect, trust, transparency, and reciprocity, which permeates every decision. To develop sustainable self-governance, it respects agreed sustainability standards and creates mechanisms to deal with conflict of interests to ensure all S1s address their operational, social, and environmental *responsibilities.*

- *Ensuring S1's accountability and synergies:* An effective context for self-organisation requires clear 'rules of the game,' and distributed and transparent access to relevant information for System 1. System 3 develops an overarching view of the cluster of Systems 1 to promote cooperation and synergies, i.e., by sharing knowledge and resources; and mentors them in finding ways for improving their performance.

- *Developing learning and adaptive capabilitiesto deal with critical v&s issues, at every level of recursive organisation:* System 4 should facilitate development of operational capabilities for responding coherently to both local and global v&s challenges and pressures and promote a rich context to implement innovations for developing healthier patterns of interaction with the local and the global niches.

- *Providing closure on core v&s issues:* To develop closure we also need to revisit periodically our identity, sustainability policies, strategies, and processes design. Only when core v&s issues have been embedded in the organisational identity, ethos, and processes design can we expect strategies and operational activities to be fully aligned with it. This is the role of the S3/S4/S5 homeostat (homeostat E in Figure 2.14): to agree and clarify v&s policy and criteria.

Recursive Governance

Developing cohesive and responsible sustainability standards at all levels of embedded viable systems is fundamental for environmental management (Espinosa et al., 2008; Schwaninger, 2015). Complex, nested organisational networks need to develop sustainable self-governance at each level of recursive organisation. This requires designing meta-systemic governance roles and mechanisms to observe and measure the essential variables for sustainability and implementing effective monitoring systems, to continuously assess progress towards sustainability standards. We have described elsewhere how to use the VSM to fully map sustainability standards and have offered examples of using the VSM for mapping ISO 26000 standards (Panagiotakopoulos et al., 2016).

Example: Sustainable Self Governance in a Socio-Ecological System

Figure 6.1 represented an example of 10 networked communities and industries (C1 to C10) with their meta-systemic management (the diamond shapes), co-existing as System 1 in a shared socio-ecological system (e.g., an ecoregion). They are permanently relating to each other (represented by arrows in the figure) and co-evolving with their niches ('E1 to E10,' the cloudy shapes). In any particular ecoregion, the communities, industries, and other public and private institutions could self-organise to co-manage their niche's socio-environmental health more intentionally and more effectively.

For sustainable self-governance, it is necessary to coordinate self-governed networks taking responsibility for the SES's essential variables for sustainability; otherwise, individual efforts will not have a permanent effect. Understanding multi-stakeholders' viewpoints and roles in caring for a particular SES is highly relevant to progress towards sustainable self-governance in socio-ecological systems. For example, it is not enough to develop self-governance in a river basin (e.g., by preventing water pollution) if the neighbouring region down the river doesn't act with the same standards and achieve similar results (the next chapter offers an example of using the v&s in this context).

If we represent each community or industry, and the whole network, as a viable network (as suggested in the previous chapter), then we can map them by clarifying their joint purposes, doing recursive analysis, and v&s mapping the different types of roles and interactions (i.e., Systems 1 to 5) in the chosen system in focus. As an example, D. Guzmán[3] developed MOSES,[4] a systemic methodology to analyse the quality of relationships between key stakeholders in a SES and their capabilities for dealing with sustainable self-governance issues (Guzmán, 2015).

He compared two big lakes in the Andean Cordillera in Colombia, both of which are extremely vulnerable to the impact of global climate change: Fuquene and Tota. Fuquene is one of the most important diary regions in the country, but its SES has suffered dramatic effects from climate change, and it is in risk of collapse. Tota is better preserved, with local industries focused on fisheries, onions, and eco-tourism. Following the MOSES analyses, Guzman facilitated several workshops in both SESs with representatives from SES' industry, community, and government. He found out that the nature of the social networks was very distinct in both SES (Espinosa and Walker (2017 pp. 269–318)).

- In Fuquene, there were no effective institutional arrangements operating to prevent or mitigate climate change risks: regional management (mostly influenced by dairy farmers) used a top-down approach for deciding on environmental actions to prevent climate change risks. There were dislocated views of the social and ecological processes and poor consciousness of the need for adaptation. Its capabilities for eco-services provision were badly deteriorated (e.g., no longer providing good enough water for human or industry consumption; and there was little capability for regulating water flows).

- Tota was a better preserved and healthier lake; it had more active participation of fishermen, local farmers, and tourism small and medium enterprises (SMEs) and a more democratic decision-making scheme. There were ongoing community efforts to protect the healthiness of the lake.

In a later study, we made a v&s analysis of the networks of stakeholders in each lake, and we found out that in Tota the meta-systemic management of the SES had a clearer System 4 role, providing collective intelligence and better capabilities for self-governance. Its System 3/4/5 included representatives of the System 1s – fisheries, tourism SMEs, onion farmers – as well as the regional government, and was making collective and timely decisions to preserve the lake.

We found that the more acute SES's conflicts are, the more difficult is it to engage people in preventive actions to care for the SES's health. The study confirmed the relevance of 'aesthetics' as an attractor for stakeholders to join actions to prevent and mitigate impact of climate change. In v&s terms, it is a very powerful S5 (ethos)/S2 (values) mechanism to support self-organisation. We finally concluded that creating effective context for conflict solving, negotiation, and collective decision making is very important for developing social capital, i.e., the society's capability to draw common strategies to fulfil collective goals – see details in Guzman and Espinosa (2015).

There follow more detailed examples of v&s analysis of sustainable self-governance in communities – represented as complex organisational networks, who are collectively taking care of their socio ecological system. In the next chapter, we will reflect on how specific efforts to improve self-governance in complex institutional, societal, and/or socio-ecological systems may be reinforced by an intentional systemic change design.

Assessing Self-Governance in an Indigenous Community in the Amazon *(with C Duque)*

In 2010, Jon Walker and I pioneered a self-transformation process in an eco-community in Ireland, which allowed us to clarify the methodology, and to test it and learn by doing with the community members on the application of the v&s approach to communities (Espinosa & Walker, 2013). After three years of mentoring the community through v&s workshops, we witnessed significant improvements in the communities' capabilities for self-organisation and sustainable self-governance. The participants in the project confirmed the project resulted in improved communications and more effective capabilities for self-governance (Espinosa et al., 2011).

Building upon this work, I worked in 2016 with C. Duque,[5] in analysing the governance structures of the *'Yurupari Jaguars'* – a traditional indigenous community in the Amazon – through v&s workshops. They inhabit the Pirá-Parana region, one of the most remote and unexplored regions in the Amazon jungle. They have managed to keep their own traditions and culture and they maintain a legitimate conversation with the Colombian government for the recognition of their rights as an indigenous community. The ACAIPI[6] selected representatives from different communities to attend our workshops.

C. Duque and I designed the v&s workshops to dialogue with them about their self-governance dilemmas, and she then led several field visits to their communities. During these visits, she facilitated highly participatory workshops to agree on their main self-governance dilemmas and paradoxes and on actions to improve them.[7] There follows a brief recount of the work and the learning it brought us and the participants – more details in Espinosa and Duque (2018).

Background on Their Governance Structures

There are four Indigenous people in the Pirá Parana River basin in the Amazon jungle who share the same ancestors, language, and culture, while keeping clear geographical borders for their own lands. Their life philosophy – Hee Yaia Keti Oka – is based on collective respect for all forms of life inhabiting their territories, including the 'sacred places' (e.g., those where water originates) and in general, those providing ecosystemic services (ACAIPI, 2015).

Following the Colombian Constitution, which protects indigenous rights to live and care for their original territories, ACAIPI was created in 1990 to support self-governance of the Pirá-Parana's communities. It includes a *'captain,'* representing each one of the communities, and representatives from each community's health, education, and inter-cultural activities. It also includes representatives of the traditional authorities: the *'Hee-Gu,'* the highest spiritual authority of each ethnic group (world healers); and the *'Kubus',* the holders of traditional knowledge (i.e., natural healing) and political advisors for each indigenous community. While the Kubus represent their cultural heritage, the *captains* are normally younger people, capable of speaking both their language and Spanish, the official language in Colombia.

Core to their self-governance principles is their '*ecological calendar*,, which explains the natural order and natural forces that must be acknowledge and respected by every member of the tribes. Activities like getting food from the jungle, collecting wild fruits, fishing, hunting, and growing food in their fields (chagras) are ruled by sound ecological principles. Such principles have traditionally been learnt by the children from their parents, in a learning by doing approach, by being involved in such basic survival activities.

Other primary community activities include building/maintaining community houses (Malocas), participating in community rituals, and defending their territories. A Maloca represent the universe as a pattern of relationships between everything that exists in the Jungle. Its four corners represent the natural cycles and this sacred knowledge is held by the *Kubu*. The *Kubu* leads the traditional rituals to maintain spiritual and eco-systemic balances. There are other forms of shared community work. For example, during cropping time in any family's '*chagra*' (family allotment), other community members collaborate to collectively gather every crop.

VSM Analysis of Their Governance Structures

We adjusted the STM to overcome the language gap that the v&s application may create for the indigenous participants, aiming to ensure adequate participation and to facilitate the self-governance diagnosis – see Espinosa and Duque (2018, p. 2012). There follow details of the activities and learning from each stage, by including an additional stage on 'boundary critique,' following Midgley and Ochoa-Arias (1999), with the intention on further analysing the relevant stakeholders to invite to the project. There follows a briefing on the learning regarding self-governance, gained through the different analytical stages of the STM.

Boundary Critique

To design the workshop agenda and identify relevant participants (using Midgley and Ochoa-Arias's (1999) boundary critique), we first drafted a recursive analysis of the communities' primary activities. We aimed at including varied representatives of the different roles from ACAIPI and from each community, making sure to have a good balance between community members doing S1 activities, and others doing meta-systemic roles. We chose representatives from 14 (five small, three medium, and six large) communities, out of a total of 28 communities from the four ethnic groups. We then designed simple questions inspired by the 'framework to assess self-governance' to guide the workshops with the indigenous.

Rich Picture – Agreeing on Identity

During the first workshops, we asked the participants to discuss their answers to our self- governance questions in their own language, and to represent their answers as rich pictures. The participants produced dozens of paintings containing particularly valuable responses to the questions – see Figure 7.1 for examples of such rich pictures.

Recursive Analysis

Based on C. Duque's 10 years' experience working with these communities, her understanding of their worldview, and the way they traditionally have organised their society and their economy, we produced first a recursive mapping (see Figure 7.2). At recursion '0,' we represented all the Yurupari Yaguars communities in their SES (The Pirá Parana Region).

At recursion 1, we described the three sub-ecoregions inhabited by different Indigenous tribes. At the Upper Pirá Parana River basin, the Tatuyo and the Eduria; in the Middle Pirá Parana, the Barasano; and in the Lower Pirá Parana, the Makuna, Bara, Carapana, Tuyuca, and Itano tribes. The size of the circles is approximately proportional to the number of inhabitants in each tribe. At the third v&s workshop, C. Duque discussed with the participants the definition of these primary activities, and the way they happen (or not) in each community.

The criteria for mapping self-organised community groups, at recursion level '2,' was to focus on those primary tasks self-organised community members do to survive; their primary survival activities, such as hunting and gathering wild fruits; growing food (*Chagras*); providing shelter; maloca (which include all community gatherings); education; health and Earth care. Some of them they do individually or with members of the family (e.g., hunting), but most of them work collectively, like when they organise a shared community project to support collection of a crop in a *chagra* (the equivalent of an allotment) when it is ready.

We were originally including 'health' and 'Earth care' as independent S1s, but when discussing it with them in the second workshop, we understood that in their life philosophy – *Hee Yaia Keti Oka* – an individual's health is inextricably linked to the health of the Earth and the two aspects cannot be separated. Consequently, we grouped them into one S1: *Health & Earth Care* In their worldview, damaging, for instance, the sources of water (one of their *sacred places*) will make nature ill, and her illness will also cause individual illnesses.

For them, having a healthy environment is the root for having a healthy community and vice versa: They are two sides of the same coin. Also, their rituals – led by the *Kubu* in each community, and by the the '*Hee-Gu*' in the

Figure 7.1 Self-governance dilemmas

(Illustrations adapted by Juan David Alonso from original drawings)

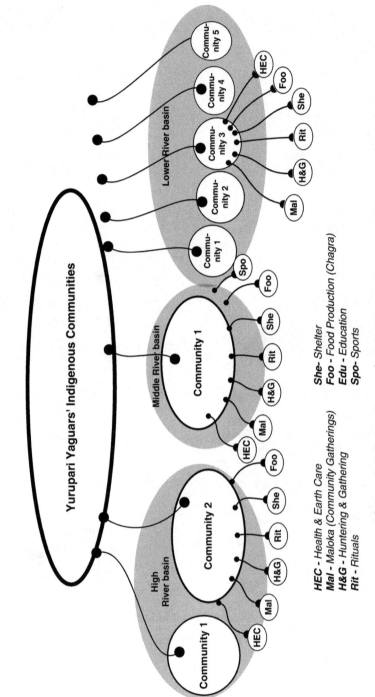

HEC - Health & Earth Care   She - Shelter
Mal - Maloka (Community Gatherings)   Foo - Food Production (Chagra)
H&G - Huntering & Gathering   Edu - Education
Rit - Rituals   Spo - Sports

Figure 7.2 Recursive analysis – Yurupari communities

(Illustration by Jon Walker)

whole territories – are a fundamental way for maintaining or restoring in-dividual and community balances with nature and for maintaining their social order, so we mapped them as a S1. As shown in Figure 7.2, only the biggest tribes are organised for every one of the primary activities, so the lowest level of organisation has small differences for each community.

VSM Diagnosis

We then worked intensively with C. Duque, interpreting the rich pictures, and mapping the identified roles and self-governance dilemmas, at the ap-propriate level of recursive organisation, following v&s criteria. We codified the diagnostic issues in a table at each level of recursive organisation and agreed on a preliminary v&s diagnosis which was then discussed and clarified with the project's participants. See, for example Figure 7.3, with a VSM mapping at a medium-size community from the High River Basin. It provides some examples of identified roles and mechanisms for S1 to S5 (*mechanisms* in italics). There follow a few examples of the identified self-governance di-lemmas – see a complementary analysis of a large-size community in another region at Espinosa and Duque (2018):

- Power conflict between captains and traditional authorities (Kubus) regarding decisions on socio-economic development projects (D7). While captains' core criteria for decision-making was economic, the Kubus' values and ecological principles will prevail in strategic deci-sions (D4).

- Children who were then attending government funded schools, managed by themselves but following both their own and 'Western' school curriculums, (e.g., having access to internet Kiosks), have lost interest in traditional social practices (D5). This was creating an open loop on their learning of the traditional wisdom (e.g., for producing food (D3)); healing, taking care of Earth (D2)); on their skills for self-sufficiency (D8); and on their adherence to traditional values and rituals (D6).

- Lack of collaboration in shared community projects (e.g., for building houses and sites, growing and collecting food), resulting in loss of trust, lost crops, imbalances in the diet, and more dependency on 'imported' food (D1).

Self-Transformation Projects

Following the framework for assessing self-governance (Table 7.1), we summarised issues which revealed room for improvement: There were still issues they need to address in the way of managing their shared community

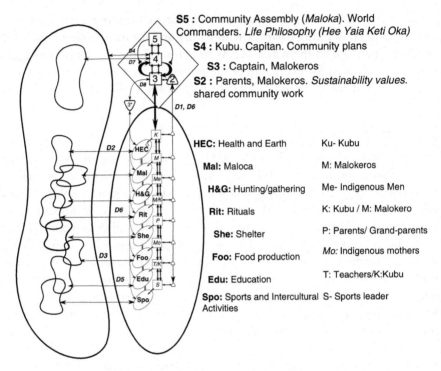

S5 : Community Assembly (*Maloka*). World
Commanders. *Life Philosophy (Hee Yaia Keti Oka)*

S4 : Kubu. Capitan. Community plans

S3 : Captain, Malokeros

S2 : Parents, Malokeros. *Sustainability values.*
shared community work

D1, D6

HEC: Health and Earth   Ku- Kubu

Mal: Maloca   M: Malokeros

H&G: Hunting/gathering   Me- Indigenous Men

Rit: Rituals   K: Kubu / M: Malokero

She: Shelter   P: Parents/ Grand-parents

Foo: Food production   *Mo:* Indigenous mothers

Edu: Education   T: Teachers/K:Kubu

Spo: Sports and Intercultural S- Sports leader
Activities

Figure 7.3 VSM Amazonian community

(Illustration by Jon Walker)

projects and therefore their capability for ensuring their food security; slow decision making in core issues for sustainability, due to lack of communication among the tribes; and the need for stronger and clearer rules for managing conflicts.

After summarisin,g the final v&s diagnosis in a simple language, C. Duque led the final workshop to discuss it with them and to decide how to act upon it. The participants then agreed, at the ACAIPI's annual meeting, specific action plans to address the most significant issues. A final visit –months later – demonstrated that several of the main agreements had been actioned and were beginning to show positive results.

For example, they decided to work on developing more effective communication mechanisms among the different communities, and appointed a few representatives to walk across the communities, and to agree on actions to improve the recognised governance dilemmas. The first tracking across the communities had resulted in agreements to empower the Kubus, to choose more representative captains, to enforce development of shared community projects, and to re-establish a more representative democracy inside each o the communities.

Learning from the v&s Project (by C. Duque)[8]

After the v&s project, ACAIPI continued in its process of strengthening its own government, and their socio-environmental governance for the following years. In 2018, the Government of Colombia recognised Indigenous Councils as government structures to self-govern Indigenous territories. It allowed the Indigenous peoples in their territories to define their representation mechanisms, policies, and local programs according to their uses and customs recognized by the state. ACAIPI registered their legal representative for the Pirá Paraná River's Indigenous Council, initiated the process of territorial delimitation, and requested government funding for its self-government programs. This empowered the indigenous peoples to be recognised and to strengthening their decision-making capabilities over their territory. Due to the recent COVID-19 pandemic, ACAIPI has decided to isolate itself while the pandemics ceases, and they know better how to combat it. Meanwhile, they are performing rituals and doing traditional work, which has allowed them again to focus on their internal processes and to strengthening their traditional self-government processes. In a few years, we may be able to analyse how this change of government from association to indigenous council affected or potentiated the dynamics of ACAIPI's self- government and its effect in managing the COVID-19 pandemics.

Sustainable Self-Governance in an Afro-Caribbean Community (with C. Duran)

There follows a summary of C. Durán's action research case-study using the v&s approach to support sustainable self-governance, in Orika, an afro-Caribbean community (OC), based in the Rosario Islands, part of the Rosario and San Bernardo Coral Reef National Park in Colombia.[9] It provides insights on the main challenges of sustainable governance for this type of ethnic organisations; and on their learning on ways to implementing a co-management model, for more effectively addressing such challenges.

Past and Present of the Orika Community Council (OCC)

The Orika community inhabits the hinterland of a marine protected area and their economic activities (fishery, tourism services, artisanal crafts) depend on the exploitation and conservation of natural resources. It has been struggling for the recognition of its ethnic minority rights since the early 2000s. Orika Community Council (OCC), their self-governed, grassroots organisation, represents a collective territory of almost 300 hectares and 900 people in Isla Grande and Isleta, two of the main islands of Islas del Rosario.

This community has evolved as a complex organisation aiming to self-govern its territory and its economy in a sustainable way. Its main goal is to develop a co-management model of their marine protected area, by addressing collective land property rights, recognising cultural diversity, protection of their environment, and promoting their self-development. This community's history is marked by their African cultural heritage and by lack of trust in government authorities (commonly white people from the mainland). In 2013, the Colombian government adjudicated a collective title to this community; in 2014, the OCC formulated their Life Plan,[10] which defines their guidelines, development strategies, and projects for sustainability and wellbeing.

In 2018, when the study was undertaken, the main environmental challenges this community faced were related to resource exploitation, garbage disposal, intensification of touristic affluence, population growth, and the need for reinforcing regulations against robberies. Their community organisation also faced internal challenges, such as lack of youth participation, need for leadership renovation, and lack of legitimacy of their actual authorities. There follows a summary of the way this v&s study – led by C. Durán – helped them to clarify ways to improve their sustainable self-governance capabilities and the learning achieved (see details in Durán, 2019).

Assessing Sustainable Self-Governance at Orika

Following the steps from Espinosa and Duque (2018) and from (Durán, 2011), we aimed to model the community as a v&s system and to analyse its capabilities for sustainable self-governance in both their marine and terrestrial ecosystems. We adjusted the STM using qualitative research tools like ethnography, depth interviews, and focal groups. C. Durán developed six interviews with community leaders, and two focal groups between October and December 2017. During the final visit in 2018, he facilitated discussions on the diagnosis with the OCC board and team leaders and reached agreements on desired and feasible improvements to their self-governance capabilities and their community organisation.

Orika's Identity

During the first focus group, the participants agreed on the following definition of the OCC's identity:

> *The Orika Community is an ethnic territorial community that exercises its own government and watches over the wellbeing of the native inhabitants and the care of our territory.* (Focus Group 1, 2018)

The OCC was created as a territorial ethnic authority – following Law 70 (1993) established for ethnic groups and endogenous communities in Colombia – which gives self-governance power to each ethnic community, in accordance with principles of self-determination and self-jurisdiction. It has a Community Board Council that exercises territorial control and order and has the power to guarantee social order and coexistence among its members, based on their own cultural principles. The Community Council responds to the collective character that encompasses the entire community and designates a management team (the Board) to exercise its self-government.

Before the v&s workshops, Durán interviewed the OCC president and legal representative, and several community leaders, to identify the main dilemmas faced by the community in its relationship with their ecological and socio-economic environment. During the first workshop,[11] he asked the participants to represent pictorially their current problems – see example in Figure 7.4. He even developed with them theatrical exercises and used other forms of artistic representation to open a creative space for public dialog.

The participants agreed on their main challenges as follows: a) population increase due to the entry of new inhabitants; b) disputes over the allocation of land and the construction of new homes; c) ignorance of the authority and roles of OCC executives; d) apathy in participation and lack of renewal of leadership; e) inappropriate behaviours regarding the care of the environment; f) concentration of power, weakness of the board, and lack of clarity on decision-making processes; and g) thefts from tourists and people from the community.

Recursive Analysis

During the first workshop, C. Durán facilitated development of a recursive mapping of the community, with the participants, by identifying self-organised activities and teams as System 1 – see Figure 7.5 – with the agreed mapping. Once more, the criterion for mapping community self-organised clusters was to focus on the main primary activities for their survival, and in this case, the associated community groups doing the different types of productive activities and providing social services. While trying to identify System 1 as those self-organised teams responsible for primary activities, we first noted that several of the identified teams were not always well-structured. Many of them were not well-defined entities, interacted more as a neural network, and operated under horizontal schemes of collective decision-making.

The main sources of income were related to eco-tourism, fishing, hotels, restaurants, ecological tours, and artisanal sales, which were clustered as *eco-tourism*. Participants clustered main social services like health and education, sports, and music as *individual and community wellbeing*. Several ongoing environmental conservation activities like preserving mangroves and coral reefs were clustered as *care for the territory and the environment*. Other productive

Figure 7.4 Cartoon Orika
(Illustration by Juan David Alonso[12])

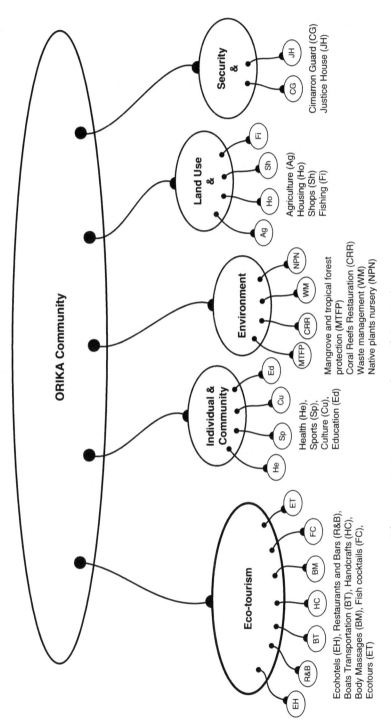

Figure 7.5 Recursive analysis of the Orika community

(Illustration by the Jon Walker)

activities like agriculture, housing, shops, and fishing were clustered as *land use and production*. Finally, activities related to guaranteeing social security and justice, like the local guard and house of justice were clustered as *land use and production*.

As Figure 7.5 shows, the first level of organisation in the system in focus is the entire community, composed of five System 1 operational units as follows:

1 *Ecotourism*: involves all individuals and eco-businesses carrying out productive activities in the tourist economy, with emphasis on ecological tourism. Eco-businesses include 10 eco-hotels, several restaurants and bars, and informal teams offering eco-guides, body massages, boat trips, beach snacks, and handmade crafts. They are allied as '*Orika Ecotourism Alliance*' (OEA), which is not legally constituted, nor does it have a visible head, but is rather a space for coordination and mutual support. The interaction within the subsystems is informal or results from specific alliances generated to offer services.

2 *Individual and community wellbeing*: this includes services like health, education, culture, and sports. The health services are not integrated, while the education services (including early childhood care) are coordinated through the Educational Board of the Schools. They aim to also create an elderly care unit. In sports, there are different teams and individuals who lead communal activities (e.g., championships). In culture, there are two traditional music performers (Traditional Gaita and Marímbula), as well as DJs, champeta[13] composers, and a dance group – some of them coordinated through the *House of Culture*.

3 *Care for the territory and the environment* includes individuals and teams with special interest in the care of marine and terrestrial ecosystems promoting conservation activities.

4 *Land use and production* concerns productive activities like housing and use of the terrestrial and marine ecosystems. There is a (meta-systemic) housing committee and the 'land use' legislation, which rules on the acceptable way to carry out these activities.

5 *Security and justice*: operated by the *Cimarrons* Guard group, which is a team of 10 people, responsible for ensuring compliance with safety and coexistence community regulations for both the community and visitors. The House of Justice – planned but not yet established –was expected to be a core mechanism for conflict resolution and for guaranteeing the rights of the islands' population.

At the lowest recursive level, we mapped the existing self-organised teams, institutions, and/or businesses responsible for developing the primary community services. Community members may develop operational activities in more than one S1; for instance, some can work (part-time) at an eco-hotel, part-time as a *Cimarrons*-Guard; and be a member of the Educational Board of the School.

VSM Diagnosis

Over the following workshops, Durán interviewed key roles at each level of recursive organisation and then facilitated the process of mapping the community at different levels as a v&s system. There follow examples of the v&s mapping at recursion level 0, and of core diagnostic issues identified with the community members. See Figure 7.6 for the agreed on v&s mapping and the identified diagnostic issues.

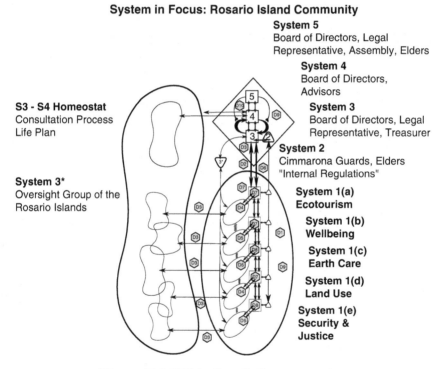

System in Focus: Rosario Island Community

System 5
Board of Directors, Legal Representative, Assembly, Elders

System 4
Board of Directors, Advisors

S3 - S4 Homeostat
Consultation Process
Life Plan

System 3
Board of Directors, Legal Representative, Treasurer

System 2
Cimmarona Guards, Elders
"Internal Regulations"

System 3*
Oversight Group of the Rosario Islands

System 1(a)
Ecotourism

System 1(b)
Wellbeing

System 1(c)
Earth Care

System 1(d)
Land Use

System 1(e)
Security & Justice

Figure 7.6 VSM of an Orika community

(Illustration by Jon Walker)

At recursion level 0, the whole community is led by the OCC and its Board of Directors (BoD). Other meta-systemic roles include different volunteer and/or elected roles – some formal, like the legal representative, the BoD – and some more informal – like community members leading specific operational teams. The assembly, the BoD, its advisers, and the treasurer develop S3, S4, and S5 roles. The BoD is supported by the 2016 *Life Plan*, which defined the strategic lines and projects for the community (S4). People from the *Cimarrons* Guard, the BoD and elder adults from the community implement S2 and S3 functions.

All System 1s have emerged as self-organised networks between individuals and/or companies, by following the objectives established in their Life Plan's document, but some of them are not legally constituted or have permanent leaders. They are mostly independent in their decision making and manage their own budgets; only in critical situations, or when establishing larger alliances or projects, S1s request authorization from the board and the OCC's legal representative.

The board is unable to manage all projects as there are too many going on; many of them don't have permanent meta-systemic roles, nor any planning instruments, nor explicit strategic goals or indicators to monitor effectiveness of productive activities (D1). As the distribution of resources is tied up to specific funded projects, S3 does not have an adequate model of operations or any mechanisms for monitoring results and generating synergies (D2). There is an incipient S3* system through an informal space called "*Oversight Group of Rosario Islands*" – a space on Facebook to review the management of the OCC, open to participation by the island's population (D3).

Ecotourism, wellbeing, and land use include commercial establishments and natural persons who share economic activities or interests. They make alliances and complement each other within each production chain (e.g., between an ecohotel, a guide, a fisherman and a boat owner). When competing in the same economic activity, they establish competition agreements (eco-hotel rates or boat passages, for example) (D4).

The *internal regulation* is the main anti-oscillatory mechanism (S2) defined by the OCC to guarantee coexistence and avoid conflicts in the S1s, but it hasn't been fully developed. Before it was put in place, there were cultural mechanisms of social organisation for coexistence and for the management and resolution of conflicts. It was evident that there was a need for more support from community authorities, i.e., the *Cimarrons* Guard, which is not yet fully operational (D5). For example, agreements on land use are the most important S2 mechanism to control over-exploitation of resources. However, there are no effective monitoring instruments for the co-management of the socio-ecological system; there are no actions other than verbal persuasion for people who, for example, pollute or overexploit natural resources (D6).

S4 includes the BoD, advisers, the assembly, and the legal representative who carry out informal activities to analyse the environmental niche and to formulate strategy. Through the implementation of the Life Plan, and prior consultation processes, S4 identifies trends, opportunities, and threats in relation to external local and regional actors, but it is an informal and unsystematic exercise based on rumour, intuition, and conjecture (D7). S1s also have project ideas and scan the environment to locate potential partners or sponsors, but there isn't a mechanism to input those into an annual planning of community activities (D8).

There is some accountability during public meetings, but it doesn't happen through a formal and systematic debate. The exchange of ideas and proposals between S3 and S4 is limited because S3 is very weak, does not have a person in charge, and does not generate strategic information to decide on adaptive responses. S4 identifies many opportunities and dreams of projects, but S3 has no way of executing projects or channelling S4's work (D9). As a community member put it:[14]

> We are full of dreams, but when it comes to materializing, it is a bottleneck: we know neither how nor when nor with whom to realise them.

S5 operates through the assembly, which includes the entire community for collectively making strategic decisions: It requires the participation of at least half plus one of the representatives of each family from the islands, but many times has difficulty achieving a quorum (D10).

Self-Transformation Projects

Having identified both the formal and informal Orika organisations implementing primary activities, Durán led another workshop with the project's participants to analyse possible ways to address the main issues identified. Following the framework for sustainable self-governance, presented at the beginning of this chapter, they jointly agreed on the following proposals to improve their organisational limitations and improve their capabilities for sustainable self-governance:

- Appoint representatives from each operating team. Promote *responsible* autonomy in S1 (S1 accountable to S3), by developing their internal management capacity and generating periodic reports of results.
- Follow up on the implementation of internal regulations; promote collective workspaces for S1 teams to converge around common goals (as the competitions agreements between ecotourism and land use). Reinforce cultural mechanisms for coexistence e.g., fully implement the *Cimarrons* Guard (S2).
- Create a project bank to manage resources and generate synergies. Design a mechanism to implement land use agreements and to punish pollution and over exploitation (S3).
- Establish an annual meeting to: review ongoing S1 projects in compliance with the Life Plan and to prepare an annual investment plan (S4); identify

and document S1 adaptive responses; create a context analysis team (S4) to continuously analyse environmental, social, economic, and cultural issues; share information on potential projects and partners; enhance oral transmission of learning and other forms of communication (audio-visual, written, theatrical, etc.) to enhance learning from OCC's adaptive experiences.

- Expand the BoD to include delegates from S1s who will communicate their achievements and needs. Incorporate participatory decision-making methods to give the assembly dynamism: The use of social networks (WhatsApp or Facebook groups) and the creation of zonal committees can be useful (S5).

Implementation of these projects would require collaboration between the management team and S1s' leaders, in clarifying roles and mechanisms, and taking responsibility for them. Also, in implementing more effective mechanisms to manage internal conflicts, for creating synergies among S1s, and for creating a more robust S3/S4/S5.

Learning from the Case Study (by C. Duran)

A big challenge for a v&s researcher is to use a simple language, understandable to participants, to allow their appropriation of ideas and improve the possibilities of effective implementation. It is noteworthy that the use of the VSM metaphor on living systems and neurological networks helped the understanding by those attending the focus groups in this community as they also use several examples of human living system as learning tools. Throughout the v&s workshops, people fully engaged and creatively contributed to proposals for organisational innovation. This is relevant given academic criticisms of the VSM's abstract and complex language (Jackson, 1988), as in this case the VSM distinctions proved to offer high explanatory simplicity through metaphorical thinking, which is inherent to human learning – a point also argued by Pfiffner (2010).

Identifying the recursive levels of the OCC allowed us to understand how this community has developed its different social and economic activities, in self-organised teams, even if not all of them were permanent or had a proper internal organisation. Given the history of resistance of this community, the participants resonated well with basic principles of 'responsible' autonomy – reflected in S1s' autonomous behaviour and their desire to remain cohesive around the OCC and to demonstrate ecological conscience in the development of its business and communal activities.

However, autonomy was not always ensured, since for certain areas of life the colonial experience of paternalism and dependency persists, as shown by some S1s waiting to act for some "boss" orders; or assuming that the solutions should come from those who rule and not from themselves. Even at this level, the project demonstrated them their capability of acting autonomously and cohesively with their Life Plan and their sustainability ethos. There follows C. Durán's testimony on the learning from the case study and its impact in the community.

CD's testimony

> *V&S theory was useful for diagnosing the core issues risking sustainability of the Orika community and for promoting necessary adjustments. Most recommendations produced in the focal groups were later introduced by the organisation's leaders in self-paced and organic processes. Two years after the fieldwork activities, the researcher has been informed that some of the positive changes the OCC introduced in the management of its operational units (S1) proved fundamental for effectively responding and adapting to the adversities that the COVID-19 pandemic brought to them. For example: a health committee was created (as a new S1) with the inclusion of young leaders who became more visible and accountable, since they represented each sector of the island as S1's operational-managers. The renewed committee organized activities such as keeping a daily registry and follow up of the most affected families to provide them the humanitarian aid received from private organisations and the Colombian government. In parallel, the management board of the OCC created a WhatsApp group that involved members from all the families of the community and created a Google Survey to address the main proposals to define S2 measures to protect the community against COVID-19 transmission. This online communication became S3* good practices and were positively accepted later for limiting the number of boat transports from Cartagena to the islands per week; and for restricting these transports exclusively to community members. These restrictions prevented the number of COVID-19 infections in the islands while protecting the whole community. Although the eco-tourism economy (S1) was highly affected by the confinement and global travel restrictions, traditional economic activities such as fishery, agriculture and exchanging goods and services (bartering) were jointly adopted by the islands' families to adapt and survive. New and young leaderships emerged and became visible. By December 2020, a new board was elected, with two young professional women elected as legal representative and president. This board has been acclaimed for refreshing the leadership style and the management models of the OCC while being more accountable and committed to internal regulations' compliance. This crisis offered an opportunity to introduce and adapt other agreed recommendations from the v&s project and to continue learning collectively about more effective structures to co-evolve with their niche.*

Conclusions

In this chapter, we have reviewed traditional ways of understanding governance, introduced the v&s understanding of sustainable self-governance, and compared the main differences between the v&s and other approaches to governance. Traditional governance studies investigate governance from a linear causality perspective (e.g., analysing correlation between key variables for good governance, like correlation between stakeholders' participation and agency).

Instead, the v&s approach sees organisations as complex systems, whose dynamic behaviour results from circular rather than linear causality. Rather than searching for causal links between variables, we suggest tools for collectively mapping their own organisation and analysing their governance dilemmas. They allow communities to make collective sense of the complex situations they may be facing, and to develop their capabilities for self-steering, while respecting their basic rules for sustainable co-existence between them and their ecological niches.

This and previous chapters have offered examples of v&s applications, which demonstrate how this theory allows us to identify governance dilemmas and paradoxes, address them collectively to redesign our organisations and to improve their governance structures. In particular, the M* Clean case study (Chapter 4), the ELF case study in Chapter 5, and the N^2BN case study in Chapter 6 illustrated examples of governance dilemmas in complex organisations and networks as well as the power of the v&s approach to analyse governance in businesses.

We briefed in this chapter Guzman's comparative analysis of the self-management of two socio-ecological systems affected by climate change in Colombia, which illustrates the positive influence that a bottom-up, collaborative network strategy to deal with the impact of climate change in a vulnerable eco-region may have. And the dilemmas resulting, on the contrary, when the economic interests of a few prevail over the collective interests of the many stakeholders. In particular, when the way of addressing climate change threats is co-opted by authoritarian, centralised structures, rather than devolved to cooperative self-managed structures.

In both community case studies here, we analysed at nested levels of organisation, their self-governance dilemmas and paradoxes and involved stakeholders to discuss possible actions forward. In both cases, we confirmed the relevance of recognising and including in the process a multiplicity of actors to develop a self-governance structure that promotes sustainability. In both cases, we complemented the STM with other systemic tools (e.g. boundary critic) and other anthropological research tools (i.e., ethnography). It allowed multistakeholder participation and involvement from a variety of ethnical and cultural perspectives. The decision to run practical workshops was carried out with simple language, using metaphors, and encouraging creative representation of the participants perceptions, allowed participants to seed the v&s concepts into everyday experiences, and to fully get involved in the learning process.

We have seen that the framework to assess sustainable self-governance can be used to compare governance dilemmas in organisations of different scales such as businesses, communities, and SSEs – see also Espinosa (2015) for a comparative analysis of capabilities for self-governance of three organisations that have gone through a VSM intervention. Both the OCC's and the ACAIPI's experiences are not far from the daily experience in companies of handling the paradox of operating between hierarchical structures based on control and requiring more autonomy and trust for effectively interacting with their niches. In every case, strengthening operational units' autonomy to adaptively co-evolve with their niche, without losing community cohesion, is one of the main challenges for complex organisations aiming to sustainably self-govern.

As in all processes of complex organisational transformation, the challenge of implementing proposals relies on the level of commitment of participants: In every case study in this chapter, it was the careful inclusion and re-presentation of multi-stakeholders, and their full involvement with the v&s workshops, that made it more likely to see results coming from the action research projects.

As the previous testimonies suggest, by continuing implementing of the v&s proposals, the communities have improved their capabilities for sustainable self-governance. In both cases, the skills developed during the process of designing and implementing self-transformation projects provided them with capabilities to better address sudden environmental changes, as it was demonstrated in their recent reactions to the COVID-19 pandemic. We also witnessed a similar learning from ELF schools.

These examples provide some evidence that the STM and the v&s learning process may be replicated to other similar organisations. It is important to acknowledge that, in communities, this possibility of replication requires an anthropological look at each organisation, since solutions must be built from within the community itself so that they are effectively implemented within the culture and norms of each community.

These self-governance studies in communities also contribute to ongoing research in what Ostrom (1990) and colleagues call 'polycentric governance,' which aims at expressing and consolidating community views with re-presentatives from the government to fulfil their collectively agreed purposes. The adapted STM offers an example of participatory tools to facilitate community agreements on strategic actions to address SSE vulnerabilities and to self-organise by identifying and implementing strategic meta-systemic roles to improve their capabilities for sustainable self-governance.

The case studies demonstrate the power of the VSM to deal with a variety of highly complex situations: from a network of businesses to a river based social economic system, to various communities. The VSM has the ability to model the situation, and its principles of effective organisation opens the door to a range of practical solutions. The power of the VSM is its possibility to reveal the nature and dynamics of social interactions in organised human activities in ways that are not 'visible' by other management (and even sociological or anthropological) research approaches.

Notes

1 https://orcid.org/my-orcid?orcid=0000-0002-5200-7613
2 In the EPSRC-funded project 'Defying the Rules: How Self-Regulatory Social Systems Work' (2007–2010), we compared the organisation of an ant's colony, a robots laboratory and a social community – using the VSM – and concluded that what we call attractors in complex adaptive systems is the equivalent of *primary* tasks (System 1) in viable systems. See details in Arcaute et al. (2009).
3 A former PhD student I supervised at Los Andes University (Colombia).
4 Model of Symbiotic Socio Ecological Systems (MOSES).
5 C. Duque is an anthropologist then doing an MSc on environmental management in Los Andes University in Colombia.
6 Spanish acronym for the Association of Traditional Indigenous Authorities of the Pirá Paraná River.
7 Carolina Duque's collaborators, Nelson Ortiz y Jorge González led with her the fieldwork.
8 Thanks to ACAIPI and GAIA Amazonas for their support in this research project.
9 C. Durán (carliDurán@gmail.com) is a former MSc student from the Centre for Innovation and Sustainability, of Externado University's School of Management, in Colombia, where I am an Invited Professor since 2018. I supervised this work and we collaborated in producing this case study.
10 Consejo Comunitario de Islas del Rosario -Orika. (2014). 'Plan de vida de la comunidad negra de las Islas del Rosario.'
11 Focus Group, November 5, 2018.
12 Adapted and translated from the original cartoon done by the participants in the focus group.
13 A well-known Colombian musical genre.
14 Eika de la Rosa, personal communication, September 21, 2018.

References

ACAIPI (2015). *El territorio de los jaguares del Yurupari. Hee Yaia godo-Bakari.* Bogotá: Ed Panamericana.
Andrade, G., Espinosa, A., Guzmán, D. y, & Wills, E. (2012). 'Towards a framework for the observation, understanding, and management of socio-ecological systems: Insight from socio-ecological, institutional, and complexity theory', *Emergence and Complexit (EcO)*, 14(1), pp. 15–30.

Arcaute, E., Christensen, K., Sendova-Franks, A., Dahl, T., & Espinosa, A. (2009). 'Division of labour in ant colonies in terms of attractive fields', *Ecological Complexity*, 6(4), pp. 396–402. ISBN 1476-945X.

Beer, S. (1979). *The Heart of Enterprise*. Chichester: John Wiley and Sons.

Bryson, J. M., Crosby, B. C., & Bloomberg, L. (2014). 'Moving beyond traditional public administration and new public management', *Public Administration Review*, 74(4), pp. 445–457.

Bula, G., & Espejo, R. (2012). 'Governance and inclusive democracy', *Kybernetes: International Journal of Systems and Cybernetics*, 41(3/4), pp. 339–347.

Durán, C. A. (2011). 'Dificultades de etnografiar el estado: una experienca de campo en las Islas del Rosario', in Chaves, M. (ed.), *La Multiculturalidad Estatalizada: Indígenas, Afrodescendientes Y Configuraciones De Estado*. Bogota: Instituto Colombiano de Antropología e Historia, pp. 181–192.

Durán, C. (2019). *Aplicación del enfoque de Viabilidad y Sostenibilidad para fortalecer la gobernanza ambiental del Consejo Comunitario de Orika en Islas del Rosario, Cartagena*. MSc dissertation, Business School. Bogotá: Externado University.

Drucker, P. (2003). *A Functioning Society*. New York: Transaction Publishers.

Espinosa, A. (2015). 'Governance for sustainability: learning from VSM practice', *Kybernetes: International Journal of Systems and Cybernetics*, 44(6–7), pp. 955–969.

Espinosa, A., Harnden, R. y., & Walker, J. (2008). 'A complexity approach to sustainability: Stafford beer revisited', *European Journal of Operational Research*, 187(2), pp. 636–651.

Espinosa, A., Cardoso, P., Arcaute, E. y., & Christensen, K. (2011). 'Complexity approaches to self-organisation: a case study from an Irish eco-village', *Kybernetes: International Journal of Systems and Cybernetics*, 40(3/4), pp. 536–557.

Espinosa, A., & Walker, J. (2013). 'Complexity management in practice: A VSM intervention in an irish eco- community', *European Journal of Operational Research*, 225(1), pp. 118–129.

Espinosa, A., & Guzman, D. (2015). 'Self-governance and symbiosis: A systemic approach to Socio Ecological Systems resilience', in *Proceedings of the ISSS Conference, Agosto 1–4, 2015*. Berlin: ISSS.

Espinosa, A., & Walker, J. (2017). *A Complexity Approach to Sustainability: Theory and Application*. 2nd edition. Imperial College Series on Complexity Science. Vol. 5. Singapore: World Scientific Press. pp. 117–138.

Espinosa, A., & Duque, C. (2018). 'Complexity management and multi-scale governance: A case study in an Amazonian Indigenous Association', in Special Issue on Community Operational Research, Midgley, G. and M. Johnson (eds), *European Journal of Operational Research*, 268, pp. 1006–1020.

Faguet, J. P. (2012). *Decentralization and Popular Democracy in Bolivia: Governance from Below*. Ann Arbor MI: University of Michigan Press.

Farrell, K., Kemp, R., Hinterberger, F., Rammel, C., & Ziegler, R. (2005). 'From *for* to governance for sustainable development in Europe', *International Journal of Sustainable Development*, 8, pp. 127–150.

Freeman, E. (1984). *Strategic Management: A Stakeholder Perspective*. Englewood Cliffs, NJ: Prentice-Hall.

Gnan, L., Hinna, A., Monteduro, F., & Scarozza, D. (2013). 'Corporate governance and management practices: Stakeholder involvement, quality and sustainability tools adoption', *Journal of Management and Governance*, 17(1), pp. 907–937.

Gunderson, L. H. y., & Holling C. S. (2002) *Panarchy: Understanding Transformations in Human and Natural Systems*. Washington, DC: Island Press.

Guzmán, D. (2015). *Autoorganización en Sistemas Socioecológicos Para la Gestión del Cambio Ambiental: Lineamientos Metodológicos y Aplicaciones.* Tesis Doctoral. Bogotá:Universidad de Los Andes, Facultad de Administración.

Howard-Grenville, J., Buckle, S. J., Hoskins, B. J., & George, G. (2014). 'Climate change and management', *Academy of Management Journal,* 57(3), pp. 615–623.

Jackson M. C. (1988). 'An appreciation of Stafford Beer's viable system viewpoint on management practice', *Journal of Management Studies,* 25(6), pp. 557–573.

Kooiman, J. (2003). *Governing as Governance.* London: Sage Knowledge.

Leach, M., Bloom, G., Ely, A., Nightingale, P., Scoones, I., & Shah, E. (2007). *'Understanding Governance: Pathways to Sustainability',* STEPS Working Paper 2. Brighton: STEPS Centre.

Levi-Faur, D. (2012). *The Oxford Handbook of Governance.* Oxford: Oxford University Press.

Malik, F. (2011). *Unternehmenspolitik und Corporate Governance. Wie Organisationen sich selbst organisieren.* Frankfurt: Campus Verlag.

Midgley, G., & Ochoa-Arias, A. (1999). 'Visions of community for community OR', *Omega,* 27, pp. 259–274.

Midgley, G., Johnson, M. P., & Chichirau, G. (2017). 'What is Community Operational Research?', *European Journal of Operational Research,* 268, pp. 771–783.

Morlidge, S. (2007). *The Application of Organisational Cybernetics to the Design and Diagnosis of Financial Performance Management Systems.* PhD Dissertation. Kingston upon Hull: Hull University Business School.

Ostrom, E. (1990). *Governing the Commons: The Evolution of Institutions for Collective Action (Political Economy of Institutions and Decisions).* Cambridge: Cambridge University Press.

Panagiotakopoulos, P., Espinosa, A., & Walker, J. (2016). 'Sustainability management: Insights from the Viable System Model', *Journal of Cleaner Production,* 113(1), pp. 792–806.

Pfiffner, M. (2010) 'Five experiences with the viable system model', *Kybernetes: International Journal of Systems and Cybernetics,* 39(9/10), pp. 1615–1626.

Pfiffner, M. (2020). *Die dritte Dimension des Organisierens: Steuerung und Kommunikation (German Edition).* Frankfurt: Springer.

Schwaninger, M. (2015). 'Organizing for sustainability: A cybernetic concept for sustainable renewal', *Kybernetes: International Journal of Systems and Cybernetics,* 44(6/7), pp. 935–954.

Schwaninger, M. (2019). 'Governance for intelligent organizations: A cybernetic contribution', *Kybernetes: International Journal of Systems and Cybernetics,* 48(1), pp. 35–57.

Teece, D. J. (2012). 'Dynamic capabilities: Routines versus entrepreneurial action', *Journal of Management Studies,* 49(8), pp. 1395–1401.

Tihanyi, L., Graffin, S., & George, G. (2014). 'Rethinking governance in management research', *Academy of Management Journal,* 57(6), pp. 1535–1543.

Tricker, B. (2015). *Corporate governance. Principles, Policies, and Practices.* 3rd edition. Oxford. Oxford University Press.

Türke, R. E. (2008). *Governance. Systemic Foundation and Framework.* Heidelberg: Physica Verlag.

Vester, F. (2007). *The Art of interconnected Thinking. Ideas and Tools for Tackling Complexity* Munich: MCB Publishing House.

Wallis, J. J., & Oates, W. E. (1988). 'Decentralization in the public sector: An empirical study of state and local government', in Rosen, H. (ed.), *Fiscal Federalism Quantitative Studies.* Chicago: University of Chicago Press, pp. 5–32.

Waltner-Toews, D., Kay, J., & Lister, N. M. (2008). *The ecosystems approach: complexity, uncertainty and managing for sustainability*. New York: Columbia University Press.

Williamson, O. E., (1979). 'Transaction-cost economics: The governance of contractual relations', *The Journal of Law & Economics*, 22(2), pp. 233–261.

Williamson, O. E. (1996). *The Mechanisms of Governance*. New York: Oxford University Press.

Chapter 8

Facilitating Systemic Change with the VSM

Systemic Change: What It Is and How It Can Be Done

Using systemic, transdisciplinary approaches to facilitate massive, systemic change has been the ambition of many complex systems researchers. Studying the complexity of social, ecological, and economic interactions in a socio-ecological system (e.g., community, city, eco-region, nation) requires a systemic, multiagency approach to mapping and analysing the complex patterns of interaction among their agents. Previous chapters showed examples of v&s action research in complex organisational systems, which demonstrated how this approach facilitates the collective learning process of stakeholders to identify more viable and more sustainable ways of self-organising to implement their own purposes or strategies. Here we reflect on how this approach helps to intentionally facilitate systemic change towards more sustainable ways of interacting in large-scale, complex systems.

Systemic change is understood as a heuristic to explore patterns and dynamics of massive social change in societies and regions. Wolfram and Frantzeskaki (2016) summarise the preferred epistemologies to facilitate systemic change for sustainability in cities: to analyse cities (or regions more broadly speaking) as places shaped by and shaping interactions between multiple socio-technical and social-ecological systems; to focus on inter-agency relations across systems; and to offer transdisciplinary approaches for experimentation. Systemic change is emerging as a highly transdisciplinary field including studies in development: the multi-level perspective (MLP), strategic niche management (SNM), and transition management (TM).

The MLP explains coevolution between an existing socio-technological regime and emerging social innovations in niches. This leads to pathways for transformation, which (can) result in new system configurations. TM has proven to be a useful heuristic to facilitate systemic changes by natural leaders (front-runners, border crossers, incumbents) in a 'transition arena' by jointly orientating, setting agendas, activating social changes, and reflecting upon them (Loorbach and Rotmans 2010). SNM enables the experiential learning

 DOI: 10.4324/9780429490835-9

of natural leaders in a particular niche, aiming to enhance the transformative impact of community initiatives in grassroot niches (Folke et al., 2002). All these approaches also share a strong concern for governance innovations, experimentation, and social learning (Davies 2012).

While these research approaches have impacted the understanding of systemic change in communities, and cities Wolfram and Frantzeskaki (2016) recognise the need for cross-scale studies to address relationships between community/urban/regional and national scales. They consider that further studies exploring the interdependencies and change dynamics between complex socio-ecological systems at different scales would be highly desirable to complement and enrich these existing approaches. More emphasis on comparative research (both qualitative and quantitative) would also be very relevant to make these emerging fields of knowledge more robust.

The number of crises and emergencies that the COVID-19 pandemic brought to us is obvious for many businesses and government institutions. But it has also been an opportunity for learning and self-organising by developing more conscious decisions on how to be more viable and sustainable in our individual lives, our households, and our primary service organisations. It has certainly made us more aware of the need for massive systemic change in certain sectors, like the health sector, worldwide.

The following sections reflect first on the results and the (sometimes unexpected) impacts of a few large-scale VSM applications aimed at facilitating massive systemic changes in specific places and niches. By reflecting on these historical examples, it then comes back to review the current challenges brought by the COVID-19 pandemic, by reflecting on three experiments in different places and contexts where the VSM has been used to analyse organisational responses to the pandemic. It concludes by making it more clear how Beer's original ideas are required more than ever, and how they offer clear criteria and tools to facilitate some of the massive systemic changes urgently required.

The Cybersyn Project

Beer's most renowned example of implementing the VSM to lead a systemic change in the national governance system was in the Cybersyn project in Chile (Beer, 1981, pp. 268–278; Espejo, 2009). In 1971, Chilean (socialist) President Salvador Allende was in the process of devolving control of the means of production (i.e., the publicly owned factories) to the workers, and wanted to implement a revolutionary socialist (technology supported) governance system. He invited Beer to lead the Cybersyn project, supported by a team of Chileans.

The Cybersyn project aimed at devolving control to each level of organisation from the individual to the factory and finally to the nation to encourage real-time, agile self-governance. It developed a Cyberfilter – a VSM-inspired performance management system – to support self-regulation and real-time performance management of each viable system in the industry. It began by doing a recursive mapping of all the state-owned industries – from the factories to the national level – and then focused on developing their self-governance systems.

At each level of recursive organisation in the (state-owned) industries, each viable system was expected to design and monitor their key performance indicators (KPIs). They involved all staff in a participatory process to identify the 'essential variables' for viability in each of the factories, using quantified flow charts to model the operation vs environment interaction and to decide their KPIs. The Cyberfilter software analysed KPIs' behaviours and produced exception reports and 'algedonics' (alarm signals) at each level of recursive organisation. This information was immediately passed on to the factory and or the industrial unit, which was the source of the data, thus encouraging self-organisation and local autonomy.

At the presidential palace (la Moneda), they set up an 'operations room,' where the president and the ministers made decisions based on real-time observed behaviours at each level of organised industrial activity when alerted by an important algedonic signal in any region or industrial sector. The project also designed a communication network (Cybernet) to share the information at each level of organised industrial activity, e.g., factories, public enterprises, industrial sectors, up to the state level. Each level of recursion had a certain amount of time to address their algedonic signals, which could be zero in an emergency. All algedonic signals didn't go straight to the top but were filtered.

It also ran a simulation model of the Chilean economy (Checo), inspired by systems dynamics, to analyse and forecast possible economic behaviours, using real-time information. Finally, the Cyberfolk project (also called 'the People's project'), focused on implementing a system to measure the citizens' well-being and their approval of ongoing state's policies and actions. It worked by designing an algedonic meter, to measure 'eudaemony' (people's wellbeing), with the very rudimentary technology available at the time.

Both the required educational and technological platforms were highly ambitious, but extra-ordinary progress had been made in all aspects during the 18 months up until August 1973. Unfortunately, the project finished abruptly after the 11th of September 1973s coup, which ended Allende's life and his government. In this project, Beer pioneered, 50 years before his time, what nowadays are called 'agile systems,' which are increasingly used worldwide. He also pioneered the idea of distributed control in complex organisational systems as the best strategy for managing complexity. This was well before the modern complexity theorists further developed these ideas with the newer theories of complex adaptive systems.

Given its visionary nature, the Cybersyn project has remained in the minds of people around the world, as an example we could still follow. There have been several efforts to relate the whole story and make it available for the wider public.[2] A few critics of the project saw it mostly as a technocratic dream of a few scientists and officials, which aimed to control the workers (Medina, 2006). But they seem to have missed the core spirit of the project, as an inclusive social experiment, aimed at promoting a more self-regulated, distributed, and democratic society.

Even if, during these early days, ideas of systemic change were not yet in the mainstream literature, Beer was clearly aware of their nature. Cybersyn was an ambitious project to facilitate a massive systemic change in the governance systems at the national level. Its design included the different elements of a systemic change approach widely recognised today:

- It 'analysed a *whole nation* as a place shaped by and shaping interactions between multiple socio-technical systems.'

- It focused on *inter-agency relationships across systems* (i.e., individual, economic, and political).

- *It offered transdisciplinary approaches for experimentation* (including organisational cybernetics, systems dynamics, political innovations, as well as many information and communication technology innovations).

- *It* also had a '*strong concern for governance innovations, experimentation and social learning,*' as the initial results obtained widely demonstrated.

Several of Beer's followers have continued applying and developing these ideas (Schwember, 1977; Schwaninger, 2006; 2019; Espinosa 2006; Espejo, 2009; Espinosa & Walker, 2017, pp. 139–149).

The next section reflects on several projects the author led in Colombia in the 1990s, also designed to produce systemic changes in different sectors at the national level, inspired by Beer's work in Chile.

Strategic Information Management at the Colombian President's Office (1990–1992)

The original version of the STM resulted from my own PhD research, inspired by Beer's Viable System Model. It adapted the Viplan methodology (Espejo et al., 1999) to create a systemic way of linking strategy, structure and information systems(Espinosa, 1995). The PhD project included a case study analysing the Strategic Information Systems Plan (SISP) at the Colombian Presidential Office (CPO) between 1990 and 1992, when I was the director of the Informatics Secretariat. It demonstrated how by following the STM, a complex SISP process could be refined to have more of a chance of success at the implementation stage.

I first developed a VSM mapping of the Colombian state inspired by Beer's work in Chile, which helped to clarify the meta-systemic roles of the CPO as a System 5 role at the national level (recursion level 0/1). They included leading policy formulation and monitoring and creating the context for effective development and performance of the public sector. Then I developed a VSM diagnosis of the CPO focusing on understanding how effective the relationship between the CPO and the public organisations were when implementing presidential policies and programmes.

The main diagnostic issues I found included centralised management at the CPO, control dilemma (attempting not to lose control, senior executives supervised every transaction made which resulted in overloaded System 3 roles, excessive documentation, and out-of-date information). Also, top-down resource negotiations and performance measuring systems resulting in long delays and a culture of lack of trust. There were ineffective (or non-existent) mechanisms for generating algedonic signals in the core sectors of communities and industries.

Mapping the complexity of the state and analysing the way the CPO was (or was not) effectively managing such complexity helped to clarify the strategic information systems needed to support the CPO in developing its leading (S5) role of the nation. Inspired by the VSM, I did a retrospective analysis of a (then) recent consulting project to design the CPO's strategic information systems using a more traditional systems analysis methodology. I understood that the consultants' SIS plan was far too abstract, technologically inspired, and overly ambitious, which not surprisingly, proved too difficult to implement.

A first learning from this case study was about the relevance of designing a SIS portfolio, in a more participatory and process grounded approach, by first analysing the organisational structure, strategy, and existing technology as the basis for designing a SIS portfolio to effectively support critical areas for organisational viability.

The final stage of the analysis focused on analysing the performance management system of the CPS/CPO. Given the interagency nature of presidential programs' coordination, the required PMS needed to be designed and implemented jointly at the national, regional, and local levels. At the time, the public institutions responsible for Systems 3 and 4 requested independently detailed information to each public organisation about their use of public funds, this way generating duplication and unnecessary extra work. In particular:

- The Finance Ministry (FM) (S3) was responsible for negotiating and sourcing operational budgets for each public institution;

- The National Planning Department (NPD) (S4) was responsible for designing the national development plan and negotiating developmental resources with them; and

- The National Auditing Office (NAO) (S3/S3*) was responsible for auditing overall public expenditure.

However, none of these had an integral systemic view of operational performance of each of the regional or local budgets, or of each of the service or industrial sectors: They all monitored financial performance using different types of financial indicators. The CPO and the public organisations were missing a more 'cybernetically sound performance management system,' with performance indicators of each of the primary activities in the public sector, industry, and communities. Without a proper performance management system, the CPO had to continue leading the country using only secondary information coming from long and complex public reports produced by the NAO, the FM, and the NPD.

I then led a joint project with the CPO, the National Planning Department, and the National University's Economic Research Centre to develop a systemic oriented performance management system to monitor the effective implementation of development programs in all public organisations in the country. We designed and ran a pioneering system to monitor KPIs on the effect of all publicly funded development programs that evolved later as the 'Synergia' project. It ran effectively for several years after and has been improved and redeveloped several times since then. It contributed to developing a culture of measuring performance in the public sector.

This project ended up with a national conference on performance management systems in the public sector where we invited institutions to present their innovations in the field.[3] We then published an edited book with the 'state of the art' in performance management systems in the country at the time (Molina & Espinosa, 1993). This project seeded a culture and awareness of the need for more systemic approaches to improve and assess public services performance, which contributed to several later cybernetic developments, as described below.

Re-Engineering the National Auditing Office (NAO) in Colombia

In 1993, I was invited by the auditing office in Cali, Colombia, to assist them in re-engineering their structure. For a year, I worked with representatives from all its offices to jointly develop a leaner and more agile structure to guarantee more effective public control in the city. This project inspired a similar but more ambitious project a year later, to re-engineer the National

Auditing Office (NAO). We initiated the project with G. Bula, who a year later became the deputy director of the NAO. I designed and led the project from 1994 to 1997.

The project was financed by the United Nations Development Program, and we hired a team of academic consultants from Los Andes University, including A. Reyes, E. Lleras, and R. Zarama. We later invited R. Espejo as an international advisor, who came for short visits three or four times each year. I was also personally coached by Stafford Beer at each stage of the project. We invited S. Beer, R. Espejo, and H. Von Foerster to a national event in 1996, where we presented the project to the main public institutions.

Redesigning the NAO

The ambition of the project was to create a massive systemic change in the control culture and processes of the Colombian Public Sector and to re-engineer the NAO, which was well known for being inefficient and lacking transparency – and even being corrupt – in the auditing processes. We aimed to introduce the idea and practice of self-regulation in the involved public institutions and distinguish between 'first-order control' (i.e., done through a traditional audit) and second-order control – guaranteeing the internal control system of each public organisation was working effectively and transparently. We called this effort the development of the *'new control speech.'*

In my previous job at the president's office, I collaborated in the process of creating a new Constitution for the country, and one of the distinctive features of the 1991 Constitution was the creation of internal control offices in the public organisations, and the realisation of the need to promote second-order control. Nevertheless, there were not yet any mechanisms to implement these ideas, so we aimed at this project at creating such mechanisms and providing successful examples of implementation.

Also, following from my learning at the CPO, and inspired by Beer's Cybersyn project, I wanted to continue looking for better ways to develop 'cybernetically sound performance management systems' in the Colombian Public Sector. The NAO's way of measuring public performance was to confirm that the public institutions spent their allocated budgets on what they had promised to do, in the expected time. They audited public institutions doing financial, environmental, physical, and technological audits. There was however, no attempt to assess whether the services offered to the public had been developed effectively and with the expected quality.

When we started the project, we reconfirmed the need for a more systemic integral, and effective way of measuring performance so we spent the first year introducing VSM criteria to the management of NAO and confirming with them their need for re-designing the organisation and the auditing process Over the first few years, I led the diagnosis of structural problems in NAO and coached implementation of their main 'self-transformation projects' using the VSM. Later, we redesigned the auditing process into what we called the 'systemic auditing process,' also inspired by the VSM. We used Viplan and Espinosa (1995)'s methodology to support the structural and auditing processes' redesign.

The Model of the State

By following VSM criteria, it was clear that the NAO, whose main role is to regulate public expenditure, should have requisite variety to regulate the activities of the state. Conant and Ashby (1970) have said that every good regulator of a system must be a model of that system. Accordingly, as the NAO was a state regulator, this implied that the NAO should develop a model of the state that had requisite variety. This wasn't the case when we started the project (they only had a model of public offices' expenditure) and thus to develop a richer model for the NAO, we clearly needed to provide it with a far richer model of the state than the one in use. I worked for several months with representatives from 40 public national organisations to jointly produce a cybernetic model of the Colombian state, following Beer's example in Chile.

We first developed a recursive analysis of the nation-state by identifying at the national level, all public organisations working directly on providing basic public services (System 1), and those offering meta-systemic services (Systems 2 to 5). The distinction in VSM terms is fundamental, as we can't estimate the public sector's performance unless we distinguish those public organisations that directly add value to the national development from those who offer meta-systemic services to the state. We mapped several levels of recursion, down to individual institutions at the national level, including hundreds of 'primary organisations' in the state.

We then produced a massive spreadsheet including information on two essential variables: operational budget and number of employees for both primary and meta-systemic institutions. These cybernetic mappings allowed us:

- To re-organise the internal structure of the NAO and to map the state model more effectively (i.e., by clearly matching the sectorial divisions with those primary sectors identified in the model of the state).

- To observe the distribution of the public budget between primary and support institutions and to analyse their capacity to implement the national development plan (Espinosa & Walker, 2017, pp. 150–155).

- To provide a richer analysis of public expenditure to guide top-level conversations in the state with the parliament, the NDP, and other institutions leading development programs.

In parallel with the process of implementing the suggested adjustments to the broad structure of the NAO, we have begun to focus on the micro level in the current auditing practices and their needs for improvement. Inspired by VSM criteria and using insights from Viplan and the STM methodologies, we agreed on what we called the *'systemic auditing'* process, which integrated financial, systems, environmental, and physical audits around a VSM analysis of the audited institution. From 1995 to 1998, we first prototyped the new auditing process and then massively disseminated it.

Implementing the 'Systemic Auditing Process'

Based on the state model, we chose a sample of 60 national organisations that became systems in focus to implement the newly designed systemic auditing process. One of the main learnings from the project at that stage was understanding the difference between 'primary' (S1) and 'support' (meta-systemic) public organisations. As a meta-system is not a viable system in itself (that will result in pathological autopoiesis according to Beer (1979, pp 408), then we needed to map the primary sector it serviced as a viable system and do the VSM diagnosis, understanding the meta-systemic roles of particular public organisations operating in that sector. For primary organisations (S1s), we will do a more traditional VSM diagnosis. When deciding on the sample of organisation to include in the project, we made sure to choose a balanced sample of primary and meta-systemic type of organisations in the different sectors of the state.

A major difference with more traditional auditing processes was that in our *'systemic auditing,'* each 'auditing team' involved both auditors from the NAO and representatives of the audited organisations to *co-develop* the auditing process. Rather than seeing the auditing as a process of collecting information about the organisational performance in specific issues (use of financial resources, compliance with environmental standards, etc.), we saw it as a coached learning process where the organisation and its external auditors will learn together on ways to improve the organisational performance.

We first developed two prototypes, one in the (then) Agricultural Bank – which I led – and one in the National Registry Office, led by A Reyes. The prototypes worked very well, and we clarified and improved the original design of the *'systemic auditing'* process and began the process of generalisation For that purpose, we provided systemic training to all the people implementing the new auditing process, through facilitated workshops. In total we trained nearly 600 auditors between 1996 and 1998. We experimented by also providing computer-supported training, using Espejo's Viplan's learning software,[4] but we faced serious resistance to change from the auditors. So, we finally relied mostly on the face-to-face training and on facilitated working sessions with support from VSM experts.

We invited both a team of NAO auditors and representatives from the audited organisations to facilitated VSM workshops aimed at learning and sharing the assessment criteria, and at coaching them and the auditors to co-develop a VSM assessment of their own organisation and its performance. Once we concluded the auditing report with the findings and recommendations, we facilitated conversations between managers from the NAO and the audited organisations (from the next level of recursive organisation in both the audited organisation and the NAO) to agree on core adjustments to structure and performance.

Learning from the Project

The new (VSM inspired) structure from the NAO eliminated several bureaucratic layers, simplified and made more precise communications between primary areas, and contributed to develop a culture of trust and transparency. The new *systemic auditing* practice importantly reduced the length of the auditing process, improved the quality of its results, and contributed to developing new relationships of trust between the NAO and the audited organisations. From 1995 to 1998, we implemented systemic auditing processes in about 60 organisations, mostly with very positive results. Some of them began to be shared in massive media (TV, radio, and press), aiming to increase public awareness about the need and convenience of having more effective and transparent auditing practices.

In 1996, we organised a national conference on Cartagena with participation of top public officials in the country, to share the results of the ongoing project. We invited Stafford Beer, Raul Espejo, and Heinz Von Foerster as our international guests. Beer's words in the opening of the conference reflect the spirit of the project and the main learning from it:[5]

> *intrinsic control or self-control can be designed to achieve more effective control and the problem of corruption would be automatically solved in that process ... Corruption is a product of the system; corruption is not an entity in itself ... . If the system is corrupt, it's because it's designed to be corrupt. So, let's redesign it.*

A year later, we had progressed in the re-structuring of the NAO, we had trained hundreds of auditors in the new systemic auditing process, and we were beginning to have an impact on some of the audited organisations. Some of them who have co-designed with us their self-transformation process implemented their agreed self-transformation projects and began to show positive impacts from them in terms of improved effectiveness and performance. In parallel to this project, in 1996, I created an MSc course on (VSM-inspired) performance management systems[6] at Los Andes University in the Industrial

Engineering Department, called ESICO. It ran for several years after we finished the project, and we continued to educate hundreds of postgraduate students in the VSM approach and other systemic approaches to performance management.

I was hoping that the new structure and processes would directly fight with corruption in the NAO and more generally, in the Colombian public sector, but unfortunately the problem of corruption was deeper than we suspected at the time, even inside the NAO.[7] The NAO project ended in 1998, and the new leaders of the NAO (who came with the new government) didn't progress further the cybernetic project. Our team produced several publications on the project's results, including five co-authored books printed at the NAO press office in 1998, and several academic papers and book chapters (Espinosa, 1998; Andrade et al., 2000, pp. 2–75; Espejo et al., 2001; Espejo & Reyes, 2011; Bula & Espejo, 2012, Espejo, 2022).

The ideas remained alive at Los Andes University and inspired not only the ESICO MSc, but also several systemic modules on the master of industrial engineering; jointly, these postgraduate courses graduated hundreds of students with a deep understanding of systemic and cybernetic theory and practice for at least one decade (1995–2005). And more than a dozen PhD students followed this path in the following decades, from Los Andes University in Colombia, and from Hull University and Lincoln University in the United Kingdom, both of which were close collaborators of us.

Monitoring the Impact of National Programs to Reduce Poverty in Colombia

The Reunirse[8] project, sponsored by the CPO and the International Development Bank (IADB), aimed to design and implement an innovative system to monitor the impact of the presidential program to fight poverty in Colombia – the Social Solidarity Network (SSN) from 1994–1998. The CPO and the SSN commissioned the Regional Development Research Centre (CIDER) in Los Andes University to innovate more systemic ways of monitoring the impact of the massive investment in reducing poverty. I led the Reunirse project during the design and first few years of implementation.

We created an action-research network including eight universities, more than 40 researchers, and 140 undergraduate students to monitor and produce early alerts on impacts of the investments to fight poverty. We supported the SSN design of its projects, based on an understanding of poverty inspired by Max Neef's (1991) ideas of human scale development. With our partner universities, we designed a fair and transparent methodology to ensure the SSN resources were allocated where they were more needed.

For each type of program (e.g., housing, employment, education, health, food), we identified KPIs (some quantitative some qualitative) and developed an information system to collect and analyse local data (where the social projects were being implemented) on KPIs behaviours. The software produced early alarms if any program or project was unable to deliver what was expected in a timely and effective manner. Reunirse responded to such alarms in as close as possible to real time by activating a self-regulatory structure at the municipal or regional level when immediate action was needed. This structure included representatives from the beneficiaries of the projects, the local authorities, educational institutions, and local businesses.

We developed a training package for the students operating the monitoring system to introduce SSN's beneficiaries to our approach to self-governance and to coach them in the design and development of local projects. They were also trained to facilitate local meetings to collectively assess the progress of ongoing projects' implementation and to address any obstacles they may be facing. Their reports and reflexions on their individual experiences counted as the equivalent of an undergraduate dissertation.

The monitors developed close relationships with local people and sent data to Reunirse's monitoring system, which analysed it and produced early alarms when there were situations arising that might result in poor performance. In such cases, the students, supported by leading academics from the regional universities would facilitate real-time decisions at the SSN's local or regional committees to address those issues in real time.

We also supported the SSN in developing a participatory decision-making scheme, in each local and region where they operated. The 'Solidarity Roundtables'[10] included representatives from the community, the industry, and the government. At these spaces, SSN representatives facilitated collective decisions on both the final distribution of resources at each town or region, and the collective assessment of their impact in each one of the areas of investment. Reunirse academic staff (supported by the monitors) facilitated the meetings in the Solidarity Roundtables when the monitoring system raised alarms about delivery or assessment of an investment.

From 1994–1998, Reunirse facilitated and monitored interactions between thousands of people from the poorest communities in the country and many public and private organisations implementing development projects to alleviate poverty. Empowering beneficiaries to participate in decisions about the best use of financial resources to support development projects in the poorest towns had a cathartic effect on people. Not only did they manage to feel ownership of their projects and therefore were highly committed to effectively implement their resources, but they also learned to contribute to (endogenous) development projects' design.

A remarkable example was in northern Guajira, where the local indigenous were about to receive funds to buy shoes (which they didn't traditionally use) and jointly with Reunirse monitors, they decided to re-orient the funds to buy goats, their main source of income. This brought far more wellbeing to this community than the originally designed investment program (designed by technicians from IADB misunderstanding the real needs of local communities).

A main innovation from Reunirse was to design and use 'cybernetically inspired' democratic self-governance structures, systems, and mechanisms, including early alarms, to improve the impact of investment resources. A survey conducted with more than 122 towns' minors revealed that more than 70% considered the impact of the SSN in their places had been significant in terms of effectively addressing core poverty challenges and had allowed effective and participatory governance of the programs (Espinosa, 1997, 2006; Espinosa & Walker, 2017, pp. 367–381).

In 1998, I led a Syntegration to assess Reunirse's effectiveness, with representatives from all SSN stakeholders: 92% of the participants considered Reunirse had left them with a better understanding of the main issues of poverty and of the impact of the SSN on affected areas. Not only had Reunirse demonstrated an effective way to close the control loops in development programs, but it also contributed to building local and regional capabilities for self-governance and encouraged democratic and transparent performance management systems for massive public investments.

Reunirse was undoubtedly an innovative experience in democratic and participatory governance in which people became more conscious of their capabilities and experienced the meaning of being 'in control of their government.' This project had a lasting effect on the culture of monitoring performance and supporting local development: see for example a current initiative for a citizen-led itinerary Assembly in Bogota.[11] Currently there are also a series of development projects led by students from Ibague University supporting core local development needs (Reyes, 2019).

Redesigning the National School System (NSS) in Colombia

In 1999–2001, I co-led an educational reform program, the 'New School System' (NSS) sponsored by the Ministry of Education and the Inter-American Development Bank (IADB), to design a systemic school system for the whole country, aimed at addressing the existing gaps in educational services in the country, both in coverage and quality of education. German Bula, the ex-deputy director of NAO had then been appointed as the Minister for Education, and he again invited some of us to lead the project.[12]

The project supported the regional and local institutions in a group of counties (5–8), municipalities (100–160), and public schools (500–800) to design their educational self-transformation programs and to finance and monitor their implementation. The NSS aimed to achieve universal net coverage of basic education and guarantee the quality of educational services by the promotion of autonomous educational institutions – *complete schools* – associations of geographically close schools that together could offer a complete basic education service with the capacity to offer a complete basic primary (and hopefully also secondary) education, with control over their financial and human resources, and full responsibility for their results. An additional aim was to make the municipal and departmental educational systems more effective.

With a group of researchers and consultants, fully supported by the Ministry of Education (ME), we first produced a recursive analysis of the education sector (Figure 8.1) and then did a VSM diagnosis to analyse the current limitations of the existing schools and the educational authorities (Figure 8.2).

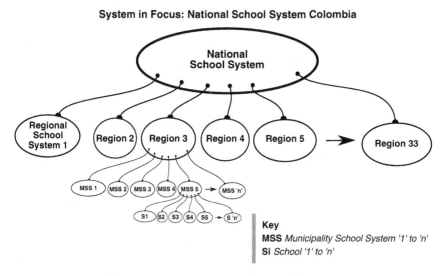

System in Focus: National School System Colombia

Key
MSS *Municipality School System '1' to 'n'*
Si *School '1' to 'n'*

Figure 8.1 Recursive analysis of the NSS

(Illustration by Jon Walker)

The preliminary VSM diagnosis of the NSS – see examples in Figure 8.3 – showed clear disparities in the way of distributing resources (D1); a top-down allocation of educational resources (D2); reduced community participation at all levels (D3); unequal quality of educational offerings (D4); deficient evaluation systems for students, teachers, managers, and schools (D5); lack of local decision support systems (D6); and a need for more effective instruments for monitoring and evaluating the impact of ongoing educational policies and programs (D7).

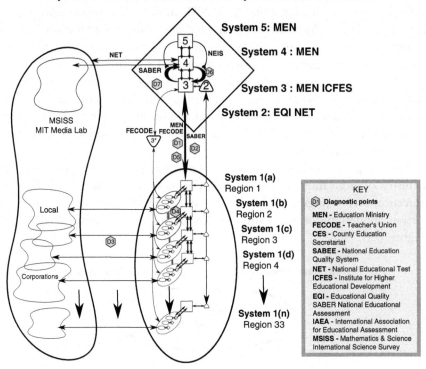

Figure 8.2 Preliminary diagnosis of the NSS

(Illustration by Jon Walker)

Based on this diagnosis, we then developed two prototypes of *complete schools* with the educational authorities of Quindío and Risaralda's counties in central Colombia, introducing alternative models of learning in the schools. For the prototypes, we organised workshops with representatives from several local schools, and the regional educational authorities. We designed and ran the prototypes in collaboration with the Media Lab from MIT. I led the team doing the organisational diagnosis and the process of identifying self-transformations for each school (the project offered a significant budget to implement their self-transformation projects). Together with D. Cavallo, the Media Lab's expert, we designed prototypes for using computers in the classroom to introduce a systemic approach to learning, supported by the then 'state-of-the-art' teaching software.[13]

A preliminary diagnosis of the effectiveness of educational services at the school level confirmed several diagnostic issues (see Figure 8.3). These included failures to produce satisfactory average academic achievement (D1); transmit relevant knowledge to children (D2); effectively promote interest in learning and research (D3); and to educate active and toleran citizens for peaceful coexistence in society (D4). Regarding the schools' management, there were serious and generalised limitations, such as lack of control over financial resources (D6); insufficient essential administrative services to support headmasters (D7); operating in precarious and deficient establishments without sports facilities, laboratories, and libraries (D8); and lack of accountability for those providing school government and stewardship (D9).

In each prototype, about 60 people participated actively in the development work, mostly through workshops with the consulting team, including schoolteachers, headmasters, and educational managers from the municipal level. The workshops facilitated the process for agreeing the conceptual, methodological, instrumental, and financial guidelines for planning and implementing the programme. They also created a context for dialectic solutions of current tensions through participative action.

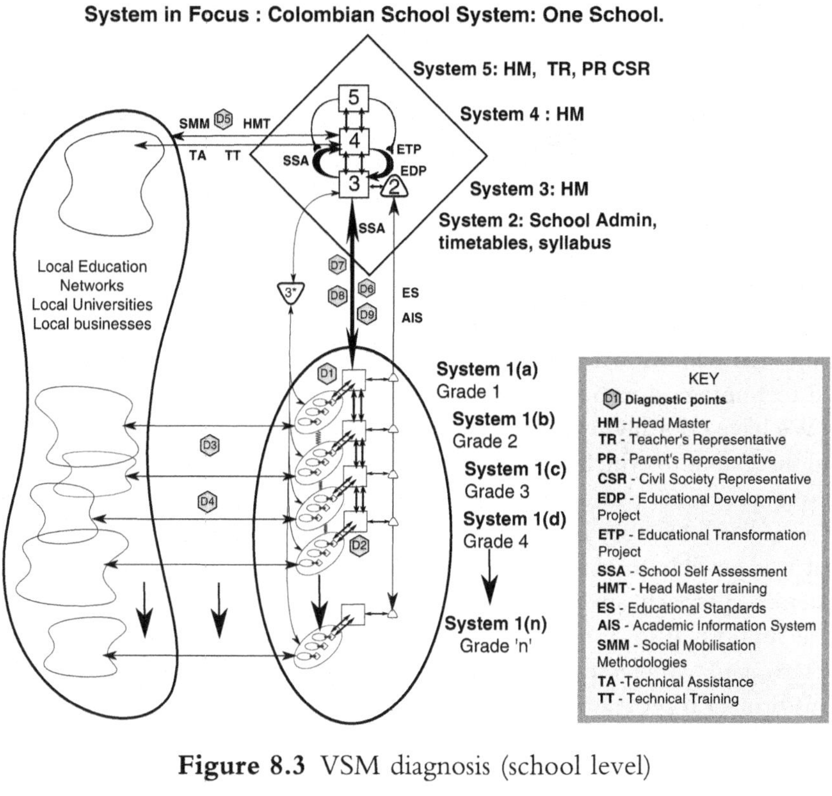

Figure 8.3 VSM diagnosis (school level)

(Illustration by Jon Walker)

The strategies to improve educational performance in the schools included increasing the participation of children and parents in developing knowledge and ensuring links to community development; improving relationships between the educational community and the municipal educational authorities; developing an incentive programme based on clarifying economic contracts among the agents of the educational system to improve the school system's performance in terms of quality, coverage, and equity; and involving the local community in social mobilization processes around collectively agreed initiatives for local educational transformation.

To implement the NSS, the complete schools would have a school government – the School Education Board (SEB) – made up of headmasters, teachers, and representatives of students, parents, and civil society. There was to be an open invitation to universities, mixed corporations, and NGOs to provide technical assistance to the organisation of the complete schools. We wanted the education provided to be more closely related to community development for it to make sense to people and gain their support.

By July 2000, there was a detailed design available to present to the Board of Directors of the programme, who accepted the proposal on proviso that more details would have to be provided in terms of action plans, mechanisms for using the resources, and specific transformation plans for the departments where the prototype activity would take place. We expected to facilitate a gradual change process, with the respective authorities joining the program at their own pace. Our hope was that the program would eventually have an impact on the whole of the basic education system.

Unfortunately, for political reasons, the project didn't conclude as we expected as a new administration took over the Ministry of Education. The new minister shifted the focus and approach of the project back to a more traditional educational reform process, with emphasis on managing financial and technological resources for educational development.

We have critically reflected elsewhere on the systemic nature of this project and the extent to which we managed to include participation and to rebalance power structures through this experience in Espinosa and Jackson (2002). Even if the NSS story may not be considered fully successful, it demonstrates that it is possible to change an educational system in the direction of a more systemic approach, given enough (and more permanent) political and technical support. Also, it offers more evidence on how the VSM can guide the design and implementation of a highly complex educational self-transformation program at the national level of a country.

Developing the National Environmental System (NES) in Colombia

Three of the systemic auditing projects that I led in the National Auditing Office project were from the environmental sector: the Ministry o

Environment, the Environmental Research and Development Institute,[14] and the Regional Environmental Corporation.[15] These projects resulted in further systemic interventions in this sector: (a) the Gorgona Syntegration – applying Team Syntegrity (TS) to design the organisation of the National Environmental System (NES) (Espinosa & Harden, 2007); and (b) the National Environmental Information System (NEIS) project (details in Espinosa and Walker 2006, 2017 pp. 256–267). As made clear in the respective publications, both were successful and innovative projects, which had lasting impacts in the way the Colombian environmental sector developed in the following decade. The core agreements on the ethos and organisational principles of NES remained used in this sector for several years afterwards.

Together with A. Reyes, we pioneered a Syntegration on the Gorgona island, with representatives from a large group of stakeholders from the environmental sector in the country. It included those leading environmental legislation and projects, representatives from environmental agencies, environmental research and education institutions, the private sector, and Afro-Caribbean and Indigenous communities. The opening question was

How should public, private, and voluntary sector organisations be organized

in order to preserve the national environment?

The *Gorgona Syntegration* made an important contribution to agreements on the ethos and organisational principles of the SINA which they called *the Gorgona Manifesto*, which remained active for several years (Espinosa & Harden, 2007). It helped those responsible to look for more systemic ways of understanding a shared reality among environmental organisations, and on ways to decide and act in this shared reality in the medium and long term.

A few years later (1999–2001), I was appointed to advise the Ministry of Environment and the Environmental Development Agency to suggest a systemic design for the National Environmental Information System. The project included supporting NES to develop more systemic and participatory approaches to planning and a collective way of mapping their organisations and understanding alternative ways to address core environmental challenges in the most strategic ecoregions of the country.

In (Espinosa & Walker, 2017, pp. 256–269) we provided an example of mapping the Magdalena River's socio-ecological system. It is the second most important river in Colombia, crossing eight counties. We first mapped the Colombian Nation as a v&s network of communities and industries, as they co-evolved within their strategic eco-regions where they live – see Figure 8.4.

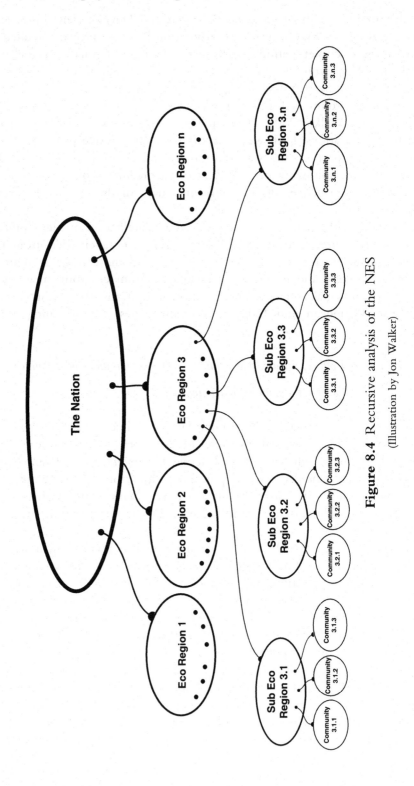

Figure 8.4 Recursive analysis of the NES
(Illustration by Jon Walker)

Then we choose as the system in focus, the Magdalena River eco-region, and produced a VSM analysis at this level. The VSM analysis helped to clarify the role of civilian and environmental agents responsible for this ecoregion's management, and the need for transcending existing political and administrative jurisdictions to clarify the SES boundaries as the river goes across 8 of the 33 counties in the country. The study suggested sharing investments i.e., in strategic information systems (S4), systems for monitoring the river's health (S3*), long-term programs to clean the river (S4), and in creating community and environmental committees with representatives from the local government agencies, not-for-profit organisations, industries, and communities to coordinate and implement these agreements (S3/S4/S5).

This project resulted in interesting learning and opened new questions. It proved the advantages of doing a v&s diagnosis of a large national sector by facilitating participatory mapping of the whole sector, providing more focus, and sharing a meta-understanding of the main dilemmas and paradoxes faced by key actors in a socio-ecological system. This was done from an eco-regional perspective, rather than by distracting political and administrative boundaries.

This allowed the administration at the time to create a learning context that favoured the emergence of collective understanding and knowledge on the strategic ecoregions of the country. All of our previous experiences in the environmental sector confirmed how the VSM (and the v&s in particular) was useful to come to agreements on long-term changes in complex organisational networks like the National Environmental Network.

The Relevance of 'Beer's Legacy to Facilitate Systemic Change

Previous case studies have illustrated historical examples of using VSM-inspired approaches as useful heuristics to facilitate systemic change. Like the other multi-agent approaches to systemic change mentioned before, the v&s is a systemic approach to support collective learning and experimentation concerning complex systems. It facilitates a focus on specific places shaped by coevolution between socio-technical and SESs; it analyses interagency activities across systems and observes the resulting pathways for transformation which may produce new system configurations. It is able to operate in transition arenas, activating social changes and reflecting upon them and enabling experiential learning among natural leaders in a niche. We have seen examples of it being used in local contexts, aiming to enhance community initiatives in grassroot niches, and to promote a clear focus on governance innovations, experimentation, and social learning.

In contrast with other approaches for systemic change, the v&s offers a robust theoretical framework for understanding organisations as self-organised, complex social networks. It offers robust methodologies to map and analyse pathological configurations among multi-agents' networks that lead to a lack of resilience, viability, and/or sustainability. It offers a meta-language to engage multi-agents in meaningful conversations to improve their organisation or network's effectiveness. It allows them to produce a collective mental model of the organisation that emerges from their interactions, which eases and focuses conversations and joint thinking on more viable and sustainable ways of interacting.

Each one of the historical examples of massive social and institutional transformations achieved important outcomes in terms of social and technical learning. The Cybersyn project, even if never concluded, is still inspiring massive interest and research insights. It certainly pioneered many of the contemporary socio-technical innovations and has not yet (to the author's knowledge) been overcome by a more complete social experiment in participatory governance. The NAO project contributed to create a more effective, collaborative, and transparent auditing structures and processes in the Colombian Public Sector. Reunirse offered a unique example of (VSM inspired) collaborative governance to address poverty in the country, which has a very positive effect in the SSN overall performance in 1994–1998.

The NSS introduced the idea of systemic education massively in the education sector in the country and educated hundreds of educational officers in this idea, some of which continued implementing the idea up to now. The NEIS project contributed in several levels to implement sustainable self-governance values and participatory planning in the environmental sector of the country and offered a new way of understanding sustainable eco-regional governance. These is only a sample of examples, from my own experience, that prove that the governance experiments Beer led continued to be an inspiration to follow in democratic businesses and institutions around the world.

Now we have the required communication (internet and mobile technology which allow real-time distributed information) and technological platforms (robust performance management systems like balanced score card, business intelligence, enterprise architecture model, etc.) to fully implement a Cybersyn type of project. Some of Beer's followers have certainly done it in many businesses and industries worldwide; e.g., Schumann (1993); Malik (2006); Brewis et al. (2011); Pfiffner (2020).

The interlinked examples of using the VSM in the Colombian Public Sector during the 1990s illustrate how the same language and tools can be used to analyse a complex organisation (e.g., the CPS, the PO, the NAO, the SSN, the NES, the ME) interacting with its socio-economic or socio-environmental niches. In every case, the VSM helped to design and roll out massive systemic change: From reorganising a specific national institution

(CPO, NAO), to improving a national governance system (NPD, NAO), reforming a national school system (NSS, ME), or developing the national environmental sector (NES).

The fact that several systemic change experiments continued during that decade in the CPS is not a coincidence. Those of us leading one experiment also inspired other institutions to try similar experiments (such as the local and the national auditing offices; and the several v&s projects in the environmental sector). These experiments, developed as action research projects led by academics, brought lots of social learning, through coaching and training. Throughout the process, we were seeding and feeding the emergence of a new generation of systemic leaders (through our systemic courses at universities), many of whom have since led other systemic innovations (e.g. Reyes, 2019).

Even if not every project concluded as expected (e.g., the NSS), they contributed to build upon ideas that have started earlier in the public sector, demonstrated practical relevance, and put them at the core of national policy and strategy; see Bula (2001). For example, the NSS left behind a learning trajectory that was later appropriated by old and new leaders and ended up confirming the route for new systems configurations.

For example, one of our collaborators in the NSS project continues very successfully to lead the "New School Foundation,"[16] an NGO that aims to develop and demonstrate the impact of a new model for school education, based on the same systemic principles pioneered by the NSS. They include seeing the teacher as a facilitator of a student's learning, promoting creative cooperation, participative and people-focused learning; linking the school to its niche; and educating for peace, solidarity, and democracy. This NGO has had an important impact on Colombian Schools over the last few decades and has also inspired similar projects in several countries. Recently, the Finish NGO HundrED listed this NGO as 1 of the 100 more innovative and inspirational educational programs worldwide.

The Need for Massive Systemic Changes to Improve Response to the COVID-19 Pandemic

The COVID-19 pandemic has opened new opportunities for intentionally implementing systemic changes, as demonstrated in the NHS's case studies in Chapter 4. The combined learning from these and the above examples offer food for thought regarding desirable and feasible improvements to the health services locally, which may be scalable to other trusts in the United Kingdom and globally. An overview of a recent VSM analysis of the Swiss response to the pandemic shows similar patterns found in different places, which opens the path for deeper understanding of the systemic changes required to develop more resilient health organisations.

While doing the LEHT study (Chapter 4), we also led a larger project to assess the effectiveness of a local trust in dealing with the COVID-19 pandemic during the first two waves. Like in the LEHT project, we identified major organisational challenges due to a highly centralised management culture and structure in the NHS (England), which impacted the capability to respond to this (and other) local trusts in England.

Over five months, our team[17] did more than 60 interviews with a large variety of stakeholders and ran five v&s workshops to jointly map and analyse the effectiveness of the trust's organisation to deal with the COVID-19 pandemic. We found out that the trust operated in a very rich context, where collaboration with the local community and other NHS organisations was excellent, and the support from local communities to the trust was outstanding.

We witnessed the outstanding strength, humane spirit, camaraderie, and mutual support among staff, even if it brought also enormous personal and family costs. The 'command structure' put in place by the NHS was effective in managing the hospitals during the peaks of the pandemic in a crisis management mode. It achieved a fast and effective transformation of processes and practices, like highly effective digitalisation of services and communications with patients and relatives; reorganisation of the physical spaces; redesign of patient pathways; redeployment of doctors and nurses; development of capabilities for the management of respiratory diseases and the use of protective equipment.

Nevertheless, there were many unsolved dilemmas affecting the final response, like exhausted staff and shortages, an extremely old hospital infrastructure that was inappropriate to protect against nocosomial infections; lack of more pro-active management styles at operational levels of the structure; and continuous (and sometimes contradictory) changes in the government guidelines.

The VSM analysis of the trust allowed us first to clarify the 'system in focus' for the analysis and then to map the complexity of the interactions between those members of staff directly dealing with COVID-19 patients. Figure 8.5 presents an overview of the VSM of the 'system in focus,' which focuses on those clinical units and roles directly dealing with COVID-19 patients in the trust.

The diagnosis of Systems 1 to 5 of this system in focus was discussed and prioritised with representatives from all the areas through VSM workshops. Based on it, we agreed on recommendations for improvements in the organisation for a future wave of the pandemic, which included: a) promoting self-organisation and self-governance in the COVID-19 wards; b) more distributed, real-time information for adapting to the increasing demand from patients; c) development of capabilities for self-governance at this level, including the management of algedonics. We also recommended to improve information and communication at this level (e.g., by using localised

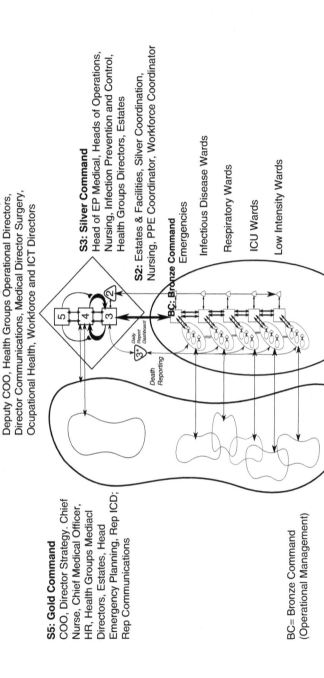

S4 Silver Comm: Head Emergency and Planning, Deputy COO, Health Groups Operational Directors, Director Communications, Medical Director Surgery, Occupational Health, Workforce and ICT Directors

S3: Silver Command
Head of EP Medical, Heads of Operations, Nursing, Infection Prevention and Control, Health Groups Directors, Estates

S2: Estates & Facilities, Silver Coordination, Nursing, PPE Coordinator, Workforce Coordinator

BC: Bronze Command

Emergencies

Infectious Disease Wards

Respiratory Wards

ICU Wards

Low Intensity Wards

S5: Gold Command
COO, Director Strategy. Chief Nurse, Chief Medical Officer, HR, Health Groups Mediacl Directors, Estates, Head Emergency Planning, Rep ICD; Rep Communications

BC= Bronze Command
(Operational Management)

Figure 8.5 VSM diagnosis – an English health trust

(Illustration by the Jon Walker)

dashboards, and daily emergency meetings) and between this and the next level of management.

More widely we strongly suggested to re-distribute existing knowledge on infectious disease control and on crises management, to all staff in the hospitals, as well as knowledge on state-of-the-art innovations in the patient and disease management. Also, to disseminate 'COVID-19 golden rules' for dealing with patients in all public spaces, to clarify guidelines for online working and to foster a culture of 'responsible autonomy' (i.e., empowering staff to make informed local decisions, and to be accountable for them) at all levels in the organisation.

We suggested to promote more pro-active management at all levels – which meant empowering local decisions and fighting the traditionally hierarchical structure and culture in the NHS. For example, we provided detailed recommendations for enhancing the command structure by decentralising the culture and decision making, (while preserving accountability) and distributing responsibilities for innovation to support decision making at all levels. Encouraging local autonomy in decision making will contribute to improve organisational resilience and their capabilities for dealing with emergencies and crises. It will also release management roles for focusing more on S4 and S5 types of activities.

Also, we recommended to disseminate and encourage innovation at all levels, which was mostly concentrated on the top levels of the structure. And qualifying the governance structure at the policy and strategic levels, by including a more balanced representation from a diversity of experts and managers throughout the hospitals, and rebalancing participation from managers and clinicians in strategy and policy decisions.

While finishing this book, this trust is in the process of implementing recommendations and adapting its organisation and processes to be more resilient in facing future waves of this or other pandemics. We have recently heard of a very positive outcome from the impact of this project. In the trust chief medical officer's words:[18]

> *Your (v&s) analysis of staff feedback, comments and suggestions has provided us*
>
> *with a valuable toolkit to improve our response to future pandemics,*
>
> *which will be a positive legacy for our local population.*

As there are many other trusts in the United Kingdom also aiming to do a self assessment of their performance, there is some hope that the learning from this pioneering project may be shared with others. We hope that cross-fertilisation will happen in adopting a systemic approach to promote massive change in the NHS, which it urgently needs to face the enormous challenges the pandemic has brought to it.

A systemic change in the NHS could well be designed to replicate this experiment in specific places, reflect on the identified pathways and actions for transformation of specific medical units and/or hospitals, and enable more opportunities for experiential learning for natural leaders. This would contribute to the reinforcement of successful community initiatives supporting the NHS during the pandemic and to focus on governance innovation, experimentation, and social learning. By replicating these v&s successful experiences, we may contribute to provide directions for further public health policy making and for improving organisational resilience in the whole of the NHS.

Schwaninger and Schoenenberger (2021) recently published a similar study analysing the management of the COVID-19 pandemic for a year and a half, in the Swiss Federation, using the VSM. A main dilemma of the Swiss Federation is that the Cantons, and at the next level, the municipalities, are self-contained and largely autonomous, so the VSM analysis asked if such a decentralised structure could potentially threaten the effectiveness of the pandemic management. Nevertheless, the statistics showed the opposite: i.e., regarding COVID-induced deaths per 100,000 population per country, Switzerland performed 20% better than the European average.

Even if there were fewer lockdowns or constraints for citizens in Switzerland than in any other European country, Swiss citizens had an embedded self-responsibility of everyone towards society, which meant that they mostly complied with the recommendations of the authorities and adapted their behaviour. Also, the economy didn't suffer too much and rapidly recovered as the crisis subsided. The authors concluded that the apparently complex structure and political process of the Swiss warrants requisite variety and ensures better results in the management of a pandemic, because decisions are more broadly based. Their study demonstrates that the Swiss Federation complies better with VSM principles than other countries in the European Union (and the United Kingdom).

In conclusion, the routes through which massive systemic innovation self-replicates over time are always unpredictable and surprising. But it is always reinforcing to discover that seeds that we sow years ago were somehow diffused by the social winds of innovation. And it is highly satisfactory to realize that they contributed to awake consciousness and desire to change in many people, which over time, produced new systems configurations.

Hopefully this book will help people who desire to contribute to the massive systemic changes that our civilisation so badly needs, to design and lead the required social and organisational changes. The final chapter will suggest that Beer's visionary theories and tools are more than ever an inspiration for the development of more robust and resilient governance systems. It will offer some final thoughts on open research paths for further developing the v&s approach to support massive systemic change.

Notes

1 https://orcid.org/my-orcid?orcid=0000-0002-5200-7613
2 See Cybersyn project.
3 'Seminario-Taller internacional 'Sistemas de Seguimiento y Evaluación de planes y programas de desarrollo'. Santa Marta, Colombia, 1992.
4 http://syncho.org/wordpress/
5 The forum was called 'The new National Auditing Office for Colombia in the XXst Century'. Its proceeedings were published by the NAO Press.
6 'Especialización en Sistemas de Control de Gestión – ESICO' – in Spanish.
7 I left the project in 1997, when the NAO Director, D Turbay, ended up in prison for curruption. The last 12 months of the project G Bula took over the NAO Direction, R Zarama took over the leadership, and R Espejo continued advising the project team with sporadic visits until its end in 1998.
8 Reunirse in Spanish means 'meeting together.'
9 after the third year D Restrepo co-lead the program with me and continued doing so when I left it in 1997.
10 In Spanish, 'Mesas de Solidaridad.'
11 Ideemos
12 R. Zarama was the program's administrative director, and I was the technical director.
13 David Cavallo from the Media Lab (technological Institute of Massachusetts, USA) ran the prototypes, using Logo, an educational software they have developed and were testing in several countries at the time.
14 'Instituto de Desarrollo Ambiental' – IDEAM, in Spanish.
15 'Corporación Ambiental Regional' – CAR, in Spanish.
16 Escuela Nueva
17 The team included Gerald Midgley, Maya Vachkova, Jon Walker, and the author.
18 Email communication with the author.

References

Andrade H., Diner, I., Espinosa, A., López Garay, H., & Sotaquira, R. (2000). *Pensamiento Sistémico. Diversidad en Búsqueda de Unidad*. Bucaramanga. Colombia: Ed. Universidad Industrial de Santander. ISBN: 9789589318782.
Beer, S. (1979). Heart of the Enterprise. Chichester: John Wiley & Sons.
Beer, S. (1981). *Brain of the Firm*. Chichester: John Wiley & Sons.
Brewis, S. J., Papamichail, K., & Rajaram, V. (2011). 'Decision-making practices in commercial enterprises: A cybernetic intervention into a business model', *Journal of Organisation Transformation & Social Change*, 8, pp. 35–49.
Bula, G. (2001). 'Observations on the development of cybernetic ideas in Colombia: A tribute to stafford beer', *Kybernetes*, 33, pp. 647–658.
Bula, G., & Espejo, R. (2012). 'Governance and inclusive democracy', *Kybernetes*, 41(3/4), pp. 339–347.
Conant, R. C., & Ashby, W. R. (1970). 'Every good regulator of a system must be model of that system', *International Journal of System Science*, 1(2), pp. 89–97.
Davies, A. (2012). *Enterprising Communities: Grassroots Sustainability Innovations; Advances Ecopolitics*. Bingley: Emerald.
Espejo, R., Bowling, D., & Hoverstadt, P. (1999). 'The viable system model and the viplan software', *Kybernetes*, 28(6/7), pp. 661–678.

Espejo, R., Bula, G., & Zarama, R. (2001). 'Auditing as the dissolution of corruption'. *Systemic Practice and Action Research*, 14(2), pp. 139–156.

Espejo, R., & Reyes, A. (2011). *Organizational systems: Managing complexity with the viable system model*. London: Springer.

Espejo, R. (2009). 'Performance management, the nature of regulation and the CyberSyn project', *Kybernetes*, 38(1/2), pp. 65–82.

Espejo, R. (2022). 'The Cybernetics of political communications and social transformation in Colombia: the case of the National Audit Office (1995–1998)', AI & Soc 37, 37, 1255–1267. https://doi.org/10.1007/s00146-021-01352-4

Espinosa, A. (1995). 'Strategic information systems at the colombian president's office: A managerial cybernetics' perspective'. *Doctoral Thesis. Aston Business School*. Birmingham: Aston University.

Espinosa, A. (1997). 'A Monitoring System for a social development program in Colombia'. *Systems Practice*, July Issue. ISBN 1094-429X

Espinosa, A. (1998). 'Organizational change. a colombian case: The cybernetic re-engineering project at the national comptrollership office' in *Proceedings of "2nd World Multiconference on Systemics, Cybernetics and Informatics"*. Orlando: World Organisation of Systems and Cybernetics (WOSC).

Espinosa, A., & Jackson, M. C. (2002). 'A systemic look at educational development programs: Two perspectives on a recent Colombian experience', *Kybernetes*, 31(9/10), pp. 1324–1335.

Espinosa. A., & Walker J. (2006). 'Environmental Management revisited: Lessons from a cybernetic intervention in Colombia', *Cybernetics, and Systems: An international Journal*, 37(1), pp. 75–92.

Espinosa, A. (2006). 'A Cybernetic Re-evaluation of Socio-economic Development Programs', *Kybernetes*, 35(1/2), pp. 30–44.

Espinosa, A., & Harden, R. (2007). 'Team syntegrity and democratic group decision making: Learning from experience', *Journal of the Operational Research Society*, 5(8), pp. 1056–1064.

Espinosa, A., & Walker, J. (2017). *A Complexity Approach to Sustainability: Theory and Application*. 2nd edition. Imperial College's Book Series on Complexity (5). Singapore: World Scientific Press.

Folke, C., Carpenter, S., Elmqvist, T., Gunderson, L., Holling, C., & Walker, B. (2002), 'Resilience and sustainable development: Building adaptive capacity in a world of transformations', *Ambio: A Journal of Environment and Society*, 31, pp. 437–440.

Loorbach, D., & Rotmans, J. (2010). 'The practice of transition management: Examples and lessons from four distinct cases', *Futures*, 42, pp. 237–246.

Malik, F. (2006). *Effective Top Management*. Weinheim: Wiley-VCH.

Max Neef, M. (1991). *Human Scale Development*. London: Zed Books.

Medina, E. (2006). 'Designing freedom, regulating a nation: Socialist cybernetics in allende's chile', *Journal of Latin American Studies*, 38, pp. 571–606.

Molina, J. P., & Espinosa, A. (eds). (1993). *Proceedings of the International Conference 'Monitoring and Assessment Systems for Development Plan and Programs*. Bogotá: Servigraphic Ltd.

Pfiffner, M. (2020). *Die dritte Dimension des Organisierens. Steuerung und Kommunikation*. St Gallen: Springer.

Reyes, A. (2019). 'Introduction to the special issue: Rethinking higher education for the 21st century: a cyber-systemic contribution', *Kybernetes*, 48(7), pp. 1373–1374.

Schwaninger, M. (2006). *Intelligent Organisations: Powerful Models for Systemic Management*. St Gallen: Springer.

Schwaninger, M. (2019). 'Governance for intelligent organizations: A cybernetic contribution', *Kybernetes*, 48(1), pp. 35–57.

Schwaninger, M., & Schoenenberger, L. (2021). 'Cybernetic crisis management in a federal system—Insights from the Covid pandemic', *Systems Research and Behavioural Sciences*, available online February 28th 2022 at Schwaninger 2022 online.

Schwember, H. (1977). 'Cybernetics in government: Experiences with new tools more management in Chile 1971–1973', in Harmut Bossel, H. (eds.), *Concepts and Tools of Computer-Assisted Policy Analysis*, 1, Birkhauser: Basel and Stuttgart, pp. 79–138.

Schumann, W. (1993), 'Strategy for information systems in the film division of hoechst AG' in Espejo, R. & Schwaninger, M. (eds.), *Organisational Fitness. Corporate Effectiveness through management Cybernetics*. New York: Campus Verlag, pp. 265–295.

Wolfram, M., & Frantzeskaki, N. (2016). 'Cities and systemic change for sustainability: Prevailing epistemologies and an emerging research agenda', *Sustainability*, 8(2), p. 144.

Chapter 9

An Idea Whose Time Has Come

Lessons on Using the VSM for Sustainable Self-Governance

The main argument developed throughout this book is that traditional, hierarchical, and autocratic management approaches are inadequate when it comes to dealing with the complexity of our current social, environmental, and economic realities. The volatility and uncertainty of the global market, and the dilemmas businesses and societies have been facing currently (e.g., global climate change, the COVID-19 pandemic, the Easter European war) are putting immense pressure on our organisations to become more adaptive and resilient. Many of us are of the opinion that without fundamental changes in the way we organise our world, the current headlong rush towards endangering the viability of mankind (e.g., through climate catastrophe, economic collapse, or a nuclear war) will continue unabated.

In the preceding chapters I have argued that through theory and practice, the VSM demonstrates clearly:

- We need to shift towards more networked and heterarchical modes of organisation in the complex and changeable world we are living in now.

- Highly effective, adaptive organisations must be based on operational autonomy, supported by the cohesive and supportive action of meta-systemic management.

- To support organisational viability, we need to critically learn about our interactions with ourselves, with others and with our niches.

- We must continuously co-create our organisations: viable and sustainable organisations must be learning networks, feeding on real-time information, and making agile decisions, to be capable of co-evolving with their niches.

  An effective way of collective learning is to share 'rich variety' models of what the organisation does, how we interact within ourselves to make it happen, and how we relate to other stakeholders in the environment.

DOI: 10.4324/9780429490835-10

268 An Idea Whose Time Has Come

- VSM language and criteria allow us to collectively agree on rich variety models of the organisation, its internal social interactions, and its interactions with all types of stakeholders in its niche.

- Understanding organisational values, culture, and ethos is core for properly managing organisational variety and to collectively identify and act upon feasible and desirable changes.

- Addressing power imbalances is a critical success factor for organisational performance. It can be handled by a) collectively agreeing on the boundaries of the problems to be addressed; b) choosing a balanced representation of stakeholders from both operational and meta-systemic levels; c) allowing them to actively engage in the learning process and take responsibility for implementation.

- To foster viability and sustainability, we must support radical changes at all levels of embedded organisations, from the individual to the global.

While Beer's original theory (the VSM) was intended to support private and public sector organisations to become more effective, the v&s approach aims to expand the boundaries of application of the VSM by supporting the design of organisations and networks, focusing not only on their (financial) viability but also in the sustainability of their way of interacting with their niches. It makes more explicit the need for a strong sustainability ethos, and for specific roles and mechanisms (S1 to S5) to take responsibility for designing and implementing corporate sustainability strategies and monitoring performance on key sustainability indicators.

The wide scope of case studies and applications in previous chapters also illustrates the power of the v&s approach to (re)design complex organisational networks. We have seen examples of self-transformations in different places and contexts – the most recent ones in the context of the coronavirus pandemic. In all cases, participants in the v&s projects collectively identified and implemented feasible and sustainable changes at each recursive level of organisation. By using the v&s in varied contexts and places, we have come to realise that whatever the complexity of a studied organisational network, there are always similar dilemmas and paradoxes (summarised as organisational *archetypes* in Espinosa and Walker (2017, pp. 485–492), independent of place and context.

For example, we saw several times that a typical dilemma is how to maintain cohesion while decentralising service delivery, without losing the individual node's autonomy or to the network's overall performance – as it happened both in the Omani Broadband company and the Latin American broadband network. We have also witnessed a similar dilemma typical of looser (*liquid*) networks; that each node may avoid committing to the network's strategies if they do not offer short term gains, as the UK Offshore Windmill case study illustrates.

Reflecting on the possibility that the v&s offers the means to design and support massive systemic changes, we learned that some historical applications of the VSM still inspire people all around the world – even if a few of them were never fully implemented for political reasons. These applications began experiments which resulted in collective social learning in the many people involved and facilitated the emergence of a new generation of systemic leaders, many of whom continue developing systemic innovations.

In the current global context of uncertainty and crisis, we can and should design v&s projects to create a rich context to promote massive changes, by collectively identifying pathways for transformation, co-designing a transition arena, activating social changes, reflecting upon them, and enabling experiential learning. The STM is a proven methodology that allows us to do so.

Developing VSM-Related Methodologies and Tools

The examples of applications from previous chapters reconfirm that the v&s is a robust systemic approach to facilitate collective learning, experimentation, and transformation in complex organisational systems. The varied contexts in which this theory has been used with positive results, demonstrated that the self-transformation methodology (STM) is a proven framework to facilitate learning to effectively manage organisational complexity. They also confirm the STM as a trusted methodology to map and analyse pathological configurations among multi-agent networks; and to identify improvements in self-governance structures to improve organisational resilience. This section offers highlights in complementary developments in VSM and v&s research.

VSM and Multimethodology

Several case studies in previous chapters provide practical examples of creatively combining the STM with other systemic tools like soft systems (e.g., cartoons), critical systems (e.g., boundary critique), teamwork (i.e., team syntegrity), and social networks (i.e., social network analysis). Other VSM researchers have also contributed to this field by using the VSM as part of a multi-methodological approach.

For example, Schwaninger and Perez-Rios (2008) suggest a joint application of the VSM and systems dynamics, to further explore issues of 'dynamic complexity,' as understood in systems dynamics. Their approach allows simulations of possible organisational behaviours, given a particular organisational structure and different possible strategic directions. It has proven useful to support strategic formation by analysing different scenarios and drawing on likely behaviours of critical variables of the business.

Gregory (2007) and Dominici and Palumbo (2013) explain the complementary between the VSM and lean systems. While the VSM focuses on improving organisational structures, lean systems focus on improving processes. These approaches complement each other very well as the VSM does not offer detailed criteria for redesigning business processes and lean systems don't offer criteria for organisational (re)design. A very fruitful path for VSM application research is the combination of contemporary fashionable agile models and methods (Scrum, SAFe, OKR, Canvas, etc.) with the VSM – because VSM is delivering what they are missing, which is a broader systemic theory of organisational effectiveness. They work very well together as all agile methods are based on cybernetic principles, too.

There are several innovations in systemic tools to support self-organised communities and networks working for socio-environmental purposes, like holocracy and sociocracy, which share the same cybernetic principles but have evolved into widely used practical tools. They clearly complement the VSM when used for improving self-governance, as they provide practical guidance on how to improve communication between different types of roles, and how to ensure balanced representation from operational and meta-systemic roles for effective and democratic decision making.

While network and CAS theories are getting increasingly popular, there is still lots to clarify regarding how to apply them to support self-organisation and self-regulation in complex organisational systems. We saw in Chapter 5 the power and complementarity of combing VSM with SNA for understanding structural (VSM) and dynamic (SNA) complexities. The examples provided offer the tip of an iceberg on what could be a very promising multidisciplinary research field, which is worth developing.

VSM and Team Syntegrity

Beer developed team syntegrity (TS) as a complementary tool for creatively agreeing on organisational policies, strategies, or action paths in large groups of people. In his own terms, TS offers an effective way to manage the explosive variety in the S3/S4/S5 homeostat. Several ongoing experiments aim to combine VSM and TS to support organisational strategy formation and implementation (e.g., Malik on Management's 'Super Syntegrations'[2]).

Chapters 5 and 6 showed a few experiments combining VSM and TS to manage organisational complexity, with very promising results (i.e. Magdalena University and the 2gNBN). TS can be used as the environment to do a VSM diagnosis (the Malik Super Syntegration approach); or as a mean to engage key people to fine-tune a VSM designed organisation (the STM approach). Either way, this is also a very rich field for further exploration and development of Beer's theories.

Recently, a group of pioneers from the Metaphorum,[3] a not-for-profit organisation developing S. Beer's legacy, has successfully run an online Syntegration[4] (ESyn 2030) with nearly 40 participants and is in the process of producing a Creative Commons license to promote public access to this powerful social technology, if issues of copyright can be resolved.[5] Using TS and the VSM supported by web-based platforms and software is also a fascinating challenge which some of us, Beer's followers, are taking seriously and can offer also very promising results.

There is no doubt that given the uncertainty and unpredictability of the world we live in at this moment, combining the strengths of complementary systemic approaches to manage organisational and societal complexity is a highly desirable path to take.

Addressing Traditional Criticisms to the VSM

Undoubtedly, the VSM is one of the most popular and inspirational systemic approaches in management. Not only has it become more widely available through academic and practitioners' publications and reports, but its popularity begun to rise in the 2010s and continues to do so, exponentially. While the original field of application was on business performance, Beer's work opened the way for wider applications in the public sector, communities, and nations, as we have seen in previous chapters.

We have also seen in previous chapters a number of applications of Beer's theory, which demonstrate how the academic criticisms discussed in Chapter 2 do not stand up to deep scrutiny. The case studies provided fully address cultural, political, and power issues, include multiple perspectives, and promote an emancipatory approach to management, which challenges the status quo and established power structures.

Nevertheless, we also should accept the purpose and limitations of a model. The VSM tells us about the organisational structure that must be in place for ensuring viability. No more and no less than that. It tells us *what* decisions must be made, *who* should be involved and *where*, and *how* to decide, but not *what to decide*. To expect the VSM to serve specific political paradigms or beliefs or to assume that it should prevent us from wrong decisions would be wrong. It's a model for organisational structure and not for content. That's why the combination with other methods and models can be useful.

Through continued practice, it is becoming clearer that the VSM offers a particular perspective on complexity management in organisations, which shares many of the grounding principles with other complex systems approaches but offers clearer and more robust methodologies and tools to (re) design organisations (Bohórquez and Espinosa, 2015). Compared with other systemic approaches to management (e.g., soft systems methodology, systems dynamics, lean systems, critical systems heuristics), the VSM offers the most robust theory for managing complexity in organisations.

Although an early critic, Jackson has become more and more supportive of the VSM as one of the most rigorous and scientific systems approaches to deal with complexity. In his own words:

> *The VSM is a model of the key features any viable system must exhibit.*
>
> *This provides a radical alternative to 'mechanistic' thinking and*
>
> *suggests organisational forms that are more appropriate to today's*
>
> *turbulent environment.*
>
> (Jackson, 2019, p. 340)

Previous chapters also exemplified effective ways to fully use the v&s apparently complex language and tools in multi-cultural and diverse contexts by carefully including multi-stakeholders in facilitated workshops by using alternative languages (e.g., cartoons, or drama) to collectively picture the participants perceptions. It is done by fully involving participants in the learning process and building up the collective consciousness that emerges to implement more effectively agreed self-transformation projects.

Hopefully the readers of this book have now found enough evidence that the VSM not only promotes autonomous, self-motivated individuals, decentralised and heterarchical governance systems, but also distributed control among individuals and subsidiary organisations. As in Pickering (2010), we can conclude that much of the previous criticisms – like the ones mentioned in Chapter 2 – demonstrate a denatured understanding of the VSM and continue to be overcome by practitioners.

VSM Research Landscape

Undoubtedly Beer's work needed several decades to be properly acknowledged and understood. But the time has finally come, and we can witness a continuously growing amount of quality research and practice inspired by the VSM. Recently, Schwaninger and Scheef (2016) demonstrated that the claim that the VSM provides the necessary and sufficient precondition for the viability of any organisation is well justified. They carried out a broad survey and pertinent quantitative analysis, and could not falsify that claim on empirical grounds, which corroborates the effectiveness of the model.

The process of further testing the power of the model in different organisational and cultural contexts continues to produce an ever-increasing number of publications. This suggests that this model is beyond a managerial fad, and that it conveys a sound and reliable knowledge on how to manage organisational complexity. A quick overview in the number of published VSM books in Google Scholar shows around 14 in the 1990s, 16 in the 2000s, 25 in the 2010s, and at least 10 since 2020.

The number of published VSM papers shows a similar exponentially increasing trend. For example, Vahidi, Aliahmadi, and Teimoury (2019) studied a sample of more than a hundred and 50 papers on the VSM from more than a thousand publications, since Stafford Beer published his original work. Major fields of application include organisational transformation, governance, performance management, strategy implementation, operational and supply management, strategic information management, knowledge management, sustainability, community operational research, education, and innovation. Undoubtedly VSM applications' research is still the most prominent field of research and there is an unexplored potential of comparative research and closing the loop of learning from practice and challenging or further developing the original theory.

From another perspective, it is not a coincidence that some of the most fashionable methods now available for improving organisational performance, like agile models and methods (Scrum, SAFe, OKR, etc.), are also based on cybernetic principles. And they complement the VSM, which offers a broader and more inclusive theoretical framework to ensure a robust structure is in place, which offers the best possibilities for improving organisational viability.

While the original field of application was on organisational design and business development, Beer's pioneering work in Chile opened the way for a large number of applications in the public sector, and in regional and national governance. The scope of VSM application at different scales, from the individual to businesses, communities, nations, and even global organisations continue to expand. We are seeing also an increasing number of works using the VSM in citizens and communities' governance, multiagency, and networks design. The versatility and universality of VSM criteria allows us to use it in fields as diverse as health, education, ICT, energy, infrastructure, regional development, and so on, as previous case studies demonstrate.

Today, it would be highly desirable and possible to extend the original theory, e.g., with state-of-the-art developments in neurophysiology and cognition and in organisational theories, as in the past 20 years there has been an explosion in the understanding of neurophysiology and its practical applications in many fields, including management. Beer himself acknowledged and supported work to further develop the original theory. In our last meeting in Toronto, in 2000, he introduced me to Candance Pert's work – The Molecules of Emotion (Pert, 1999). He was extremely excited about the possibilities that her work – confirming the existence of peptides – the molecules directly responsible for managing emotions in the body – would bring to further development of the VSM original theory.

Sabir (2014) has now tested (in dozens of companies in Pakistan) the correlation between emotions in the workplace and each one of the basic VSM principles. Her pioneering work opens a new research field which can potentially enhance the existing theory of viability by clarifying the role of emotions in augmenting and reducing complexity at the workplace (Sabir, Espinosa, and Vidgen, 2014). Sabir's findings confirm the hypothesis that the VSM is a useful framework to develop a more holistic view of affect-oriented work events and their impact on employees' attitude and behaviours. She found that it is possible to further develop VSM criteria to include the balance of 'inhibiting' and 'enabling' workforce emotions not only at the individual but also at the departmental and systemic levels. It is worth continuing the study of how the VSM can further contribute to comprehension and management of workplace emotions.

Several case studies showed the power of the v&s and the STM to inspire well-focused, quick, and sometimes dramatic changes in organisations experiencing chaotic changes in their niches, as happened in many sectors during the COVID-19 pandemic. For example, we saw that a few successful experiments of using the v&s in the U.K. health sector confirm the need to contribute to further governance innovation, experimentation, and social learning in the NHS. It is technically possible, if there is political support, to replicate these experiments to improve the organisational resilience of the NHS and comparable health providers in other countries further and more massively. Managing organisations in the middle of emergencies and crises is a highly relevant research direction to follow.

The case studies analysed in Chapter 7 showed that the v&s criteria help to enhance the resilience of self-governed communities by facilitating their representatives to strengthen self-organised groups, by addressing gaps in their self-governance structures and developing their capabilities to co-evolve with their niches more adaptively without losing community cohesion. Further exploring the use of the VSM to strengthen communities' resilience would be a fruitful effort.

Several case studies in this book explained how to use the v&s to (re) design complex, fluid organisational networks by strengthening the networks' metasystem inspired in v&s criteria; thus, reducing the possibilities of ending up with a fragmented, disintegrated network. This contributes to a growing field of research for designing multi-agency organisational networks to address complex societal issues requiring a unified approach (e.g. pandemics, natural disasters, and international terrorism). For example Sydelko, Midgley, and Espinosa (2021) offer an example on how the VSM combined with boundary critic, can be used to design a multi-agency to deal with international drug traffic.

A prominent field of research that has evolved from complex adaptive systems and social network analysis is the field of big data analytics, thanks to the raise of supercomputers and artificial intelligence. These tools allow powerful analysis of stakeholders' narratives in complex networks, which reveal otherwise indistinguishable social behaviours, values, and attractors in ways that were unthinkable a few decades ago.

This has, among other applications, created the context for the field of political marketing to grow, which is having a notorious impact in the current way of doing politics, although not always with positive outcomes. Scandals like the one from Cambridge Analytica (Berghel, 2018) are raising alarms, regarding the need for clearer ethical regulations of the use of these approaches and techniques. This is still an open debate, and more urgently needs to be researched and done to find effective ways to prevent it to continue happening. Combining the VSM with SNA and other innovative technologies like Decentralised Autonomous Organisations (DAOs) would allow us to design massive systemic changes in the way of self-organising communities, and in finding creative and robust ways of using social media for the benefit of citizens, rather than as a political marketing tool, e.g. manipulating their will to vote.

Applying the VSM research for further understanding the complexity of self-organised social groups is another exiting research field. Huxley's (2015) exploratory analysis of the viability of groups with salient social identities using the VSM model demonstrates the validity of core VSM principles to support more effective social networks cooperating for specific purposes. Similarly, Cardoso and Espinosa (2020) clarify how to observe and measure relevant aspects of the structure and dynamics of self-organising social systems, and how to value organisational capabilities to manage complexity, as originally described by Arcaute et al. (2008). It also contributes to the study of organisational pathologies (Perez-Rios, 2012; Espinosa and Walker, 2017, pp. 485–492), another promising open VSM research field.

Conclusions

This book hopefully contributes to establishing the usefulness of the VSM in general, and the v&s approach specifically, to address broader challenges of sustainability and self-governance in businesses, communities, and regions. It has shown that the v&s and the STM (supported when required by complementary systems approaches) could be used as a useful heuristic to facilitate systemic change.

Because the VSM was inspired by the extra-ordinary efficiency of the workings of the human body, a diagnosis will always be followed by a clear direction in which to proceed. The five systems must always be present, equipped with the capacity they need to fulfil their role and, as Beer puts it, intricately interconnected in the appropriate manner. If our current organisation looks like *this*, we can decide what needs to be done to make it look more like *that* – the pattern of relationships that defines the VSM.

Human societies are not only viable systems, but also (potentially at least) evolutionary learning societies, and therefore able to decide on their ethos, history, and foreseeable futures, and to make conscious decisions on preferred trajectories to new states of evolution. While some aboriginal societies have survived since immemorial times, as artistic and archaeological evidence demonstrate, whatever they learned in terms of best ways to self-organise for keeping their societies alive, it is not a knowledge that is easily deciphered over the echoes and lacunas of historical data. But even in that context we saw how we can use the VSM to support an indigenous community (in the Amazon) to reflect on their contemporary self-governance dilemmas and to find effective ways of self-organising to address them.

Undoubtedly, both at local and global levels, we urgently need to develop requisite variety on decisions concerning sustainability of our organisations and societies. What we learn from the v&s approach is that this requires of the sharing of a strong sustainability ethos; democratic and inclusive networking; real-time sustainability measurement systems; effective decision-making mechanisms; and a proper context to encourage synergies among people and institutions responsible for local and regional environmental policies and strategies.

The paradox is that, while we continue to worship at the altar of economic growth, the only control loops operating are the financial ones. Such a single control loop falls woefully short of providing requisite variety at a time when evidence of environmental, social, and political instability is increasing. Thus, none of this desirable context for promoting sustainable self-governance is yet possible.

From a v&s perspective, a first step is that each organisation and society must decide to address and solve the most urgent issues for its own sustainability locally. The next step is generating robust, global meta-systemic management to deal with essential issues for sustainability of human life on earth, for which the v&s criteria would be essential, at each level of recursive organisation. An important aim of this book is to inspire other researchers and practitioners who have the desire to contribute to the required social and organisational changes and to design and lead the massive systemic change that our businesses, communities, governments, and global organisations are so badly needed.

In short, the VSM presents a quantum leap in our way of understanding management that transcends many of the limitations of more traditional command-and-control approaches and solves the most important organisational dilemmas that current approaches still are dealing with. It is increasingly relevant to a world where organisations must evolve in the context of the ecosystems in which they operate, where innovation is required at all levels, and where collaboration is at least as important as competition. See Figure 9.1.

Figure 9.1 An idea whose time has come

(Illustration by Thom Igwe-Walker)

Notes

1 https://orcid.org/my-orcid?orcid=0000–0002-5200–7613
2 Malik's Super Syntegration. Available at: https://www.malik-management.com/malik-solutions/malik-tools-and-methods/malik-supersyntegration-mss/
3 Metaphorum. see https://metaphorum.org/
4 Esyn-2030. see https://metaphorum.org/esyn-2030
5 Team Syntegrity is copyrighted to Malik on Management (Switzerland).

References

Arcaute, E., Christensen, K., Sendova-Frank, A., Dahl, T., Espinosa, A., & Jensen, H. (2008). 'Division of labour in ant colonies in terms of attractive fields', *Ecology and Complexity*, 6, pp. 392–402.

Berghel, H. (2018). 'Malice domestic: The cambridge analytica dystopia', *Computer*, 51(5), pp. 84–89.

Bohórquez, L. E., & Espinosa, A. (2015). 'Theoretical approaches to managing complexity in organizations: A comparative analysis', *Estudios Gerenciales*, 31(134), pp. 20–29.

Cardoso, P. P., & Espinosa, A. (2020). 'Identification of organisational pathologies. Exploration of social network analysis to support the viable system model diagnostic', *Kybernetes*, 49(2), pp. 285–312.

Dominici, G., & Palumbo, F. (2013). 'Decoding the japanese lean production system according to a viable systems perspective', *Systemic Practice and Action Research*, 26(2), pp. 153–171.

Espinosa, A., & Walker, J. (2017). *A Complexity Approach to Sustainability: Theory and Application*. 2nd edition. Singapore: World Scientific Press.

Gregory, A. J. (2007). 'Target setting, lean systems, and viable systems: A systems perspective on control and performance measurement', *Journal of the Operational Research Society*, 58, pp. 1503–1517.

Huxley, J. (2015). 'An exploratory analysis and synthesis of the viability of groups with salient social identities using Stafford Beer's VSM model'. *PhD Dissertation*. Portsmouth: University of Portsmouth.

Jackson, M. (2019). *Critical Systems Thinking and the Management of Complexity*. London: Wiley.

Pickering, A. (2010) *The Cybernetic Brain*. London: The University of Chicago Press.

Pert, C. (1999). *Molecules of Emotion*. London: Pockets Books.

Perez-Rios, J., (2012). *Design and Diagnosis for Sustainable Organisations: The Viable System Method*. Heidelberg: Springer.

Sabir, I. (2014) 'A Holistic Emotions Measurement Model: Using the Viable System Model to Diagnose Workforce Emotions'. *Doctoral thesis, Business School*. Hull: The University of Hull

Sabir, I., Espinosa, A., & Vidgen, R. (2014). 'What Beer's theory of viability can offer to the field of workforce emotions', *International Journal of Work Organisation and Emotion* 8(3), pp. 169–184.

Schwaninger, M., & Scheef, C. (2016). 'A test of the viable system model: Theoretical claim vs. empirical evidence'. *Cybernetics and Systems*, 47(7), pp. 544–569.

Schwaninger, M., & Perez-Rios, J. (2008). 'Systems and cybernetics: A synergetic pair' *Systems Dynamics Review*, 24(2), pp. 145–174.

Sydelko, P., Midgley, G., & Espinosa, A. (2021). 'Designing interagency responses to wicked problems: Creating a common, cross-agency understanding', *European Journal of Operational Research*, 294(1), 2021, pp. 250–263.

Vahidi, A., Aliahmadi, A., & Teimoury, E. (2019). 'Research status and trends of management cybernetics and viable system model', *Kybernetes*, 48(5), pp. 1011–1044.

Index

Printed in the United States
by Baker & Taylor Publisher Services